Soviet Perceptions
of the U.S. Congress

Soviet Perceptions
of the U.S. Congress

The Impact on Superpower Relations

Robert T. Huber

Westview Press
BOULDER & LONDON

Westview Special Studies on the Soviet Union and Eastern Europe

Published in 1989 in the United States of America by Westview Press, Inc., 5500 Central Avenue, Boulder, Colorado 80301

Library of Congress Cataloging-in-Publication Data
Huber, Robert T., 1955–
  Soviet perceptions of the U.S. Congress : the impact on superpower relations / Robert T. Huber.
    p. cm. — (Westview special studies on the Soviet Union and Eastern Europe)
  Bibliography: p.
  Includes index.
  ISBN 0-8133-7603-3
  1. United States—Foreign relations—Soviet Union. 2. Soviet Union—Foreign relations—United States. 3. United States—Congress—Public opinion. 4. Public opinion—Soviet Union—History—20th century. I. Title. II. Title: Soviet perceptions of the US Congress. III. Title: Soviet perceptions of the United States Congress. IV. Series.
E183.8.S65H833 1989
327.73047—dc19   88-17595
                                                                                                          CIP

Printed and bound in the United States of America

The paper used in this publication meets the requirements of the American National Standard for Permanence of Paper for Printed Library Materials Z39.48-1984.

10   9   8   7   6   5   4   3   2

Contents

Acknowledgments

The study of Soviet attitudes towards the role of Congress in U.S. foreign policy concerns an area of Soviet foreign policy considerations that has received little attention by Western scholars and that offers valuable new insights for the study of Soviet foreign policy and U.S.-Soviet relations. As such, this initial treading onto empirical virgin lands has required the thoughtful, meticulous, and in many instances indispensable guidance and support of a number of individuals.

At the outset, I wish to express my deep appreciation to F. Jackson Piotrow and Nicholas Onuf of the American University and to Thane Gustafson of Georgetown University, whose guidance with respect to research method, epistemology, internal organization, and substantive development of this study were invaluable. Similarly, in the collection and compilation of research materials, intellectual and logistical suggestions, and in his thoughtful evaluation of the study, Joseph Whelan of the Library of Congress deserves my special gratitude and mention.

A number of helpful stylistic and substantive suggestions were offered by William Inglee and Michael Poloyac of the House Foreign Affairs Committee staff. In suggesting research orientations, pointing out empirical cul-de-sacs and shortcomings, and for his constructive ruthlessness in critiquing this study, special thanks goes to John Hardt of the Library of Congress.

A special word of thanks also goes to Rep. Dante Fascell (D-Fla.), the chairman of the House Foreign Affairs Committee. His encouragement and moral support, as well as his willingness to be interviewed for this study, demonstrated in an important way the value of a thoughtful, wise, and sensitive superior.

I am also deeply indebted to Dr. Iurii Alexandrovich Ivanov, Section Chief of the Political-Military Department of the Institute of the USA and Canada, USSR Academy of Sciences. Dr. Ivanov, one of the Soviet Union's preeminent scholars on the U.S. Congress, was a most gracious and helpful sponsor during a visit to the Institute in May-June 1987. His input, and willingness to arrange a variety of important meetings with other Soviet americanists studying the Congress, provided an invaluable and irreplacable contribution to this study and helped to verify and revise important judgments made about the scope and direction of Soviet studies of the Congress in the last two decades.

Far too often, the thankless but essential tasks of typing, proofreading, collating, and preparing manuscripts are ignored by self-important authors. In this regard, I am deeply indebted to the superb work of a number of friends and colleagues. First and foremost, Beth Ford was an invaluable assistant in this endeavor. She did editing, manuscript preparation, and textual organization with a rare and consummate skill and intelligence. She also provided irreplaceable moral support during those inevitable times of frustration in preparing a study of this nature. Carol Glassman, Jennifer Grant, Deborah Hickey, and F. Marian Chambers also provided valuable assistance.

Finally, and most importantly, my most special appreciation goes to my wife, Lois, and my sons, Jeremy and Joshua, who bore the brunt of the creation of this manuscript and the long hours, interrupted weekends, and too often cantankerous husband and father. Only they know how much I depended on them.

Robert T. Huber

1

Western Studies of Soviet Foreign Policy

Studies of the Soviet Foreign Policy Process

In recent years, Western studies of Soviet foreign policy and the political system have focused on what has been called the input side of politics. Scholars have attempted to discern the relationship of the political authorities to demands and the supports generated in the political process. In particular, scholars have attempted, through a number of case studies, to demonstrate that Soviet foreign policy has been influenced by the ability of foreign policy specialists in the Academy of Sciences and Soviet party and government institutions (the foreign policy establishment) to help determine leadership policy decisions.

This scholarly effort has had both empirical and normative purposes. It has been empirical in its attempts to demonstrate systematically comparative political phenomena between the Soviet Union and other political systems and demonstrate "the advantages and indeed the indispensability of a comparative approach to the study of Soviet politics."[1] In tandem with this empirical effort has been a normative objective. American scholars have argued that, since the death of Stalin, Soviet foreign policy has changed from a totalitarian, ideological, confrontational posture to a more pluralistic, pragmatic, and negotiable posture.

For example, studies of Soviet foreign policy specialists have attempted to demonstrate influence and impact on policy formulation and implementation. In one such study, Soviet specialists on India in the late 1960s offered specific recommendations concerning economic development that were subsequently adopted by the Soviet leadership as reflected by Soviet aid programs to India.[2] In another study of specialist influence on Soviet foreign policy, it has been argued that a number of Soviet foreign policy specialists on the Third World have all but rejected the simplistic notion of a "natural alliance" between the Soviet Union and the Third World against Western imperialism. For many Soviet specialists, reality has become much more complex and a variety of roads to development, including non-socialist ones, are now acknowledged with a stress on improving relations with emerging capitalist states in the Third World.[3] Soviet foreign policy specialists have recommended great care in selecting client states as a way of saving aid resources and preventing Soviet association with unpopular, unstable regimes, and that increasing domestic economic requirements argue for a reevaluation of current Soviet aid policies to the Third World.

It is argued by Western scholars of the Soviet Union that the skepticism and sophistication of foreign policy specialists regarding Soviet prospects for enhanced political influence in the Third World have influenced the Soviet leadership, which in the 1980s, has "set upon a course of restraint and caution in their policy towards the Third World."[4] In line with the advice of foreign policy specialists, Soviet leaders in recent years have appeared to downplay Third World gains and have put in its place a renewed commitment toward seeking arms reductions, lowering East-West tensions and settling regional disputes peacefully.

Other efforts to demonstrate the influence of foreign policy specialists have included studies on Soviet decisionmaking concerning the invasions of Czechoslovakia in August, 1968 and in Afghanistan in December, 1979.[5] In a study on the Czech invasion, Soviet foreign policy specialists saw the intervention in Czechoslovakia as too costly to Soviet relations with Western communist parties and trade unions, as a threat to the international conference of communist parties scheduled for November, 1968 and as detrimental to the beginning of SALT negotiations. Soviet foreign policy specialists generally saw Czechoslovakia's Communist Party leader Alexander Dubcek as a moderate, particularly when compared to discredited Czech hardliners and "anti-Soviet" forces in the Czech political process. They urged caution and sought to persuade Dubcek to limit internal political reforms so as to inhibit Soviet decisionmakers in the military and some elements of the Soviet party apparatus who were counseling the invasion option.

In the case of Afghanistan, Soviet foreign policy specialists were less cautious in their advice concerning the invasion option. Specialists in the Ministry of Foreign Affairs and the Party's International department were pessimistic about the prospects for U.S.-Soviet relations before the invasion, concluding that the SALT II Treaty by December, 1979 was headed for defeat or indefinite procedural postponement. Prospects for a reliable partnership with the Carter Administration were considered very dim. Foreign policy specialists also advised Soviet leaders that U.S. policymakers were too preoccupied with the hostage crisis in Iran (which developed in November, 1979), to challenge or react strongly to a Soviet invasion of Afghanistan.

Other studies of the Czechoslovakia and Afghanistan invasions seem to produce an uncertain pattern of specialist influence on Soviet foreign policy. Foreign policy specialists seemed to have had only limited influence in the case of Czechoslovakia, where the decision to invade was delayed but eventually taken against the recommendation of foreign policy specialists. In the case of Afghanistan, specialist influence is difficult to discern because the preferences of those specialists were consistent with those of other institutional actors involved in the decision.

In addition to case or issue area studies attempting to demonstrate specialist influence in the making and conduct of Soviet foreign policy,

American scholars have undertaken studies of foreign policymaking institutions to demonstrate continuous, day-to-day influence. For example, the Soviet Communist Party's International Department (ID) has been seen as exercising considerable influence in foreign policy formulation. The International Department is regarded by some Western scholars as an authoritative umbrella organization that requests, relies on, and synthesizes information from a variety of sources in the foreign policy apparatus in order to prepare the foreign policy agenda of the Politburo and the Central Committee Secretariat, and brief its members.[6]

In addition to this direct policy-advising role, it is argued that the International Department: coordinates and processes foreign policy support activities in Soviet government ministries; tasks research institutes to generate policy-relevant studies; supervises the conduct of covert operations, including military support of national liberation movements; represents Soviet foreign policy positions in meetings with non-communist parties and in parliamentary exchanges; and, exercises editorial control over a leading international communist theoretical journal (*Problems of Peace and Socialism*, published in the West under the title of the *World Marxist Review*).[7]

In addition to an influential role in Soviet Third World policy, the ID foreign policy specialists are credited with a major role in the determination of trade policy with the West, particularly concerning procurement of high-technology items, and the development of public diplomacy in Western Europe such as the failed effort by the Soviet Union to prevent NATO's deployment of a new generation of medium-range nuclear missiles. The International Department's foreign policy specialists are also increasingly influential in U.S.-Soviet relations generally and specifically the formation of positions at the arms control discussions in Geneva. This has become particularly true as a result of the appointment of former Ambassador to the United States, Anatolii Dobrynin, as ID chief, long-time Foreign Ministry americanist Georgii Kornienko as ID deputy chief and the creation of a new arms control unit, the first entity of its kind outside the control of the Ministry of Defense.[8]

Existing Conceptualizations of Soviet Foreign Policy

The Totalitarian Perspective

Despite numerous studies like those decribed above, the task of building an enduring empirical foundation for the study of Soviet foreign policy remains elusive. American studies of Soviet foreign policy cluster around three competing points of view: totalitarian, pluralist, and corporatist perspectives. .

The totalitarian perspective sees the Soviet Union as one type of totalitarian dictatorship, and its foreign policy as manifesting characteristics typical of a totalitarian state. Stress is placed on the existence of an official ideology, a single mass party led by a dictator, and party control of society through police terror, mass communication, armed force, and control of the economy.[9] Regime legitimacy in foreign policy is viewed in the totalitarian perspective as deriving from expressions of ultimate principles including building a new society and the final state of communism. The totalitarian view has been described as an "essentialist approach" in that it focuses its attention not on what the Soviet Union does but what it is and "defines the Soviet system as inherently evil, sees little prospect for change, and denies the benefits of piecemeal accommodation."[10]

The totalitarian perspective sees Soviet foreign policy as essentially expansionist and not particularly sensitive in its application to leadership changes or policy differences among leadership elites in the Soviet Union. Older motivations of Russian hegemony (distributions of lands, seas, and population, the search for warm water ports, etc.) are seen as merged with Marxist-Leninist objectives of world revolution to produce a preoccupation with hostile Western forces. This in turn produces an obsession with national security fears which make the amassing of military power and its use to stabilize and extend Soviet borders paramount in foreign policy.

Proponents of the totalitarian perspective see no foreign policy inputs in the system other than those initiated by the Party leadership at the highest levels. Interest groups "either do not exist or are so controlled that they lack the political resources to translate their claims into public policy."[11] Foreign policy inputs are initiated at the top and under the strict control of the General Secretary. Party organizations are established to dominate the economic and political objectives of the party and to control their implementation through the respective ministries of government.

Proponents of the totalitarian perspective on Soviet foreign policy also argue that party control lessens accountability for the consequences of foreign policy decisions. By insuring that party loyalists take control of foreign policy institutions, the prospect for factional groupings, disparate views, or popular or administrative checks and balances on decisionmaking are virtually eliminated.

Foreign policy is conducted without regard for popular forms of political participation (elections, legislative accountability, etc.) and leaders "not only will demand total devotion but will find it relatively easy to emancipate themselves from the awkward restraints of law and conventional morality."[12]

Even when disagreement about the nature and direction of foreign policy occurs, supporters of the totalitarian perspective see power struggles among leadership elites for the wielding of absolute power as the basis for such disagreement, not a reflection of genuine institutional restraints. The Soviet leadership seeks the goal of "utterly obstructing the aggregation of interests that are shared by several individuals."[13] The articulation of interests through bargaining, compromise, and incrementalism typical of pluralist political systems is seen as being suppressed altogether.

Soviet leaders are described as having a bipolar outlook. Foreign policy outputs are the product of a single monolithic actor "with a coherent long-range plan or master plan and both the intent and the capability to carry it out."[14] Soviet foreign policy under the totalitarian perspective sees nuclear war as winnable (or at least survivable) and arms control negotiations as an instrument to weaken the United States and strengthen Soviet military capabilities in a quest for military superiority.

For some of the more intense supporters of the totalitarian approach to the study of Soviet foreign policy, the relentless amassing of military power is combined with a demonstrated willingness to use it for political gain and the acquisition of "surrogate client states" like Vietnam, Angola, Ethiopia and especially Cuba. Soviet foreign policy is directed toward threatening vital Western interests; thus the invasion of Afghanistan is seen as pointed toward a strategy aimed at "encircling the Middle East" and "thereby making possible the 'Finlandization' of Western Europe, Japan and ultimately the United States."[15]

Advocates of the totalitarian approach argue that Soviet foreign policy seeks nuclear and conventional force superiority, as well as arms control agreements, not for military but for political ends, presenting the United States with the choice of surrender or defeat. The Soviet Union is not a settled nation-state seeking feasible accomodations. Rather, because of its ideological and historical experience, it seeks, like Nazi Germany, "to overthrow the present international system and to replace it with one in which its own power is dominant and its own political culture becomes the model and the norm."[16]

Adherents to the totalitarian perspective place heavy emphasis on ideology as an organizing and conditioning factor in the making of Soviet foreign policy. Soviet-style communism is seen as a system that assumes the right of total control over every aspect of life. The need to eliminate political opposition domestically produces a requirement for expansionism in foreign policy to reduce and eventually eliminate the foreign sources of that opposition.

Supporters of the totalitarian perspective emphasize highly centralized power, with policy initiative emanating from the Soviet leadership in Moscow. To explain anomalies to these assumptions, supporters of the totalitarian view see contemporary Soviet politics and foreign policy as best understood "more by the ways (foreign policy) departs from the totalitarian model than . . . through new models."[17]

The Pluralist Perspective

A far different interpretation of Soviet foreign policy is outlined in the pluralist perspective. This point of view, developed in the late 1960s as a theoretical rejection of and response to the totalitarian perspective, sees Soviet foreign policy as the product of differing perspectives in the Soviet leadership. Rather than seeing policy outputs as the product of a single unitary actor, the pluralist view assumes Soviet policymakers engage in a learning and interactive process which includes significant feedback from Soviet experience abroad and "implies the need for greater fine-tuning of analysis and policy responses and generally assumes a more pervasive interdependence between the two adversary systems."[18]

Advocates of the pluralist perspective point to the decreasing utility of the totalitarian approach, particularly since the death of Stalin, arguing that it is empirically inadequate to attempt to explain the Soviet foreign policy process as mainly a function of leadership-directed inputs and outputs. As we have seen in this chapter, "pluralist" scholars point to growing evidence that "behind the facade of the monolithic party a genuine struggle has been taking place among rival groups or factions."[19] In the post-Stalin period, supporters of the pluralist perspective point to public policy debates in which Soviet specialists have been allowed, even encouraged, to express their views and have ultimately influenced final decisions." Moreover, the nature of specialist advice (the best types of economic development programs to pursue the perils and pitfalls of building influence in the Third World, etc.) suggests that these specialists are being asked to develop optimal policy options and are not merely pawns in power-political disputes among Soviet leaders, as is argued by adherents to the totalitarian perspective.

The pluralist perspective also allows for the possibility that specialist elites can even in some instances engage in uncooperative behavior to achieve their policy objectives. Thus, one scholar has argued that the Soviet military strongly resisted attempts by then First Secretary Nikita Khrushchev to cut force levels and defense spending in the early 1960s. The cost-cutting effort failed and Khrushchev's eventual ouster was thought in part to have stemmed from this ill-fated policy. According to Kolkowicz, Soviet leaders subsequently concluded that "any political leader who persistently and profoundly threatens some of the military's basic interests invites his own political demise."[20]

To be sure, advocates of the pluralist perspective have not regarded Soviet and Western forms of pluralism as identical or even similar. Proponents of the concept of pluralism as applied to the study of Soviet politics, have stressed that the pluralist model is: (1) not a complete model of the Soviet political system or of the process of decisionmaking within that system; (2) not proposing that political interest groups are the dominant factors in the Soviet political process; and (3) not suggesting that interest groups were the primary source of political initiative or that the structure of power and authority were not central to the Soviet system. Advocates of the pluralist view also do not support the assumption, "so firmly fixed in the minds of the critics, that the recognition of the existence of interest groups . . . is equivalent to the belief that (the Soviet Union) is pluralist or is inevitably tending toward pluralism."[21]

Nonetheless, the pluralist school of Soviet foreign policy has, by the admission of one of its most notable adherents, argued that the Soviet political system contained "a number of the features of the conventional American model of pluralism."[22] These assumptions have included some familiar ones to students of the concept of pluralism in American politics:[23] (1) there is a multiplicity of interests in a political system and no particular interest emerges preeeminent; (2) the political process includes conflict and cross-cutting alliances of groups with divergent interests; (3) the state mediates these conflicts and seeks to strike incremental bargains between conflicting interests; (4) "minorities rule," with those most heavily involved and affected by a decision being the most influential in policy inputs and outcomes; and, (5) closed politics (bargaining, elite representation of mass interests, power to the interested participants, limited demands, etc.) is more relevant to policy outcomes that open politics (elections, public demonstrations, etc.) In both foreign and domestic policy, supporters of the pluralist point of view have sought to adapt the concept of pluralism to the obviously different Soviet political environment and to use this concept, derived from the American political environment, for comparative analysis.

The pluralist perspective sees Soviet foreign policy as responsive to American perceptions and misperceptions. A decision to take a certain action (as we have seen earlier in the case of the Soviet invasions of Czechoslovakia and Afghanistan) is regarded as the product of a variety of conflicting viewpoints. Intense, informed discussion and debate in Soviet ruling institutions is identified, with a host of political and economic factors at home and abroad, taken into consideration. As such, the notion of a monolithic Soviet leadership conducting a foreign policy bent on aggressive domination under an all-encompassing ideology is rejected. There exists no "blueprint" for Soviet foreign policy. The pluralist perspective places heavy emphasis on reactive elements to events abroad and in the case of U.S.-Soviet relations, American foreign policy actions toward the Soviet Union. Soviet foreign policy successes, for example, in the Third World, are seen not as the result of a conscious Soviet strategy but the result of other dynamics which benefit the Soviet Union (economic grievances, negative perceptions stemming from past Western colonial rule, etc.).

In light of the uncertainties and differences among Soviet policymakers, supporters of the pluralist view stress the management of Soviet-American relations, the search for parallel interests, arms control and other negotiations to reduce areas of disagreement. Concerning, for example, regional disputes, one of the most nettlesome and continually irritating elements of U.S.-Soviet relations, it is argued that the Soviet leadership would be amenable to developing a "code of conduct," or "rules of the game" regarding U.S.-Soviet competition in the Third World. Because of the importance of reactive elements and policy disagreements among Soviet leadership elites, supporters of the pluralist perspective argue that the "political atmosphere" or "international climate" in which Soviet foreign policy is conducted is critical to decisionmaking.

As such, adherents of the pluralist perspective "attribute importance to American and other foreign behavior as a determinant of Soviet foreign policy and reject the notion that it is entirely internally driven."[24] Unlike the totalitarian school of thought, the pluralist perspective regards Soviet foreign policy outputs and assumptions as subject to fundamental change depending on the experiences, institutional affiliation, and even the time of birth and socialization of key members of ruling institutions.[25]

Adherents to the pluralist perspective on Soviet foreign policy thus devote much greater attention than adherents of the totalitarian school to empirical analyses of Soviet elite career patterns, content analysis and interpretive studies of professional Soviet journals as well as the mass media press, because it is believed genuine policy differences can be discerned. Through newspapers, scholarly journals, and special conferences, specialists articulate institutional interests and even interests of broad societal groups.

Scholars adopting the pluralist perspective also argue that younger generations of Soviet elites at the local and central levels of the party, the government, and in the social science institutes are changing the tone and direction of Soviet foreign policy. These younger leaders are better educated, well-travelled, and less traumatized by the experiences of industrialization, the Stalinist purges and World War II. The personification of this trend is often seen by adherents of the pluralist model in current Party General Secretary Mikhail Gorbachev.[26] With the reduced role of terror and police-methods in the post-Stalin period, the opportunity for interest articulation in both foreign and domestic policy is thought to be much greater and Gorbachev and a new generation of leaders is believed to be encouraging this process epitomized by the well-publicized concept of glasnost.

Because of different personal and political experiences, the pluralist perspective sees the younger Soviet foreign policy elites as not as strongly influenced as are their predecessors by aggressive, bipolar, Stalinist views of the United States. These younger elites are generally supportive of U.S.-Soviet arms control agreements and detente, and seek cooperative solutions to Third World conflicts where American and Soviet policies are at odds. These elites are also candid about the Soviet Union's own foreign policy limitations. Finally, the pluralist perspective argues, if the willingness of these new elites to pursue a more cooperative relationship with the United States is reciprocated, improved relations will develop.

The Corporatist Perspective

A synthesis of the totalitarian and pluralist perspectives can be seen by the formulation of the so-called corporatist perspective of Soviet foreign policy. Corporatism developed from studies of political systems in Western Europe and Latin America and was seen by American scholars of the Soviet Union, beginning in the mid-1970s as an alternative to perceived deficiencies in both the totalitarian and pluralist points of view. The corporatist perspective sees Soviet foreign policy actions as the result of a state acting in its role as the promoter and planner of the common good. Foreign policy decisions are the result of

> a system of interest representation in which the constituent units are organized into a limited number of singular, compulsory, non-competitive, hierarchically-ordered and functionally-differentiated categories recognized and licensed (if not created) by the state and granted a deliberate representational monopoly within their respective categories in exchange for observing certain controls on their selection of leaders and articulation of demands and supports.[27]

The corporatist model tempers and transcends a number of assumptions of both the totalitarian and pluralist perspectives. The formulation of, and aggressive behavior sometimes demonstrated by, Soviet foreign policy in the totalitarian model is acknowledged, yet it is not represented as a "blueprint for revolution" but rather a function of system maintenance. Interest representation aspects of Soviet foreign policy in the pluralist model are also acknowledged. Such representation, however, applies only to functional institutional party organizations and government ministries who are not assumed to represent or be sensitive to broader societal forces (the mass public) but instead rather are committed to "political, economic, and social stability, and the maintenance of the prevailing distribution of political power."[28]

Finally, policy differences and dissonance among the elites in the pluralist perspective are acknowledged by adherents to the corporatist point of view but outcomes are believed to reflect consensus and cooperation, not conflict. Foreign policy institutions are organized by the state to actively promote state interests; or what has been called controlled pluralism, a pluralism confined to "official institutions, pluralism only for and among the elite, without much input from other constituencies, and finally pluralism which implicitly accepts several key unifying themes and rules of the game unchallenged."[29] Under these conditions, some scholars have chosen to identify the foreign policy decisionmaking process as corporatist because "as a way of conceptualizing Communist politics . . . it provides for particular interests to participate in the policy process without assuming competition between autonomous political groups."[30]

The corporatist perspective does not regard groups or institutions involved in Soviet foreign policymaking as independent or autonomous but rather as linked integrally with the state for access and even survival through constant interaction. The lack of planning in the pluralist model is rejected in favor of an active planning role for the state in foreign policy, which cannot retain its power without such planning. The state seeks to gain the benefit of specialist inputs while forcing compliance with whatever ultimate decision is made. Specialists do not share the final decisionmaking power. They are on tap, not on top.

The corporatist model also points to a strong element of clientelism between bureaucracies and the Soviet leadership in the making and conduct of Soviet foreign as well as domestic policy. For example, adherents to the corporatist perspective have pointed to three types of conflicts in the Soviet decisionmaking process: analytic, organizational, and systemic political.[31] In each type of conflict, a type of clientelism which helps build consensus and cooperation to resolve such conflicts is evident. In analytic conflict, there is no clash over the "correct solution," but rather over the means. In this instance, technically competent specialists attempt to convince Soviet leaders that their proposals will best achieve agreed upon objectives. In organizational conflict, there is a clash over scarce resources or jurisdictional scope of organizations. Decisions in this case usually reflect skills of both technical specialists and political heads of bureaucracies who attempt to fulfill both political and substantive requirements of a particular policy goal. Finally, in systemic political conflict, leadership factions become allied with bureaucratic institutions. Even at this level of conflict, however, the locus of decisionmaking may be at the agency or "staff level," in an effort to reduce open political conflict. Thus, the corporatist perspective of Soviet foreign policy stresses that bureaucracies are linked with their clienteles in a manner that resolves conflicts and rationalizes the policy process.

As such, the corporatist perspective can be seen as a "mechanistic" approach emphasizing preservation of the system as the primary goal of Soviet foreign policy. Soviet actions are seen as largely conservative and based first and foremost on geopolitical considerations. System maintenance objectives dictate the amassing of military power but not for aggressive purposes as adherents to the totalitarian perspective would argue, but rather to achieve greater security.

Like the pluralist view, arms control negotiations are seen as a legitimate aspect of Soviet foreign policy. But adherents to the corporatist point of view are likely to see the results of such efforts as meager given the importance of military power in preserving the Soviet political system and the institutional predominance of the military over the formulation of arms control positions in U.S.-Soviet negotiations. It has been demonstrated that the role of the Soviet military in the Soviet SALT I delegation was a major one and that the strong preference of the Soviet military for caution in disclosure of Soviet military interests and concerns "clearly contributed to the generally passive and reactive Soviet stance with respect to concrete proposals for arms limitation."[32] Nonetheless, "corporatists" believe the overarching concern with system maintenance drives Soviet leaders to seek negotiated agreements in arms control to reduce the likelihood of war.

Similarly, Soviet foreign policy in the Third World is seen in the corporatist perspective as primarily driven by the extension of influence, enhancing relations with countries and regions in border areas vital to Soviet security (while downplaying or failing to support revolutionary activity elsewhere). Soviet economic assistance, for example, is geared toward producing direct economic benefits to the Soviet Union, while military assistance is provided in exchange for military facilities and privileges that extend the reach of military power. Unlike the totalitarian view that sees such activities as part of a pattern of Soviet-sponsored revolutions, the corporatist perspective is more prudent. Activities such as support for national liberation movements, are believed by corporatists to be aimed at "the reduction of Western influence and military capabilities and the concomitant expansion of the military and political capabilities of the Soviet state."[33]

In short, the corporatist perspective of Soviet foreign policy sees Soviet actions as the result of cautious institutional actors whose primary motivations are system maintenance and their place in that system. Unlike adherents to the pluralist school, the corporatist point of view sees strong ideas and dynamic leaders to be atypical of the Soviet political system. Centrist, consensus policy outcomes are clearly the norm, with institutional and personal disagreements either submerged or its participants removed for their political imprudence. National security requirements and the strengthening of military power to achieve those requirements are paramount considerations in Soviet foreign policy since they assure the security and survival of the Soviet regime.

Theoretical Implications of New Subject Matter: Soviet Attitudes on the Role of Congress in U.S. Foreign Policy

As we have seen, the accuracy, validity and explanatory power of the three existing conceptualizations of Soviet foreign policy are still in dispute. Generally, scholars of the Soviet Union would not likely identify fully with any of the existing perspectives yet their writings can be schematically placed within this tripartite description of perspectives on Soviet foreign policy. Studies of Soviet foreign policy toward specific countries of the world, functional questions (arms control, international organizations, international economic policy, etc.), and studies of foreign policy making institutions have been conducted by American scholars. Still, a widely acceptable perspective of Soviet foreign policy has still not been formulated. In the view of one scholar, academic debates about the validity of existing approaches "usually degenerate into repetitiveness, and as a result come to be distinguished by their air of exhaustion after a short burst of initial enthusiasm."[34]

This is not to say however, that past efforts at theory formation have not had their achievements. Soviet studies and comparative politics have been at least somewhat integrated through the application of the concepts of pluralism and corporatism adapted from the study of other political systems. As a result, numerous case studies on the Soviet foreign policy process have built stronger empirical foundations. The stress pluralist and corporatist scholars have put on comparativity has enabled us to ask what aspects of Soviet foreign policy are similar to other states, what aspects are different, what the significance of these similarities and differences are, and why, methodolgically, they are important.

Furthermore, it has been accurately pointed out that "there is a tradition in the study of Soviet politics of devising some word or phrase to describe 'the system.'"[35] Admittedly, if the heuristic value of conceptualizations is replaced by the polemical value of labels, very little will have been accomplished. On the other hand, the breakout from theoretical doldrums which has been attempted by various studies of Soviet foreign policy and the effort to find a place for those studies in comparative politics and political science is sure to continue.

This study hopes to make a contribution to this effort. Its principal achievement will hopefully be the value of new, important, and theoretically-important subject matter for the study of Soviet foreign policy. While, as we have seen, Soviet foreign policy actions and objectives have been analyzed thoroughly on both a state-to-state and institutional basis, significant information gaps remain.

One such gap is represented by the lack of specific, conceptual and empirical analysis on the question of how Soviet foreign policymakers deal with the increasingly important role of the U.S. Congress in American foreign policy. Despite the critical nature of Congress' role, and the need to take this role into account in the making and conduct of Soviet foreign policy, this research question has received virtually no attention by Western scholars.[36]

Like other case studies cited in this chapter, the author has both scientific and value commitments. Many of the institutions involved in the making and conduct of Soviet policy toward the United States, and particularly toward the U.S. Congress, have heretofore received inadequate scholarly attention. Empirically, the writings of Soviet scholars on the subject of Congress and U.S. foreign policy, the relations between the Soviet Embassy and the Congress on foreign policy issues, the various means of information-gathering conducted by the Soviet Union vis-à-vis the Congress, the treatment given Congressional delegations visiting the Soviet Union by Soviet foreign policy institutions, and the attitudes of the Soviet leadership toward Congress' role in U.S. foreign policy may help to make an inductive contribution to answering the question of which perspective of Soviet foreign policy is most accurate, as well as examine some of the explanatory strengths and weaknesses of each of the perspectives.

For example, analysis of specialist attitudes on Congress and foreign policy will enable us to test the assumption of the pluralist perspective that such specialists can put forth a wide variety of opinion in their specialist journals. By examining the treatment given by Party and government foreign policy institutions to Congressional delegations visiting the Soviet Union and the way the Soviet Embassy in Washington handles day-to-day relations with the Congress, we can get a richer understanding of the trends away from a rigid totalitarian decisionmaking process, as well as the pattern of leadership-bureaucracy relations that serve the system maintenance objectives described in the corporatist perspective.

Finally, one source of information which can be used in analyzing Soviet attempts to evaluate and consider Congress' role in U.S. foreign policy are the reports which the Members of Congress often provide on meetings with the Soviet leadership, reports which can be enriched with interviews of participants in such meetings. Thus, we may have a rare opportunity to explore directly leadership attitudes on a key foreign policy issue, giving us a better sense for the way those attitudes have been shaped, and who initiates foreign policy in the Soviet political system. Useful information on this critical question could shed light on the long-held assumption of the totalitarian approach to Soviet foreign policy that policy initiative is monopolized by the Party leadership, thus contributing to the theoretical as well as practical understanding of Soviet foreign policy.

In this manner, Soviet perspectives of Congress' role in U.S. foreign policy represent new analytical ground with the potential for fresh evaluation of the cardinal assumptions of Western perspectives of Soviet foreign policy and their validity. Furthermore, the types of attitudes expressed by Soviet scholars and the Soviet leadership on the Congress may well reflect aspects of the various existing Western perspectives of Soviet foreign policy. If so, even more valuable information can be gathered.

Soviet academic writings on the Congress clearly express attitudes which each of the Western perspectives have regarded as prevailing. For example, some Soviet attitudes on Congress and foreign policy have emphasized that Congress' foreign policy role in the postwar period has weakened and the executive role has strengthened as part of "the centralization of economic power in the hands of the monopolies and their coalescence with the apparatus of the state" and that the gathering together of the "main levers of state power in the executive branch headed by the President has gone hand-in-hand with concentration of economic and political might in the hands of monopoly capital."[37] This attitude would tend to verify the official ideology and unitary world outlook described in the totalitarian perspective of Soviet foreign policy.

On the other hand, other Soviet attitudes have stressed that legal and constitutional factors are an important element of the American political system and that undue concentration of power in the Presidency "at the expense of Congress' committees and their allies in the executive departments would . . . rob the system of its flexibility and responsiveness."[38] This suggests a level of informed discussion about the separation of powers and the ongoing operation of the Congress in the foreign (as well as domestic) policy area that is consistent with the pluralist perspective of Soviet foreign policy. Disagreements have also been found concerning the scope, nature, and significance of Congress' role in foreign policy. This too reflects the intense, informed debate and consideration of issues and policy alternatives suggested by the pluralist perspective.

However, other Soviet writings on Congress and foreign policy concerning issues such as Congress' involvement in U.S.-Soviet trade have been analytically subordinated to the question of whether the output of Congressional activity was favorable to Soviet foreign policy objectives. This type of analysis confirms the explanatory power of system maintenance and security motivations outlined in the corporatist outlook on Soviet foreign policy.[39]

But aside from the theoretical considerations and objectives, this study also has normative objectives. This book is also a study for policymakers. While members of Congress and policymakers in the executive branch seldom think about theoretical constructs such as those described in the totalitarian, pluralist, and corporatist perspectives, they are clearly concerned about how Soviet foreign policy is made and carried out. Members of Congress are particularly concerned how their actions impact on U.S.-Soviet relations. It makes a considerable difference to the making and conduct of U.S.-Soviet relations on a variety of issues if Soviet foreign policy is attuned to the actual Congressional role in those specific issues. As this study will subsequently detail, Congress, particularly since the mid-70s, has reasserted its constitutional, traditional, and political role in foreign policy. As the role of Congress in U.S.-Soviet relations and foreign policy generally increases, the cost of misperceiving the importance of that role on both the American and Soviet side rises.

It is critical that both Soviet and American policymakers fully understand the "Congress factor," as Soviet analysts often describe it, in U.S. foreign policy. It must be made an effective consideration in the way superpower relations are conducted in both Washington and Moscow. Otherwise, perceptions about the "real" role of Congress will serve as a source for suspicion, which as we will see, has too often been the case in the past.

This study will provide an in-depth examination of contemporary Soviet perspectives on the role of Congress in U.S. foreign policy. Chapters 2 and 3 examine Soviet scholarship on Congress' role in U.S. foreign policy, including procedural aspects of the American foreign policy process that ensure enduring Congressional involvement, as well as Soviet views of legislative actions on specific issues. As in the case of other studies of Soviet foreign policymaking, consideration will be given to the hypothesis that Soviet foreign policy toward the United States may be partially judged or understood by an assessment of the ability of American specialists in the Soviet foreign policy establishment to influence leadership decisions on factoring the Congressional role in U.S. foreign policy.

Chapters 4 and 5 detail Soviet sources of information on the Congress. Scholarly sources and operational sources such as the Ministry of Foreign Affairs, the Committee for State Security (KGB), the Supreme Soviet, and direct interactions with the Congress are examined. Chapter 6 attempts to directly address the issue of Soviet leadership attitudes toward Congress' role in foreign policy, drawing on information from official parliamentary exchanges between Soviet leaders and Members of Congress.

The concluding chapter will attempt to synthesize Soviet attitudes on Congress and foreign policy for purposes of demonstrating the strengths and weaknesses of existing Western perspectives of Soviet foreign policy. The validity and possible complementarity of each perspective will also be examined in an effort to develop a more widely acceptable outlook. This should contribute to a deeper understanding of the formulation and implementation of Soviet foreign policy. From a U.S. perspective, this study should also build greater awareness of the effects of Soviet attitudes toward the Congress on U.S.-Soviet relations. As such, not only will an important gap be filled in our knowledge of Soviet foreign policy, but policymakers will also be able to calibrate a growing new factor in the conduct of superpower relations both in Washington and in Moscow.

Notes

1. Susan Gross Solomon, "'Pluralism' in Political Science: The Odyssey of a Concept," in *Pluralism in the Soviet Union*, ed., Susan Gross Solomon (New York: St. Martin's Press, 1983) p. 22.

2. For more information on the role of Soviet Indologists in influencing Soviet relations with India, see Richard B. Remnek, "Soviet Scholars and Soviet Policy Toward India," in *Social Scientists and Policy Making in the USSR*, ed., Richard B. Remnek (New York: Praeger Publishers, 1977) pp. 97-101.

3. U.S. Congress, House, Committee on Foreign Affairs, *The Soviet Union in the Third World: An Imperial Burden or Political Asset*, by Joseph G. Whelan of the Senior Specialists Division, Congressional Research Service, Library of Congress (Washington, D.C.: Government Printing Office, 1985), p. 45.

4. Ibid., p. 32.

5. Jiri Valenta, "Soviet Decisionmaking on Czechoslovakia, 1968," in *Soviet Decisionmaking for National Security*, eds., Jiri Valenta and William Potter (London: George Allen and Unwin, 1984), p. 170.

6. For more on the ID's services to and influence on Politburo foreign policy decisions, see Robert W. Kitrinos, "International Department of the CPSU," *Problems of Communism* (September-October 1984): 50.

7. For more on the above functions, see Kitrinos, pp. 51-65.

8. For more information on these personnel shifts, see Wallace Spaulding, "Shifts in CPSU ID," *Problems of Communism* (July-August 1986): 80.

9. For a useful summary of the assumptions of the totalitarian perspective on Soviet foreign policy, see Archie Brown, *Soviet Politics and Political Science* (London: MacMillan Press Ltd., 1974), pp. 35-41. The classic delineation of these characteristics of the totalitarian state is Carl J. Freidrich and Zbigniew K. Brzezinski, *Totalitarian Dictatorship and Autocracy* (New York: Praeger Publishers, 1956), pp. 3-17.

10. Alexander Dallin and Gail W. Lapidus, "Reagan and the Russians: United States Policy Toward the Soviet Union and Eastern Europe," in *Eagle Defiant: U.S. Policy in the 1980s*, eds. Kenneth A. Oye, Robert J. Lieber, and Donald Rothchild (Boston: Little, Brown & Co., 1983), p. 206.

11. William E. Odom, "A Dissenting View on the Group Approach to Soviet Politics," *World Politics* (July 1976): 545.

12. Andrew C. Janos, "Interest Groups and the Structure of Power: Critique and Comparisons," *Studies in Comparative Communism XII* (Spring 1979): 11.

13. Odom, p. 555.

14. Dallin and Lapidus, p. 207.

15. Norman Podhoretz, "The Future Danger," *Commentary*, vol. 71, no. 4 (April 1981): 31.

16. Ibid., p. 40.

17. Odom, p. 567.

18. Dallin and Lapidus, p. 207.

19. H. Gordon Skilling, "Interest Groups and World Politics," *World Politics* (April 1966): 440.

20. Roman Kolkowicz, "The Military," in *Interest Groups in Soviet Politics*, eds., H. Gordon Skilling and Franklyn Griffiths (Princeton, N.J.: Princeton University Press, 1973), p. 166.

21. For more on these points, see H. Gordon Skilling, "Pluralism in Communist Societies: Straw Men and Red Herrings," *Studies in Comparative Communism*, XIII (Spring 1980): 83-85.

22. Jerry F. Hough, "The Soviet System: Petrification or Pluralism," *Problems of Communism*, (March-April 1972): 28.

23. For further information and full elaboration of the concept of pluralism as applied to American politics and other political systems, a representative sample of the literature would include: Robert A. Dahl, *Who Governs?* (New Haven, Conn.:

Yale University Press, 1961); Gabriel A. Almond and G. Bingham Powell, Jr., *Comparative Politics* (Boston: Little, Brown and Co., 1966); David Easton "The Analysis of Political Systems," in *Comparative Politics: Notes and Readings*, eds., Roy C. Macridis and Bernard E. Brown (Homewood, Ill.: The Dorsey Press, 1977), pp. 93-106; and David B. Truman, *The Governmental Process* (New York: Knopf, 1971).

24. Dallin and Lapidus, p. 208.

25. See, for example, Jerry F. Hough, *Soviet Leadership in Transition* (Washington, D.C.: The Brookings Institution, 1980), pp. 1-61, and 109-131.

26. Hough writing in 1980 summarizes the pluralist model's emphasis on the importance of generational change in shaping the foreign policy outlook of the postwar generation of Soviet elites, which include Gorbachev: "A new and younger leadership is likely to be more self-confident in its international actions. It may be more willing to take risk for diplomatic gains . . . to promote arms control by sacrificing old weapons, to engage in quiet diplomacy that helps to overcome domestic political problems on both sides . . . the penalties that we are likely to incur by failing to influence Soviet cost-benefit calculations may be much more severe than they have been in the Brezhnev era." (Hough, *Soviet Leadership in Transition*, p. 167.)

27. Phillipe Schmitter, "Still the Century of Corporatism," *Review of Politics* 36, (January 1974): 93-94. A representative sample of corporatist literature with respect to other political systems includes the following: Frederick B. Pike and Thomas Stritch, eds., *The New Corporatism: Social-Political Structures in the Iberian World* (Notre Dame: University of Notre Dame Press, 1974); Alfred C. Stepan, *The State and Society: Peru in Comparative Perspective* (Princeton, N.J.: Princeton University Press, 1978); Peter J. Katzenstein, *Corporatism and Change: Austria, Switzerland, and the Politics of Industry* (Ithaca, N.Y.: Cornell University Press, 1984); and the April, 1977 issue of *Comparative Political Studies*, devoted to corporatism and policy-making in contemporary Western Europe.

28. Valerie Bunce and John M. Echols III, "Soviet Politics in the Brezhnev Era: Pluralism or Corporatism?" in *Soviet Politics in the Brezhnev Era*, ed. Donald R. Kelley (New York: Praeger Publishers, 1980), p. 6.

29. Dmitri Simes, "The Politics of Defense in the Brezhnev Era," in *Soviet Decisionmaking for National Security*, eds. Jiri Valenta and William Potter (London: George Allen and Unwin, 1984), p. 76.

30. Archie Brown, "Pluralism, Power, and the Soviet Political System: A Comparative Perspective," in *Pluralism in the Soviet Union*, ed. Susan Gross Solomon (New York: St Martin's Press, 1983), p. 75.

31. For more information on these types of conflicts in Soviet decision-making, see Donald R. Kelley, "Toward a Model of Soviet Decision Making: A Research Note," *American Political Science Review* (June 1974): 704-706.

32. For a thorough discusssion of the dominant role of the Soviet military in the Soviet SALT I delegation, and its original reluctance and gradual acceptance of arms control negotiations as a complement to Soviet military doctrine, see Raymond L. Garthoff, "The Soviet Military and SALT," in *Soviet Decisionmaking for National Security*, eds. Jiri Valenta and William Potter (London: George Allen and Unwin, 1984), pp. 140, 142-153.

33. Roger E. Kanet and M. Rajan Menon, "Soviet Policy Toward the Third World," in *Soviet Politics in the Brezhnev Era*, ed. Donald R. Kelley (New York: Praeger Publishers, 1980), p. 240.

34. Jerry H. Hough, "Pluralism, Corporatism, and the Soviet Union," in *Pluralism in the Soviet Union*, ed. Susan Gross Solomon (New York: St Martin's Press, 1983), pp. 40-41.

35. Bunce and Echols, p. 2.

36. The only two studies found by the author that devoted significant attention to Soviet perspectives on the role of Congress in foreign policy are Morton Schwartz, *Soviet Perceptions of the United States* (Los Angeles: University of California Press, 1978), pp. 46-60, 73-92, and Neil Malcolm, *Soviet Political Scientists and American Politics* (London: MacMillan Press, Ltd., 1984), chapters 1, 4, and 5.

37. I.D. Levin and V.A. Tumanov, eds., *Politicheskii mekhanizm diktatury monopolii* (Moscow: Nauka, 1974), p. 159.

38. For further discussion of the point among Soviet analysts, see Malcolm, pp. 122-123.

39. E.V. Prokudin, "Congress and American-Soviet Trade," trans, Joint Publications Research Service, *USSR Report; USA: Economics, Politics, Ideology* 85-006, (March 1985): 54-62.

2

Soviet Perspectives on the Process of Congressional Involvement in U.S. Foreign Policy

Development of Soviet Studies of Congress and Foreign Policy

Soviet scholarship on the subject of the role of Congress in American foreign policy (part of Soviet studies of the United States referred to as amerikanistika) evolved in tandem with the development of political science in the Soviet Union.[1] While the existing centers of study of U.S. foreign policy will be fully detailed in Chapter 4, the early origins of amerikanistika can be traced to the establishment of the first full-fledged international relations research institute, the Institute of World Economics and World Politics, founded in 1925 and headed by Evgenii Varga.[2]

In 1928, the Institute began the process of producing a thirteen-volume study on the United States. The attention of the Institute was, however, soon directed toward the Great Depression and only one volume was published in 1937 on the Democratic and Republican parties.[3] The chaotic effects of the purges of the late 1930's produced a brief hiatus, which was ended by the wartime alliance with the United States. This in turn created the need for widely available, polemic-free information on the American political system and other institutions. Handbooks covering a variety of subjects (geography, natural resources, economy, history, armed forces, and political system) about the U.S. were published in 1942 and in 1946, as was a historical study of American interwar diplomacy.

Self-imposed cultural isolation and the intellectually deadening effects of the Cold War soon set in, however, destroying any serious, systematic effort to explain or understand U.S. foreign policy. In 1947 Varga's institute was abolished. No books on the United States were published for the remainder of the 1940's. In nearly every case, until Stalin's death and the 20th Party Congress in 1956, amerikanistika was heavily polemical, concerned with "reaction" and "fascization" of American political life, including Congress' role in supporting a U.S. foreign policy that made it a "vicious enemy of the people." During this cold war period even Soviet academic writing assumed and retained for a few years as one scholar put it, "the unrelievedly polemical stance, to use the kindest expression, that had been characteristic of the more journalistically-oriented parts of the Soviet press."[4]

The 20th Party Congress resuscitated amerikanistika with a high-level mandate from the party leadership for a comprehensive and deep evaluation of phenomena in other foreign countries. Party leaders were intensely critical of foreign policy research and Varga's institute was reconsituted in 1957 under the name Institute of the World Economy and International Relations (instead of World Politics). This institutional revival signalled a renaissance of foreign policy studies that has continued to grow. Slowly, a basic body of literature on Congress' role in U.S. foreign policy began to form. In the late 1950's and early 1960's a number of studies on the constitutional powers and mechanisms of U.S. foreign policy were published by the Academy of Sciences' Institute of State and Law. These studies examined in detail, if somewhat formalistically, the two-party system in Congress and the inter-actions of the President and the Congress on foreign policy issues.

The mandate of 23rd Party Congress in 1966 to "put an end to the notion . . . that the social sciences have merely a propagandist significance"[5] combined with party direction to comment on theory as well as practice provided further impetus to the study of Congress and foreign policy. In 1967, a Central Committee decree ordered sweeping changes in social science research, culminating in the creation of the Institute of the USA and Canada in the (hereafter referred to by its Russian acronym ISKAN) in the USSR Academy of Sciences bureaucratic structure.

Despite these developmental benchmarks, insightful analysis of the role of Congress in U.S. foreign policy was slow to develop. In particular, Soviet experts on the United States (the so-called americanists) were not adequately prepared for the Jackson-Vanik amendment, named for Sen. Henry Jackson (D-Wash.) and Rep. Charles Vanik (D-Ohio) in 1974. This amendment, which linked the extension of Most Favored Nation (MFN) trade status for Communist countries to their performance on human rights issues and required assurances about emigration of its citizens, showed the danger of relying on a shopworn ideological framework, developed during the Cold War years, which saw the predominance of the executive branch in foreign policy as part of imperialism's deepening political crisis. It became necessary to drop the operating assumption that increased Congressional involvement in foreign policy was a development that, a priori, favored working class, democratic interests.

To be fair, this assumption appeared to be especially valid on issues where Congressional resistance to executive branch initiatives in foreign policy (Vietnam, the War Powers Resolution, amendments to cut off funds for U.S. forces in Cambodia, resistance to increased defense expenditures, etc.) were viewed as sympathetic to Soviet foreign policy interests. When, however, as in the case of Jackson-Vanik, Soviet foreign policy interests were clearly seen as being eroded by Congressional activism in foreign policy, it became clear that it was, as one Western scholar has noted "no longer possible to use a scheme of explanation which counterposed monopoly power (in the executive) to a popular struggle for democracy (through the enfeebled legislature)."[6] Moreover, the Jackson-Vanik amendment was a "sharp reminder to Soviet americanists . . . that the Congress was indeed a force to reckon with."[7]

It was also clear in retrospect that the Soviet leadership and Soviet Ambassador to the U.S. Anatolii Dobrynin had placed far too much confidence in the executive branch's ability to negotiate a trade package with the Soviet Union and get such a package through the Congress without linkage to emigration issues. By placing excessive confidence and reliance on the Nixon Administration and particularly Secretary of State Henry Kissinger during the two-year evolution of the Jackson-Vanik amendment, one well-documented study on the amendment has argued that the Soviet leadership clearly underestimated the threat of passage of Jackson-Vanik. Excessive reliance on diplomacy through the executive branch "contributed to Soviet miscalculations based on ignorance of development of other events in Congress."[8]

Accordingly, the mid-1970s witnessed a thorough revision and expansion of amerikanistika studies on Congress and foreign policy. Substantial efforts, through monographs and shorter articles in the journals of the USA Institute and three other Academy of Sciences Institutes: the Institute of State and Law (Russian acronym—IGPAN); the Institute of the World Economy and International Relations (Russian acronym—IMEMO); and the Institute of World History, examined a wide range of topical as well as legal, procedural, and constitutional issues concerning the role of Congress in American foreign policy. Thus in 1970, while Western scholars were able to find only three Soviet sources on Congress, a 1984 book on Soviet political scientists identified nearly 100 sources.[9]

Process and Procedural Issues: The Separation of Powers and Constitutional Prerogatives

Americanist Perspective

This chapter and the succeeding one explore in full detail the writings of the Soviet americanists on the role of Congress in U.S. foreign policy. The subject matter is divided into writings on the enduring procedural and process issues affecting Congress' role in foreign policy and contemporary issues which the Congress has had an impact on in the last 15 years. In each case, for purposes of comparison, contrast, and analytical quality, Soviet scholarship on particular issues will be contrasted with analyses deriving from American sources on Congress' role with respect to the issue under consideration. This juxtaposition of Soviet and American analysis on Congress' role in a variety of foreign policy issues will also serve the purpose of providing a context for judging the soundness of assumptions contained in the totalitarian, pluralist, and corporatist perspectives of Soviet foreign policy.

Specifically, this chapter will focus on the enduring process and procedural issues which are a key element of the Congressional impact on foreign policy. Specifically, analysis of amerikanistika on five issues will be provided: (1) the separation of powers and executive-legislative prerogatives in foreign policy; (2) the effects of the two party system; (3) the organization and operational procedures of Congress; (4) pressure groups and public opinion and their effects on Congress' action; and (5) the effects of joint executive-legislative responsibility concerning war powers.

The doctrine of separation of powers is the subject of intriguing analysis by americanists. The idea that power could be shared or diffused among state institutions which could both coalesce and conflict with each other is conceptually very difficult for Soviet americanists. Soviet scholars interviewed for this study argue that in the Marxist-Leninist tradition, pluralistic power hierarchies are not fundamentally acknowledged, and the doctrine of separation of powers is seen as a bourgeois propaganda device to disguise the class character of state power "and its indivisibility and singleness of purpose directed in the interests of the ruling class."[10] While a certain tactical independence between the President and the Congress is acknowledged, and disagreements clearly identified, both the executive and legislative branches are seen as "two pillars of the machinery of state of the ruling class."[11] Disagreements between the two branches are explained by the fact that the monopoly capitalist class has groups opposed to each other. However, americanists argue that class and political goals provide the foundation for cooperation between the Congress and the President, and "those forces belonging to the ruling class are interested in preserving a balance between the components of the state system."[12]

If class analysis has been maintained regarding the underlying significance of the concept of separation of powers, this has not stopped Soviet scholars from developing a rather thorough understanding of its operation with respect to legislative prerogatives and rivalry with the executive branch over the form and application of U.S. foreign policy. Americanists outline in clear terms Congress' constitutional prerogatives, including the power to declare war, raise and support armed forces, give advice and consent to treaties, approve appointments to major defense and foreign policy positions, and authorize and appropriate funds for the conduct of defense and foreign policy. Soviet scholars clearly understand the difference between U.S. and West European parliamentary systems, particularly the relatively greater power and institutional independence from the executive branch that is bestowed in the U.S. Congress. One Soviet scholar interviewed for this study regarded the separation of powers as a deeply powerful concept and Congress' powers as a representative body to be considerably greater than its Western European counterparts. Even Congress' indirect influence on foreign policy is identified through "adopting resolutions, publishing statements by Congressmen, conducting investigations and hearings in its committees and publishing documents on foreign policy issues."[13]

The ebb and flow of dominance over U.S. foreign policy by either the executive branch or the legislative branch in the course of American history has also been identified by americanists, although they disagree over its cause. Three schoools of thought can be identified. Some Soviet scholars follow an orthodox ideological explanation, tying the rise of executive power in foreign policy in the 1950's and 1960's to the imperialist phase of capitalism which required centralized state leadership to conduct an expansionist, aggressive foreign policy and which has made only tactical retreats in the face of mass public dissatisfaction.[14] Other scholars holding this view are somewhat less polemical, viewing the separation of powers as favoring the executive but seeing this development as the. natural outgrowth of the need for all executive branches, including those in socialist countries, to make rapid political and economic decisions.

In somewhat the same vein, others regard the rise of legislative power beginning in the late 1960s as a democratic response influenced by mass movements (e.g anti-Vietnam political groups) and a shift in the global correlation of forces in favor of the Soviet Union. This has led to legislative resistance to an aggressive American foreign policy and legislative support for detente. This group of scholars also attempts to correlate Congressional resistance to a President's foreign policy program with public resistance to that policy and support for improved U.S.-Soviet relations.

A third group, however, no doubt humbled by the Jackson-Vanik experience and the growing Congressional conservatism of the late 1970s which contributed to the scuttling of the SALT II treaty, has placed the weight of the explanation for legislative resurgence in foreign policy on institutional rivalry and protection of prerogatives.[15] The recovery of prerogatives lost or surrendered, the failure of the executive branch to observe norms of consultation and approval for many of its foreign policy initiatives, and the basic unpopularity of the Vietnam War are the most often cited explanations by this third group.[16] Thus, the sympathy for Congress that existed prior to Jackson-Vanik has been replaced by a more cautious analysis which sees Congress as inconsistent and even hypocritical in its approach to foreign policy issues.

This third group of Soviet scholars currently represents the most dominant trend of analysis. Institutional rivalry, prerogative protection, and the natural interest of an independent institution seeking to increase its power are seen as best explaining Congress' continuing activism in foreign policy. These factors also help illuminate its function as a "balance" or "source of flexibility" in the conduct of bourgeois foreign policy. As one Soviet scholar told me, Congress represents different streams and forces in the American ruling class and is valuable in helping those streams and forces to be articulated. Congress also helps to fulfill a role in checking the development of a too powerful executive branch, a development another Soviet scholar interviewed for this study regarded as a principal concern of the American "founding fathers."

Even within this now dominant analysis, however, one finds disagreement about the extent and importance of disagreements stemming from institutional rivalry and guarding of prerogatives. For some, conflicts between the President and the Congress over foreign policy issues has had little impact on "the fundamental relationship between the President and the legislature."[17] The diffusion of foreign policy powers between the two branches in the 1970's reflects the inherent pluralism of a complex ruling class mechanism. The Congress is viewed by these scholars as serving several functions: keeping close tabs on popular sentiment, creating the illusion of marginally responding to such sentiment through hearings and legislative oversight, and generating legitimacy through the legislative process.

In fact, the period of executive dominance in U.S. foreign policy for most of the 20th century is itself viewed as an aberration to the general pattern of executive-legislative relations in foreign policy. For most Soviet americanists Congress is viewed as the institution where oligarchic capitalist ruling centers can reconcile their foreign policy differences. Others, however, tend to view conflicts in more serious and fundamental terms, and see the Congress as a force for restraining an executive branch which is always striving to increase its power at the expense of the legislature, as a source for rejecting outmoded and dangerous foreign policy assumptions, proposing alternate courses of action, and as an institution which heads off crises caused by an arrogance of power in the executive branch.[18]

The various manifestations of institutional rivalry are thoroughly analyzed by americanists. The so-called "honeymoon" phase in executive-legislative relations, when Congress tends to support a new Administration's foreign policy initiatives in the interests of a smooth political transition has been detailed, as has the following period of "customary competition, deals and political bargaining."[19] The failure to consult the Congress prior to the submission of legislation on important foreign policy actions and its often negative consequences has also been described, as has the growing role of Congressional staff and outside consultants in providing alternative sources of foreign policy information. Thorough descriptions of the role of the Congressional Research Service of the Library of Congress, the General Accounting Office, the Congressional Budget Office, and the Office of Technology Assessment have been provided, including the key role of those agencies in providing analytical information for the legislative process, oversight work concerning the validity and effectiveness of the expenditures of foreign and domestic programs, and budgetary information and alternative budgetary plans for such programs.[20] Finally, the use of the legislative veto, which attempts to reject proposed foreign policy actions by the President through resolutions which do not require his signature has also been analyzed as a means of restraining Presidential power in foreign policy.[21]

This does not mean however, that americanists universally support the products of legislative actions stemming from institutional rivalry or protection of prerogatives. Leaks of information in Congress about the SALT negotiations have been described by Soviet sources as complicating those negotiations, a view no doubt subscribed to by the American executive branch. The inconsistency of members supporting both arms limitation and

Jackson-Vanik is described as an inability to "overcome their deeply entrenched anti-communist and anti-Soviet prejudices."[22] The drive to reinforce
legislative prerogatives in foreign policy sometimes results in the view of
some americanists in greater policy instability and a destructive, negative
quality to Congress' actions in foreign policy.

Congress is also thought to be unable to propose a "constructive program
for the restructuring of foreign policy simply because if for no other reason,
its vote is limited by its position in the governmental and political structure
of the United States."[23] While the President and the executive branch are
forced by their position to take the realities of international life into
consideration, members of Congress are seen as not bearing this kind of
responsibility as they pursue foreign policy initiatives. Some americanists
have even gone so far as to acknowledge the continuing validity of de
Tocqueville's observation that "the division of powers makes it impossible
for the U.S.A. to participate effectively in the complex process of relations
between states."[24]

In short, Soviet scholars, when faced with both the negative as well as
the positive effects of Congress' increased activism in foreign affairs on the
Soviet Union, have become increasingly equivocal and uncertain about the
explanatory factors accounting for such activism. Faced with differing types
of activism from both the left and the right in the U.S., americanists have
had to question increasingly what one Western scholar has referred to as
"traditional notions of affinity between monopoly capital and the top levels
of the executive on the one hand and the potential of legislatures as channels
of mass pressure on the other."[25] In its place is a more complex analysis,
shorn of reliance on or preference for one branch of the U.S. Government
over another.

Analysis of Amerikanistika on the Separation of Powers and Constitutional Prerogatives in Foreign Policy

As has been noted earlier, notions of shared powers or the separation
of powers doctrine creates great difficulty for Soviet analysts. This difficulty
is often explained in terms of Marxist conceptions of the superstructure
which deny any fundamental significance to the separation of powers doctrine
or the absence of a societal tradition of shared powers. Whatever the reason,
the continued search for a monopoly power center that really "runs the
show" while promulgating myths like the separation of power to confuse
and mystify the masses is still evident in amerikanistika, although many
now only make passing reference in an otherwise polemic-free analysis to
the guiding hand of monopoly capital.

However, the perceptual problems created by such concepts as the
separation of powers have not had fatal effects on the quality of americanist
descriptions of legislative powers in foreign policy. Nor has this dissonance
affected analysis on the continuing clash and interplay of both the executive
and legislative branches in foreign policy. The discussions of advice and
consent powers, the power to confirm or deny executive appointments, the

"power of the purse", and war powers and related responsibilities to raise and support armed forces are consistent with and approach the quality of American textbooks on legislative powers in foreign policy.[26] The ability to discern the difference between powers of West European parliaments and the U.S. Congress is also impressive. Foreign observers are often confused by Congress' ability to reject executive branch foreign policy initiatives even when the Congress and the Presidency are controlled by the same political party. As we have seen, indirect influences through informal methods short of enacting legislation have also been discussed in amerikanistika. The use of hearings, speeches, non-binding resolutions, investigations and publications have all been noted.

The tracing of the phases of executive and legislative preeminence in foreign policy is somewhat less impressive and uneven in quality. The remaining groups of americanists who see the rise of executive dominance in foreign policy in the early postwar period as the product of the inten-sification of authority in the imperialist phase of capitalism and see the legislative revival in foreign policy matters in the 1970s as a mass democratic response to that intensification clearly ignore a historical pattern which has seen other periods of congressional activism in foreign policy, most recently the isolationist activism of the interwar period.

Fortunately, a more dominant school of thought among Soviet americanists has developed which stresses institutional rivalry, protection of prerogatives, and the political pressures generated initially by opposition to the Vietnam War as best explaining recent legislative activism in foreign policy. There is an undeniable consensus among American scholars that "the issue which perhaps more than any other ended congressional passivity in foreign policy decisionmaking was the Vietnam War."[27] The belief is widely held among members of Congress that the concentration of power in too few hands led to the isolation from political pressure and arrogance of power, which in turn led to the policy debacle in Vietnam. This helped create an enduring view that the legislature must be both independent and forceful in its forays into the making and conduct of foreign policy.

Interestingly, the division within this dominant group of Soviet scholars about the extent and importance of executive-legislative disagreements on the conduct of foreign policy mirrors that found in the writings of American scholars on the question. Some American scholars see specific acts of assertiveness aimed at restricting Presidential powers, such as the War Powers Resolution, as provisional types of restraints. They point out that "it is one thing to enact new curbs; it is quite another to put them into practice and enforce them rigorously."[28] Similarly, in a case study of Senate responses to President Carter's negotiation of a comprehensive international trade agreement and the SALT II agreement, another scholar has concluded that "the new Congress, for all its activism and assertiveness, remains responsive to strong politically skillful executive leadership."[29]

Other American scholars see legislative actions in foreign policy as more permanent and fundamental. Some, for example, point to the reversal of unchecked executive authority in foreign policy as having extricated the nation from the Vietnam War and, "by having enacted the War Powers Resolution of 1973, decreased the likelihood of future Vietnams to mar the nation's diplomatic record."[30] Congress is credited with having checked executive branch enthusiasm for political and military commitments abroad and for democratizing the foreign policy process by demanding early legislative and popular involvement in its making.

The manifestations of institutional rivalry are adequately described by americanists. American scholars also point to the honeymoon period as an important factor driving Presidents to gain acceptance of foreign policy initiatives. The Senate's advice and consent to the Panama Canal Treaties came about in part because of reluctance on the part of some Senators to oppose President Carter early in his term. By contrast, no such reluctance existed during Senate consideration of the SALT II Treaty at the end of his term. In fact, so much political capital was exhausted by the Panama Canal vote that the Senate was ill-disposed to undertake another major foreign policy vote for the President on SALT II. Lack of consultation, as in the case of the negotiation of SALT II and the decision to normalize relations with the People's Republic of China, is also an important factor in certain foreign policy decisions. The failure to consult adequately helped to doom the prospects for legislative acceptance of the former and considerably complicated them in the case of the latter.

As americanists have noted, the dramatic increase in Congressional staff as a contributing factor in legislative activism cannot be denied. The tremendous growth in staff can be easily documented. For example, the House Foreign Affairs Committee had a total of 16 staff in 1970 and now has nearly 100. Such staff growth has clearly resulted in a growing institutional interest in the making and conduct of foreign policy, as well as an interest in putting a personal stamp on foreign policy decisions. Committee and personal staff are also supported, as Soviet americanists rightly point out, by the General Accounting Office's extensive auditing and oversight capabilities in evaluating whether funds for foreign policy programs are being well spent, by the Congressional Research Service's ability to meet long and short-term foreign policy research needs, and the Congressional Budget Office's ability to project budgetary profiles for foreign policy programs and suggest alternative means of expending such funds.

Finally, the role of the legislative veto as a means of restraining executive actions in foreign policy is also an important one, particularly with respect to proposed arms sales and sales of nuclear fuel. Amerikanistika have also come to recognize the potentially far-reaching and negative effects on legislative foreign policy oversight of the Supreme Court's decision in *Chadha vs. the Immigration and Naturalization Service*, which ruled that legislative vetoes were unconstitutional.[31]

It is also significant that the often negative americanist reaction to the effects of the legislative activism in foreign policy is shared by many American scholars of Congress' role in foreign policy. Concerns have been expressed by americanists about disclosure of sensitive information as the circle of legislative foreign policy makers widens, and the instability created by the inability of committee chairmen or the House or Senate leadership to speak for or ensure the support of the Congress on foreign policy matters. The contention that only the President has the national perspective to plan coherently and that the Congress frustrates an effective foreign policy because of special interest concerns has often been argued by American Presidents and scholars alike.

Finally, the debilitating effects of legislative conditions and restrictions on the conduct of foreign policy and the complaint that it is "still not clear who exactly in the U.S. can speak in international relations on behalf of the United States,"[32] are all criticisms found in American literature as well. Thus, the disillusionment felt by americanists as a result of Jackson-Vanik and the conservative swing in Congress in the late 1970s and early 1980s which spelled the doom of SALT II appears to have produced a more fundamental understanding of Congress' institutional shortcomings, deficiencies that can manifest themselves in ways that from a Soviet perspective, can damage U.S.-Soviet relations.

Effects of the Two-Party System on U.S. Foreign Policy

Americanist Perspective

Like analysis on the separation of powers, amerikanistika on the effects of the two-party system on U.S. foreign policy has produced spirited disagreements. Americanists produce a thorough, detailed analysis of the views of the party leaders in Congress. However, they disagree on how strong a role party affiliation plays in Congress' actions in the foreign policy field.

For example, americanists regularly analyze the results of congressional elections, especially for their effects on U.S. foreign policy. Thus, it was pointed out that the 1978 elections resulted in the loss of five Democrats in the Senate who were likely to support arms limitation. The conservative tide swept in by the Reagan landslide in 1980 and its effects on U.S.-Soviet relations has also been thoroughly discussed, as was the Democratic gain of 26 seats in the House in 1982 and the Democratic takeover of the Senate in 1986.[33] Former Speaker of the House, Thomas P. O'Neill, Jr., and his ability to work with both liberal and conservative Democrats on foreign policy has been described in detail.[34] The current Speaker of the House, Jim Wright (D-Tex.) has been referred to favorably for his views on the Iran-Contra affair, U.S. policy in Central America, and on efforts to bring changes in the Reagan administration's arms control policy.[35] The political profile of former Senate Foreign Relations Committee Chairmen Richard Lugar (R-Ind.), Frank Church (D-Idaho) and Charles Percy (R-Ill.) have been fully analyzed, as have Senate Democratic Leaders Robert Byrd (D-W.Va.) and Alan Cranston (D-Calif.), as well as former Senate Majority Leader

Howard Baker (R-Tenn.) and current Minority Leader Robert Dole (R-Ka.) and Minority Whip Ted Stevens (R-Alaska).[36]

However, disagreements continue to ensue over the role and nature of partisan politics in U.S. foreign policy. For some americanists, supporters of a "bipartisan" foreign policy, which stresses cooperation between the President and Congress, is seen as an instrument for a Cold War foreign policy, enabling foreign policy management by what is regarded as an unrepresentative Republican and Southern Democratic coalition. At the same time, when Congress opposes the President on measures favored by the Soviet Union, Congress has been attacked for its failure to be bipartisan and similarly praised for its bipartisan support of the Nixon and Ford Administration's arms control measures with the Soviet Union.

Americanists are also divided on the extent of partisan rivalry and its effects on foreign policy. For some, "the position of the President as the 'highest legislator' is significantly worse if the majority in the Congress belong to the opposition party,"[37] and during times of poor executive-legislative relations, such as during the Watergate scandal, the opposition party used foreign policy issues to strengthen its political position.[38] Some Soviet scholars interviewed for this study saw these periods of 'split government' as giving Congress an opportunity to serve as a forum for new ideas and alternative policies that enable the formulation of options and choices beyond those pursued by the executive branch. Should a crisis of confidence about Presidential leadership develop, some Soviet scholars see Congress' foreign policy powers as more influential as well. Party line votes on such issues as the nuclear freeze, aid to the contras in Nicaragua and the placing of Marines in Lebanon are also pointed to as proof of the strength of party politics. Others however, downplay partisanship as a factor pointing out that the institutional interest to be actively involved is deeper, more enduring and broader than mere partisan considerations. To prove the point, these americanists point out the difficulties President Carter had with a Democratic Congress and President Reagan with a Republican Senate on a variety of foreign policy issues.[39]

In the mid-1970s americanists tended to associate the Democratic Party almost exclusively with the anti-war sentiment of the Vietnam period, as well as with support for detente and arms control. This association is no longer made. The so-called "liberal bloc," which was associated almost entirely with the Democratic Party, and which was once thought to have the potential to fundamentally alter American foreign policy, is now not held in as high esteem. While liberal support for arms control and improved U.S.-Soviet relations is cited approvingly, Democratic criticism of Soviet human rights abuses is dismissed with the shopworn charge of internal interference in Soviet affairs. U.S. policy in the Third World as proposed by Democratic Party policy statements in the early 1980s are also criticized as viewing "U.S. relations with the Asian, African, and Latin American countries through the prism of Soviet-American confrontation."[40]

Accordingly, Soviet scholars have increasingly relied on a more sensible approach that organizes foreign policy attitudes in Congress according to loosely configured liberal, centrist and conservative factions, each with its own staff resources, floating membership, and bipartisan composition. Democratic and Republican members and their organizational structures are described as "extremely amorphous and independent of the national committees" and "not bound by the norms of factional discipline in their actions."[41] One Soviet scholar interviewed for the study regarded the two-party system as a "wonderful American political invention," ensuring policymaking flexibility and smooth operational ruling class control through the development of loose, cross-cutting ideological blocs that transcend political parties and lack political discipline or enforceable political platforms. These amorphous blocs produce political parties that are both active and passive simultaneously and enable a complex ruling class mechanism to function effectively. Because of the independence of Members from the national party organizations for funding resources to get re-elected, party leaders are seen as influential only on foreign policy issues not sensitive to constituent interests. Party leaders in Congress mediate and formulate compromises with the President regardless of the Chief Executive's party affiliation. The President conducts consultations on foreign policy with leaders of both parties (although more so with his own) and "it would be virtually impossible to determine the differences in their views on the basis of party affiliation."[42]

The conservative faction in Congress is described as adhering to the "foreign policy dogmas worked out during the years of the Cold War," and as advocating "the continuation of the arms race" and the position that "assistance should be given to any racist or dictatorial regime as long as it takes an anti-communist position."[43]

The description of the liberal faction is less simplistic and is seen in somewhat contradictory terms. While getting high marks for its position on the Vietnam War and arms control and for increasing Congress' foreign policy activism, it is criticized for its participation in anti-Soviet foreign policy initiatives, its support for Jackson-Vanik, and its unqualified support for Israel.

The centrist faction, which is seen as holding the balance of power on foreign policy decisions in Congress, is regarded as the most influential in both the House and the Senate. The party leadership posts are usually held by "centrists" who are seen as favoring consensus, compromise, and incremental policy outcomes.

Americanists also argue that the members of the three factions can even shift their positions across factional lines depending on the issue invovled. Thus liberals vote with conservatives on certain issues (Jackson-Vanik), centrists vote with liberals on other issues (arms limitation agreements and other arms control issues) while voting with conservatives on others (increasing defense expenditures). The relative strengths of each faction is seen as shifting from Congress to Congress (liberals ascendant in 1974, 1976 and 1982 and 1986; conservatives in 1978 and 1980). But for both the liberals and the conservatives "in order to push through their own legislative measures, each has required the support of at least part of the centrist bloc."[44]

Amerikanistika on the two-party system has evolved to a credible position which while acknowledging partisanship, stresses the greater importance of factional groupings that cut across party lines in explaining congressional attitudes on foreign policy issues. Nonetheless, as in the case of americanist analysis on the separation of powers issue, a final, overarching class analysis is applied which sometimes obscures the complexity of Congress' role in foreign policy. Thus, despite sometimes impressive analysis, the reader is also on some occasions confronted with an analytical search for the monopoly power center, located preferably in Wall Street, whose directors somehow ultimately determine policy outcomes.

While Western Marxist analyses have also stressed the political control exercised by the ruling bourgeoisie, analysis is much more subtle, pointing to factors such as the manipulation of public attitudes, the public education system, and various forms of citizen indoctrination. Soviet attitudes on these issues are much more crudely polemical, with far less empirical substantiation and more sweeping generalizations about the "monopoly capital state." Both parties are seen as working "exclusively in the interest of the insignificant minority of the population . . . the monopolistic bourgeoisie."[45] The difference between the two parties is seen as "tactical" with Congress reflecting the comparatively broad range of interests of various segments of the ruling class. Congress is "expected to balance these interests, smooth out differences and make the most effective, from the bourgois standpoint, government policy."[46] Nonetheless, despite these analytical shortcomings, Soviet americanists have at least qualified Marxist-based analysis and have come to recognize a much more complex U.S. foreign policy mechanism, with Congress as one of the most complex elements of that mechanism.

Analysis of Amerikanistika on the Two-Party System and its Effects on Foreign Policy

Amerikanistika on the two-party system again reflects a strong operational understanding of the effects of this factor on U.S. foreign policy combined with a less impressive understanding of the fundamental systemic significance of partisanship. Obviously, shifts in control of one or the other House between the two parties, or large gains for one or the other without a shift in control can make a major difference in foreign policy outcomes in Congress. Americanists were accurate in perceiving that the defeat of five pro-SALT Democrats in 1978 whetted the appetite of SALT II opponents interested in stopping legislative approval of the treaty. Similarly, the 1980 election swept in a much more conservative Congress (including Republican control of the Senate) that enabled a major increase in the defense budget to be approved. A pickup of 26 seats for the Democrats in the House in 1982 emboldened its Democratic leadership to schedule early consideration of the nuclear freeze resolution. Finally, the Democractic takeover of the Senate in 1986 gave impetus for early consideration of comprehensive trade legislation opposed by the Reagan administration and enhanced the prospects of legislatively-mandated changes in U.S. arms control policy being enacted into law.

The biographical sketches of the House and Senate leadership, as well as their positions on foreign policy issues, are impressive. The description of former Speaker O'Neill as a consensus builder among Democrats is generally recognized as well by American scholars who see his primary motivation as "trying to keep dangerous rifts from developing within the party."[47] O'Neill is credited with having achieved this objective on a variety of foreign policy issues including the implementing legislation associated with the normalization of relations with the People's Republic of China, the Panama Canal Treaties implementation legislation and the authorization of a U.S. troop presence in Lebanon under the terms of the War Powers Resolution.[48] In his first term, Speaker Wright has developed a growing reputation for taking on tough foreign policy issues including arms control and U.S. policy in Central America; thus americanist analysis of his willingness to oppose the Reagan administration is accurate. Similarly, the description of Republican leaders like Senators Dole and Lugar and their stands on foreign policy positions are accomplished largely without polemical overtones.

The discussion of bipartisanship in foreign policy is more transparent and far less impressive. Here support for or criticism of bipartisanship seems largely dependent on whether a bipartisan stance supports Soviet foreign policy objectives like the approval of U.S.-Soviet arms control measures. Bipartisanship as a factor in legislative-executive relations in foreign policy involves much more than simply one issue. It grew out of a consensus, admittedly an anti-communist one, which saw U.S. foreign policy interests as being advanced by a minimum of Congressional opposition to executive foreign policy initiatives. While bipartisanship as an article of faith in legislative consideration of foreign policy matters collapsed over the conduct of the Vietnam War, members of Congress from both parties are very sensitive to the charge that they might be undermining the success of U.S. foreign policy for partisan reasons.

Moreover, there are certain practical reasons why bipartisanship remains an important factor in U.S. foreign policy. First, the Presidency and the majority of one or both Houses of Congress are often controlled by different parties. Secondly, party discipline in the Congress is weak and informal. Even when the representation of the President's own party in Congress is large, he cannot ever count on total support. The President's own party leadership can and does disagree with him on a variety of foreign policy issues. Many Congressional Democrats concerned about uninterrupted imports of the strategic mineral chrome from Rhodesia disagreed with President Carter's decision to impose economic sanctions on the white minority government as a means of producing black majority rule in what is now Zimbabwe. House Minority Leader Robert Michel (R-Ill.), because of industrial interests in his district, opposed President Reagan's efforts to stop the building of a Soviet gas pipeline in Western Europe.

This does not mean bipartisanship is not without its costs to a President. It often creates a strain with the extremists within the President's party. The political extremes of both parties may also sometimes come together, as liberal Democrats and conservative Republicans did in their unsuccessful effort to defeat in the House the Lebanon War Powers Resolution, which authorized the 18-month stationing of U.S. Marines in a multinational peacekeeping force in Lebanon.

Americanists do a better job in their discussion of the effect of partisanship, as opposed to the role of bipartisanship, on Congress' consideration of foreign policy issues. Disagreement over the effects of partisanship found among americanists can also be found in American scholarship. There can be no question that partisanship does play a major role in the foreign policy difficulties a President may encounter in Congress although public statements of opposition seldom stress this factor. Americanists have properly recognized, as have American scholars, that "the prevalent impression of a President's public standing tends to set a tone and to define the limits of what Washingtonians do for him or do to him."[49]

Thus, the ability of the Congress to override President Nixon's veto on the War Powers Resolution was in large part a result of his weakened position during the Watergate scandal. President Ford's grudging acceptance of legislative restrictions prohibiting aid to Angola reflected in part his weakened status as an appointed President who was unpopular because of his pardoning of President Nixon. The decision by Senate Republicans to oppose the SALT II Treaty grew, in large measure, out of the public perception that the Carter Administration was soft on defense and "Republicans saw defense as a promising partisan issue."[50]

At the same time, americanists also seem to understand that partisanship is not a prerequisite for legislative activism in foreign policy. President Johnson's problems in Congress on Vietnam were almost exclusively the product of the Democratic-controlled Senate Foreign Relations Committee. President Carter had great difficulties with the Panama Canal implementing legislation in the Democratic-controlled House Merchant Marine and Fisheries Committee and Senate opposition to the Panama Canal Treaty was led by Senator James Allen, a Democrat from Alabama. Thus, as Thomas Cronin has pointed out, much was made of the idea that "most of the problems in presidential-congressional relations could be overcome if both branches were held by the Democrats . . . but the promised harmony never came about."[51] In short, Congress will continue to demand that it play an active role in every major foreign policy issue.

The shift by americanists to a factional approach to understanding foreign policy sentiment in Congress is also a more sensible approach to the effects of the two-party system. Members in both parties consistently support increased defense spending and there is no political mileage to be gained from seeking detente with the Soviet Union for its own sake. While Democrats tend to be more generally supportive of efforts to improve U.S.-Soviet relations, particularly on arms control questions, it is by no means a universal tendency as witnessed by the efforts of the late Senator Jackson on SALT II and the crafting of major arms control agreements by successive Republican administrations. This tendency does not apply at all to trade policy or responses to Soviet Third World policy in Afghanistan, Ethiopia, Angola or the Middle East. In fact, on trade issues, such as grain exports, farm state Republicans have been in the forefront of increased trade efforts and Rep. Michel led the House effort to vitiate President Reagan's gas pipeline sanctions. For reasons Soviet scholars have now recognized, constituent interests often drive legislative sentiment on U.S.-Soviet relations, be it defense contracts or export sales. On other foreign policy issues as well, one can identify liberal, centrist, and conservative factions far more predictably than through an analysis which stresses party affiliation.

Organization of Congress and
Its Effects on Foreign Policy

Americanist Perspective

Americanists have demonstrated a rather thorough understanding of how organizational aspects of Congress affect the consideration of foreign policy issues. The committee structure has been studied in detail, including its various abilities to hasten, delay or modify Presidential foreign policy intiatives.[52] Soviet scholars have rightly concluded that the committee systems in the House and Senate are a major structural and institutional element of Congress' foreign policy-making activities.

Bills or resolutions reported by foreign policy-related committees are thought to be seldom successfully amended and great weight is placed by americanists on the role of the chairman as to the amount, nature and form of committee business. Nonetheless, Soviet scholarship has identified a reduced role for chairmen as a result of the internal reforms of the mid-1970s which, particularly in the House, made the chairman subject to election by the entire Democratic Party Caucus rather than selection by seniority consideration alone. This has created uncertainty insofar as chairmen cannot always "deliver" their committee for the executive branch on foreign policy agreements reached between the Administration and the chairmen. Americanists are accurate but ambivalent about the effects of this changing role for committee chairmen:

> The reduced authority of the committee chairmen is introducing a new element into the interrelations between the executive branch and Congress, particularly in the area of foreign policy-making. When the committee chairmen were omnipotent, it was precisely these men who constituted the link in the congressional structure to which the administration usually turned for advice on planned measures. After gaining their consent, the White House could expect support from the necessary committee and, consequently, from Congress. Consultations of this kind on questions of domestic policy and national security made it possible, incidentally, to avoid undesirable publicity. The new status

of the chairmen threatens the existing system of communication, and although
it is still in effect, it, on the one hand, is being criticized in the Congress,
and on the other, is losing much of its value to the administration, as feelings
of good will on the part of the chairmen are ceasing to signify automatic
support for the particular action by the committee and Congress.[53]

Attention is also given to the proliferation of subcommittees concerned
with foreign policy issues. Soviet scholars point out that subcommittees are
becoming more specialized and increasingly involved in legislation. They
also argue committees generally tend to support subcommittee recommendations, and subcommittees represent the particular link in the Congressional
structure "where three sides cooperate more effectively on each specific
issue—the legislators, the related subdivisions of the federal bureaucracy,
and the representatives of the capitol's interest groups."[54]

The fragmentation of foreign policy responsibilities across a number of
congressional committees has also attracted the attention of Soviet scholars.
The fragmentation is sometimes decried as creating conditions for deliberate
delay or postponement creating "a situation in which the Capitol is capable
of intervening in the plans of the White House and even subverting them."[55]
Moreover, the fragmentation of foreign policy powers is seen as creating
"numerous groups and grouplets of Senators and Congressmen which
frequently spring up on a temporary basis to satisfy the particular requirements
of separate monopoly groups, political groups or 'pressure groups'."[56] Members of Congress are criticized for their lack of organization which results
in a utilitarian, regional and narrowminded approach to various problems,
subordinating the national interest to parochial constituent interests to the
detriment of U.S. foreign policy.

The substantive description of the various committees of the Congress
is also quite impressive. Americanists tend to regard the Senate Foreign
Relations Committee, the House Foreign Affairs Committee and the Senate
and House Armed Services Committees as having the chief roles in the
legislative discussion of foreign policy and national security issues. The
Senate Foreign Relations Committee is considered the most influential, much
more so than the House counterpart, although the late Rep. Clement J.
Zablocki (D-Wisc.) is given credit for enhancing the activism of the House
Foreign Affairs Committee while chairman from 1977-83.

In general, americanists are divided on the relative substantive and
political strengths of the Senate Foreign Relations and House Foreign Affairs
Committees. Some argue that the House generally "has always been more
inclined than the Senate to make compromises and to concede to the
executive branch in foreign policy matters."[57] These Soviet scholars point
to the unique powers reserved to the Senate regarding treaties and the
confirmation of executive appointments as well as the Senate's activism
against the Vietnam War as proof of the Senate's relatively greater influence
in foreign policy.

The Senate is also seen by some as more capable of activism on foreign
policy because of the relatively loose party discipline and procedures for

debate and amendment in the Senate as compared to the House.[58] By contrast, other americanists see the House as more democratic, reflecting less-powerful elements of the bourgeoisie and, particularly during the Reagan Administration, the House's opposition to various elements of U.S. policy in Central America has been noted.[59]

The Senate and House Armed Services Committees are generally dismissed as "bodies which invariably support the Pentagon's demands for arms buildups."[60] National security policy is seen as largely framed in the executive branch and largely endorsed by the two committees. Committee members are supposedly not driven by the examination of major problems in national security or the determination of the total size of the defense budget, but rather how many dollars will be spent in their district. The Defense Department, in turn, "is not stingy in rendering every kind of service to the influential members of the committee when it needs their support."[61]

Americanists have also rightly identified the importance of the House and Senate Appropriations Committees in legislative consideration of foreign policy issues. The authorization process, which provides Presidential authority and policy guidelines for the use of the funds to carry out foreign policy programs, is followed by an appropriations process which actually funds the programs. Since the power of the purse is central to the relevance of Congress in foreign policy matters, americanists are accurate in describing the power and prestige of service on the Appropriations Committees, particularly the Defense and Foreign Operations subcommittees of both the House and the Senate committees. The autonomy of subcommittees of the Appropriations Committees make them "more independent and influential than other Congressional bodies on this same level."[62]

Americanists detail the many functions performed by the legislative process. The lengthy process of consideration of bills and resolutions in committee, and on the House and Senate floors, is analyzed. Also examined are House-Senate conferences that attempt to resolve differences between different versions of legislation passed by the House and Senate. Soviet scholars accurately point out that all of these steps must be accomplished under annual or biennial deadlines or legislative consideration begins again. Soviet scholars also describe the so-called "subjective factor" whereby seniority on committees builds experience and political influence for Members, culminating in their accesion to chairmanship. Former Senators William Fulbright (D-Ark.) and Jackson are cited as examples of this process, with conflicting effects on U.S.-Soviet relations.

Some americanists see an enduring Congressional activism in foreign policy stemming from its organizational structure. Legislators are described as "no longer satisfied with merely giving advice" and they "insist on playing a greater role in the development and implementation of government policy."[63] Indeed, as was detailed in the previous chapter, Soviet scholars detail Congressional use of appropriations power, amendments conditioning the use of foreign assistance upon performance of certain actions by the recipient, resolutions expressing Congressional sentiment, and other organizational tools to put its mark on a number of diverse issues. U.S. defense contributions to Western Europe, U.S.-Soviet relations in all of its aspects, the size and scope of the MX missile program, as well as the defense budget in general, aid to the contras in Nicaragua, military assistance to Latin America and CIA assistance to Angola, the size, scope and type of U.S. arms sales, U.S. policy towards South Korea, and human rights standards in the provision of foreign assistance have all been affected by Congress' involvement in foreign policy.

Moreover, americanists see several benefits deriving from Congress' organizational tools in foreign policy. First, public hearings, usually held at the outset of the legislative process, provide for criticism of imprudent executive branch proposals or revelations about executive mismanagement of foreign policy. The investigation of CIA activities by the House and Senate in the mid-1970s and the rejection or near rejection of unqualified Presidential appointments to foreign policy positions are viewed as significant examples of the importance of the hearing process.

The hearing process also enables new ideas and proposals to be discussed, alternatives pursued, and differences reconciled. Congress is thus seen by americanists as vital to the operation of the American political system because it possesses flexibility and adaptability and can "reflect changes taking place both in the international situation and inside the country."[64] Arms control proposals as well as changes in the fundamental assumptions in U.S. foreign policy have been cited as two primary examples of Congress as a sounding board for new foreign policy approaches.

Nonetheless, other Soviet scholars, particularly those writing in the late 1970s and 1980s, are negative about Congress' organizational tools and their effect on foreign policy. The committee system, the proliferation of subcommittees, and the decline of centralized authority are seen as producing delay and an excessive number of foreign policy figures in Congress with whom the Executive Branch has to deal. Committees also jealously guard foreign policy information from each other. Management problems for the President and Congressional leadership increase. The protracted debate over the Panama Canal Treaty in the Senate was cited as an example of how Congress' ability to destablize the conduct of foreign policy had become particularly and harmfully evident.

Some Soviet scholars have essentially come to the conclusion that Congress' organizational structure "gives rise to a tendency toward slowing down and obstructing any new foreign policy idea or initiative, regardless of whether it has originated in Congress or has come from the administration."[65] This makes Congress effective as an instrument for delay, but ineffective as a formulator or implementer of foreign policy initiatives. As one Soviet scholar told me, Congress is simply too awkward and complicated a body to implement foreign policy. In a startling juxtaposition considering where nearly all americanists stood in the early-to-mid 1970s, a decade later "the idea that the relative autonomy of the state from the ruling class is more fully embodied in the executive is fairly widespread among Soviet Americanists."[66]

*Analysis of Amerikanistika on the Organization of Congress
and Its Effects on Foreign Policy*

Amerikanistika on the organizational aspects of Congress and its effects on U.S. foreign policy has reached a high level of analytical quality. For the most part, Soviet scholars appear to have grasped the importance of organizational factors in legislative consideration of foreign policy issues, as well as the changes that have taken place in the organization of Congress that affect that consideration.

Nonetheless, there appears to be some confusion in the analysis of the relative importance of committees. It is certainly not the case that committee-passed foreign policy legislation is seldom subject to amendment. In fact, committee chairmen often have to accept scores of amendments on the floor of the House and in the Senate, some of which fundamentally transform the content of the committee-passed version. The role of the chairman of the committee is still an important and prestigious one, but his control over the scheduling of legislation in his committee is overrated by americanists.

For example, the decision to schedule a bill is often dictated by the House and Senate leadership or by the chairman's fellow Committee members who he must now consider with much greater respect and deference than was the case prior to the mid-1970s reforms, which subjected committee chairman to election by the majority caucus. Election of subcommittee chairmen, rather than by their selection by the chairman, as was the case before the reforms, also dilutes the chairman's power. In that regard, americanists are quite accurate in pointing to the diffusion of power in the Congress on foreign policy issues, resulting from a proliferation of independent subcommittees as well as the spread of shared jurisdiction of foreign policy matters across a number of committees.

Negative comments by Soviet scholars about the fragmentation of foreign policy responsibilities are echoed by American scholars. Congress has been described as more "parochial, personal, and divided than at any time since the Senate's refusal to give advice and consent for U.S. participation in the League of Nations."[67]

Both the Senate Foreign Relations Committee under Senators Church (1979-1981) and Percy (1981-1985) and the House Foreign Affairs Committee under Representative Zablocki (1977-1983) were often torn by intra-party and inter-party bickering. Under the Carter Administration, Chairman Zablocki often had to resort to voting with the Committee's Republicans against its Democrats to get foreign assistance legislation through the Committee. While less willing to pursue such a course, current chairman Dante B. Fascell (D-Fla.) has, particularly on the sensitive issue of aid to the anti-communist forces in Nicaragua, found himself in a distinct minority among committee Democrats. Chairman Fascell has, however, engaged in consensus building with both parties to increase the committee's influence on a variety of foreign policy issues. By contrast, the Senate Foreign Relations Committee has experienced successful challenges by other congressional committees to its once preeminent position and continuing concerns over the authority and effectiveness of its current chairman, Sen. Claiborne Pell (D-R.I.). With the ascension of the deeply conservative Jesse Helms (R-N.C.), as ranking minority member, dissension and ineffectiveness within the committee has grown.

The growth of foreign policy staff, not only on committees but on the staff of individual members as well, gives Members of Congress not only independent information on foreign policy but the motivation to be more active and, consequently, the ability to do so. As Congress moves into not only the making of foreign policy but also its conduct, many American scholars, like the Soviet americanists, see Congress as unduly complicating and frustrating foreign policy implementation.

Further compounding the problem of Congress' participation in foreign policy decisions are the questions of who should be included by the executive branch in prior consultations, whether any responsibility is conferred on members who are consulted, and the uncertainty that Party leaders can speak for or gain the support of both parties for a certain course of action they may agree to in consultations. As some American scholars have justly argued, Congress has supplied little evidence to show that it is "prepared to adapt its own organizational structure and internal procedures to the demands of an active foreign policy role its members are determined to play."[68]

Americanist discussions about the relative influence of the various foreign policy and national security committees of the Congress is interesting although uneven in quality. The Senate Foreign Relations and House Foreign Affairs Committees have moved increasingly closer in their level of influence in recent years as Representative Zablocki and Representative Fascell have continued a pattern of more active participation, while their counterparts Senators Church and Percy saw a decline in their influence and credibility as major legislation approved by the Senate Foreign Relations Committee under their chairmanship subsequently failed to be approved in the Senate. Both eventually suffered electoral defeat. Senator Lugar is perceived as having restored some influence to the Committee as a result of his ability to work closely with the Reagan Administration, while still preserving the Committee's institutional independence. This influence has apparently dissipated, however, with the Democractic takeover of the Senate in 1986.

In this regard, some americanists overrate the importance of the Senate's treaty-making power as evidence of the Senate's greater influence in foreign policy. The increasing resort by successive Presidents to the use of executive agreements for the conduct of major foreign policy initiatives has diluted the Senate's exclusive power concerning treaties. As U.S. overseas commitments have expanded through executive agreements, their implementation has involved greater use of the "power of the purse." In this case, the House has tended to dominate. Finally, with the onset of the Reagan Administration, which brought Republican control of the Senate, the major foreign policy controversies on arms control, U.S. policy in Central America, and U.S. relations with the now deposed Marcos government in the Philippines have led to the Democratic-controlled House being the forum for legislative action.

The portrayal by americanists of the House and Senate Armed Services Committee is quite simplistic. While it cannot be denied that the two Committees are generally more sympathetic to Defense Department funding requests than the full House or Senate, and have tended to oppose past U.S.-Soviet arms control agreements, amerikanistika overlooks serious efforts by the House Armed Services Committee under the chairmanship of Representative Aspin to explore the full range of national security policy issues. Aspin's, as well as Senator Nunn's and Cohen's, participation in the Scowcroft Commission report that led to continued MX funding in exchange for Reagan Administration revisions in its arms control positions will be discussed in Chapter 3. Additionally, both Committees have undertaken major efforts to reorganize and overhaul the Department of Defense, often over the opposition of the Reagan Administration. Thus, while constituent interests, including defense contracts, are a major factor of consideration for committee members, and membership turnover is low,[69] the notion that committee members conduct no oversight whatsoever on Pentagon spending or defense policy is simply wrong.

On the other hand, americanists are clearly correct in stressing the importance and influence of the House and Senate Appropriations Committees. Americanists have explicit understanding of the crucial difference between authorization and appropriation bills. This difference has become ever more critical as Congress has increasingly relied on the funding of foreign policy programs through an end of the year continuing resolution. This resolution, once a device for temporary extension of funds until a regular appropriation bill could be passed for the entire fiscal year, has in recent years in the field of foreign policy become a replacement for regular appropriations. This in turn has tended to circumvent the authorization process because the continuing resolution is not subject to the prohibition contained in the rules of the House of Representatives on the use of legislative provisions in an appropriation bill.

Thus, while the authorization legislation for many foreign policy programs controlled by the House and the Senate foreign policy committees in the past set the overall policy guidelines for the conduct of programs, that role is increasingly falling to the Appropriations Committees as a result of the frequent use of the continuing resolution to fund foreign policy programs. The Reagan Administration has also acquiesced in the process, believing it is less likely to get legislative restrictions from the budget-conscious Appropriations Committee members than from the policy-conscious members of the authorizing committees, particularly in the House.

The descriptions of the many functions of the legislative process and their effects on U.S. foreign policy are also impressive and consistent with American scholarly treatments of this subject. The often tortuous procedural path a bill must travel for enactment, the positive effects of seniority on a legislator's foreign policy experience and perspective, and the likelihood that a high degree of legislative activism in foreign policy may be enduring, have been thoroughly described by both americanists and American scholars. In addition, the range of foreign policy issues in which Congress has made its mark, the importance of legislative oversight in uncovering mismanagement as well as developing policy alternatives, and the ability of Congress to reflect new trends in public opinion and incorporate them into the making and conduct of foreign policy—these are all aspects of legislative foreign policymaking that both Soviet and American scholars develop effectively.[70] As such, amerikanistika on the organization of Congress and its effects on U.S. foreign policy demonstrates a relatively high level of quality, and is accompanied by thoughtful, substantive disagreements among scholars over various aspects of the phenomena under study.

Pressure Groups and Their Effects on
Congress' Role in Foreign Policy

Americanist Perspective

Americanists have devoted considerable attention to pressure groups and their ability to influence Congressional decisions on foreign policy issues. Here, as in other process and procedural issues, Soviet scholars are divided over the importance and effect of such pressure groups for the functioning of U.S. foreign policy.

Some Soviet americanists tend to see mass protest movements (the anti-war movement, the nuclear freeze movement) as responsible for greater shifts towards more liberal influence in legislative foreign policymaking.[71] Others deny that such trends have fundamental significance for the operation of U.S. foreign policy. They argue that the liberal and subsequently conservative shifts are largely a "feedback mechanism" reflecting "the state of opinion among select ruling class groups."[72] Soviet scholars argue that these shifts of opinion help to provide balance and flexibility for the capitalist establishment and the organs of the government doing its bidding. These shifts of opinion in Congress have even been explained as a smokescreen for "the political interests of the ruling class, which does not cease depicting the representative organ as a stronghold of democracy."[73]

There also appears to be a division of opinion among americanists about the relative influence of public opinion on Congress' actions in foreign policy. Here again, some point to the popular dissatisfaction with Vietnam and later, with the Reagan Administration's arms control policy as cases where public opinion appeared to have made a difference. Public opinion is even credited by some Soviet scholars with legislative determination to "restore all of the constitutional prerogatives in the area of foreign policy that had been lost, or in some cases voluntarily turned over to the Administration."[74]

Other americanists have a different perspective of American public opinion, pointing out that in the 1980s "gigantic arms spending and crusading anti-

Sovietism were supported by the average American, who twice put the current President in the White House."[75] They also point out that such support is limited however, "on condition that this course does not hit the American public too hard in the pocket,"[76] and that there are limits to popular anti-Sovietism.

The ultimate leverage of all pressure groups and the general public against Members of Congress—the threat of electoral defeat—is also acknowledged. Legislative districts, for example, have been analyzed for their demographic profiles as a means of explaining the positions of individual legislators on foreign policy issues.[77] As has already been noted in the discussion of the effects of the two-party system, americanists acknowledge the fact that the more a foreign policy issue affects the economic or political interests of a powerful element of a Member's constituency, the less likely he is to support his party leadership or the President who may be taking an opposing position. Elections are also seen as "not merely a method of determining trends and problems and creating the necessary political coalitions, but they are also a referendum for the elucidation of positions on the Administration policy and presidential performance."[78]

Despite these acknowledgements of an "electoral factor" and even some degree of "representativeness" in Congress' views and actions on foreign policy issues, elections are by no means viewed by americanists in fully positive terms. Frequent elections are thought to lead to incrementalism as legislators "play a waiting game and refuse to make far-reaching decisions."[79] Because of election considerations, members are vulnerable to local business interests, particularly defense contractors, leading to a situation where elections produce anti-Soviet rhetoric and anti-Soviet political positions on foreign policy issues. As such, "Congress always has the potential to become an instrument for counteracting realistic steps toward detente and the improvement of Soviet-American relations."[80] Elections are also seen as producing an enduring inconsistency in the direction of U.S. foreign policy, and Congress' role in its formulation and implementation. A candidate who takes a "hardline" against the Soviet Union in order to get elected finds that a return to a more "rational approach" is not possible and the Member is "imprisoned for a long time by his own propaganda images."[81]

The primary foreign policy pressure groups are looked on by Soviet scholars with almost universal disdain. The most attention is directed toward the "military industrial complex." After a period when public opinion and a series of more liberal Congresses slowed the growth of defense spending, defense spending advocates have been seen as having regained their political strength. Defense lobbyists, as well as some Department of Defense officials and defense think tank analysts, are invariably viewed as "opponents of detente" and promulgators of the mythical Soviet threat. Their influence on the House and the Senate Armed Services Committees as described by americanists has already been discussed. The use of the Soviet threat to gain defense spending increases is detailed thoroughly as is the crucial link between jobs for local districts and support for defense spending. The influence of the defense lobby is deeply respected in amerikanistika as "one of the main centers in the American political process . . . (which) serves as an important means of directly influencing the nation's foreign policy."[82]

The so-called ethnic foreign policy pressure groups are also thoroughly examined. The 'Zionist lobby' attracts the most attention. It is credited with holding influential positions in the media, as being active and influential in the electoral process well beyond its numbers and being responsible for making domestic consideration preeminent in the formulation of U.S. policy in the Middle East.[83] Pro-Israel pressure groups are castigated for their role in noisy human rights campaigns and more significantly in the passage of the Jackson-Vanik amendment. They are also criticized for their coalition with the defense lobby against detente. The 'Zionist lobby' is considered so powerful that "the Israeli government actually conducts its policy on two levels in its relations with Washington, dealing with the executive branch and with an invariably friendly Congress."[84] Still, americanists have noted that this lobby was unsuccessful in stopping major arms sales to Saudi Arabia in 1978 and 1981, a sign of "increasing aspirations in American ruling circles to escape the 'unnecessary' dependence on their Israeli client."[85]

Other ethnic lobbies cited for their influence in amerikanistika include the so-called "Greek lobby", which is given much credit for the imposition of a U.S. arms embargo against Turkey in 1974 after that country's invasion of Cyprus, as well as Eastern European ethnic lobbies. In the case of the latter, some credit is given for their role in increasing funds for Radio Free Europe (RFE) and Radio Liberty (RL). They are derisively "credited" with "much more modest forms of support from Members of Congress—public statements of sympathy for their position, presentation of the proper speeches, or at the most, the adoption of non-binding or symbolic resolutions."[86] As a result, members of Congress are generically accused of "paying a cheap price for election support from the emigrant organizations, as he himself is quite aware of the demagogic and unproductive nature of this kind of symbolic declaration."[87]

While not a classic pressure group as such, the executive branch and some of its more political methods of influencing legislative actions on foreign policy issues have drawn the attention of americanists. The so-called "whirlpools of interest" identified in American political science literature between the executive branch, individual Members of Congress or Congressional committees as a whole, and private industry and their representatives has been outlined in amerikanistika, particularly in the field of defense policy, where this triangle of interests help fulfill economic benefits for defense industry representatives and political benefits for legislators.

The determination of President Reagan to avoid the poor relations between the executive and legislative branches on foreign policy matters which existed under the Carter Administration is also discussed in amerikanistika. Political promises to build hospitals, power plants, etc, in exchange for foreign policy support has been chronicled in the case of the sale of AWACS to Saudi Arabia. The use of Presidential phone calls as well as "influential political and public spokesmen, retired officials, personal friends of legislators, the mass media and even the Congressman's constituents"[88] to get Congressional support has been fully analyzed. Promises or the threat of withholding Presidential support for reelection to gain support or silence on foreign policy issues has also been described. The escalating amount of attention and persuasion needed to get legislative approval of foreign policy initiatives by the President is sometimes cited as proving the increasingly unwieldy nature of U.S. foreign policy institutions, which are seen as less able to deal with complex foreign policy challenges and problems.

Analysis of Amerikanistika on Pressure Groups and Congress' Role in Foreign Policy

American scholars are divided on the effects of pressure groups on Congress' actions in foreign policy, so we should not be surprised that americanists are divided on this issue. No one denies that the unpopularity of the Vietnam War spurred legislative action leading to the withdrawal of American commitments. Similarly, growing public fears about nuclear war helped to give rise to the nuclear freeze movement and subsequent Congressional consideration of nuclear freeze resolutions.

Nonetheless, the enduring effect of pressure group activity is highly variable. An event like Vietnam which aroused public opinion to an unprecedented degree and ushered in a new era of legislative activism in foreign policy is rare. By contrast, the nuclear freeze movement had far less impact. It may have helped create an enduring deeper consciousness about arms control issues in Congress, but its immediate results were minimal as indicated by the fact that shortly after the House passed a nuclear freeze resolution supported by the nuclear freeze movement, it supported additional funding for the MX missile program. Americanists are therefore perceptive in noting this type of balancing or flexibility, although they tend to portray it as ruling class hypocrisy. In any event, according to Soviet scholars, with the exception of Vietnam, the natural tendency of Congress is to compromise, paper over or blunt a definite direction foreign policy pressure groups or public opinion would like it to take. Giving a little something to everyone and reducing acrimony and contradiction is the norm.

Equally perceptive are the different characterizations of public opinion by the americanists. The American public, at least as indicated through opinion polls, tend to want both arms control and a "get tough" policy toward the Soviet Union. Concerns about "throwing money at defense" are combined with a defense adequate to "stand up to the Russians." Achieving strength and power in foreign policy is combined with an attitude of minimal personal sacrifice. As Soviet scholarship has realized, it is easy to understand Congress' flexibility on foreign policy issues when viewed in light of these contradictory popular sentiments.

The effect of foreign policy issues on congressional elections is also a controversial and easily misunderstood subject. A full discussion of the subject is beyond the purview of this study. Nonetheless, americanists are accurate in arguing that the state of a President's popularity has a significant effect on congressional elections. For example, American scholars have argued that in marginal swing districts, general voter awareness of congressional legislative activities is low and "national swings in the congressional vote are normally judgments on what the President is doing (or thought to be doing), rather than on what the Congress is doing."[89]

Americanists are also accurate in pointing to demographics as a critical factor in determining foreign policy perspectives. Large or vocal constituencies of one kind or another play an unmistakable role in influencing a Member's position on foreign policy issues. These constituencies influence Congress' foreign policy decisionmaking in several ways. Campaign contributions, or the threat of contributions to one's opponent, are the most direct means. But the picture is more complex than this. American scholars have pointed out that the existence of a defense, arms control, ethnic or other foreign policy oriented constituency will influence a legislator's position due to adherence to the principle that politicians generally get elected and re-elected by not offending people, particularly vocal, well-organized groups. Thus, direct political influence tends to be multiplied by the 'don't offend' principle. Legislators with large foreign policy constituencies may internalize arguments sympathetic to such constituencies and anticipate their positions in advance, furthering their influence as a result. Finally, legislators may be a product of the constituencies themselves or may simply believe in their positions without resort to political pressure.

The negative effects of foreign policy pressure groups on the making and conduct of foreign policy noted by Soviet scholars have their echoes in American scholarship on the subject. The unpopularity of the Panama Canal Treaties undoubtedly slowed Senate and House consideration and produced legislative reservations and conditions that on occasion very nearly led to Panamanian repudiation of the original agreements with the United States.[90] Similarly, defense constituencies have often opposed U.S.-Soviet arms control agreements and have helped to shape a general consensus among politicians that pushing detente does little for their political health. "Standing up to the Soviet Union" is a much more sensible political defense, although one must add Soviet foreign policy actions immeasurably contribute to this perception. Americanists are also on track on the negative consequences of hardline anti-Soviet campaign rhetoric, which is subsequently withdrawn in policy practice. President Carter, for example, repudiated the Vladivostok framework, then wound up returning to it as the basis for negotiating SALT II. President Reagan bitterly attacked the SALT II agreement as "fatally flawed" then wound up abiding by its terms for several years on an informal basis. In the process, years of negotiating time were lost.

Soviet discussion of specific foreign policy pressure groups is somewhat overblown and too often polemical. While defense contractors and their lobbying groups undoubtedly support increased defense spending and have high threat perceptions of the Soviet Union, the commitment to a "strong national defense" extends beyond lobbying pressure and is an article of faith for legislators of both parties. Even legislators who oppose a variety of controversial weapons (e.g. the B-1 bomber, the MX missile, binary chemical weapons) will support defense legislation when amendments are completed and the bill reaches final passage. Moreover, political action committees on defense and foreign policy issues also now include liberal groups strongly supportive of arms control, thus creating counter-pressures on members who may be in marginal districts and are undecided on showdown votes on major weapons.[91]

The description of the Israeli lobby is also somewhat simplistic. The power of this lobby cannot be denied and its chief lobbying organization, the American Israel Public Affairs Committee (AIPAC), has helped to make domestic considerations a major factor in U.S. policy in the Middle East. Americanists are accurate in arguing that a recalcitrant executive branch can often be brought into line to support Israel by that country's influence with the Congress. Congress clearly is the most pro-Israeli institution involved in the formulation of U.S. policy in the Middle East.

Furthermore, pro-Israeli sentiments are clearly exaggerated with respect to the number of Jews in the United States. The pro-Israel lobby "gets its' strength not so much from its numbers, as from its money, from the depth of its feelings, from the local prominence of some of its leading members, and from its broad base of support in public opinion."[92]

It is also true that the issue of human rights, particularly the repression of Soviet Jews has brought liberals and conservatives together in a manner disadvantageous to Soviet interests. Senate sources have also tended to confirm that, for example, passage of the Jackson-Vanik amendment was due in large part to lobby pressures and the "don't offend" principle described earlier.[93]

But there are several reasons for Congress' strong support of Israel, and lobbying and political pressure is only one of those reasons. Personal convictions in support of Israel among members of Congress is another reason. These convictions stem from the Jewish background of some Members, the experience of the Nazi holocaust and the perception that U.S. national interests are served by close relations with Israel. Many Members see Israel as a remarkably successful liberal democratic state which has survived despite hostile Arab neighbors aligned with the Soviet Union Support for the emigration of Soviet Jewry has doubtless been amplified by Soviet human rights practices which clearly regulated the flow of emigration for political purposes and engaged in a consistent pattern of harassment of Jews wishing to leave the Soviet Union. Harassment has extended from job firings to imprisonment and torture.

Finally the use of the term "Zionist lobby" by americanists is highly pejorative. Not all Jews are Zionists nor are all Zionists Jews. Zionism is a political movement which seeks to protect and sustain the idea and reality of a Jewish state. The fact that Zionist has become a buzzword for anti-Semitic polemics further calls into question the intellectual quality of amerikanistika on this issue.

The relatively brief treatment of the Greek lobby by americanists is perhaps an interesting indication of Soviet perceptions of the lobby's political decline. For example, pro-Greek lobbying groups were unable to prevent the Congress' reversal in 1978 of the arms embargo imposed against Turkey in 1974. Nonetheless, Congress' insistence on preserving the 7-10 ratio on military assistance to Greece and Turkey must be considered evidence of the continuing influence of the Greek lobby.

Americanists are, on balance, accurate in their dismal assessment of the influence of East European lobby groups. Funding for RFE and RL has been generally supported on a bipartisan basis without much need for intense lobbying. Beyond this, however, Congress' actions, outside the context of the Commission on Security and Cooperation in Europe, has been largely in the field of hortatory resolutions condemning actions taken by East European governments, most notably the imposition of martial law in Poland. An Ad Hoc Committee on the Baltic Republics that seeks to maintain the U.S. policy of non-recognition of the Soviet annexation of Latvia, Lithuania, and Estonia in 1940 has also been active. Americanists ascribe such actions by members as an effort to humor emigre organizations. It is more accurate to state that "campaign rhetoric has generally had little relationship to policies carried out by either party once in power."[94] U.S. ability to influence events in a manner consistent with the goals of East European ethnic groups is usually not possible and the influence of these groups is limited by the fact that only a small percentage of East European Americans vote primarily on the basis of "foreign policy platforms and that among organizations actively concerned with policy toward Eastern Europe there is, at times, considerable rivalry and little unity of purpose."[95]

Soviet scholars have demonstrated a thorough understanding of the role of the executive branch as a pressure group regarding Congress' actions in foreign policy. The triangular relationship between defense contractors, the Pentagon bureaucracy, and members of Congress that often drives legislative decisions on defense spending, is well documented and Soviet scholars have grasped its essence, signifcance and effects on U.S. foreign policy rather well.

The americanist perception that executive-legislative relations under the Carter Administration were strained on foreign policy, as well as domestic policy, is generally shared by American scholars. The refusal of that administration to deal with members on bread and butter constituency issues, the use of appeals to the American people over the heads of Congress, the failure to consult on key issues even with the Democratic leadership, the refusal to provide various representational and personal amenities, and the refusal to engage in horsetrading and compromise took their toll on foreign policy issues. As such, Carter's legislative victories on lifting the arms embargo to Turkey and the sale of F-15s to Saudi Arabia took place over the objections of a majority of Democrats in both houses on Congress. The Reagan Administration has corrected most of these lobbying mistakes, as americanists have noted.

Americanists also accurately describe the use of other Presidential lobbying techniques. Personal phone calls before and after votes, the use of local officials in a member's state or district, the use of interest groups and local media to support the President's position, influential public or private officials, mass mail or phone banks and other devices are identified by both Soviet and American scholars.

Still, the americanists are also correct in stating that as fragmentation of foreign policy responsibilities in Congress developed, so did the time and effort the executive branch must dedicate to lobbying Congress. This has sometimes led to an overload in lobbying circuitry that has contributed to Presidential defeats on foreign policy issues. As has already been mentioned, the intense lobbying during Senate consideration of the Panama Canal Treaties led to the lessened effectiveness of lobbying for the SALT II Treaty. Reagan's intense lobbying for the MX missile in 1982, 1983, and 1984 left little time to prevent defeat of funds for binary chemical weapons production considered in the same legislation. Lobbying for funding for the contras in Nicaragua diluted White House efforts to defeat a House-passed resolution supportive of U.S.-Soviet comprehensive test ban negotiations. Thus, we see an identification of an "overload factor" which sometimes works to Congress' advantage in rejecting executive branch foreign policy initiatives.

Constitutional Responsibilities Concerning War Powers and Treaties and Their Effect on Foreign Policy

Americanist Perspective

The War Powers Resolution, enacted into law over President Nixon's veto in November 1973, was one of the clear signals to americanists that Congress was becoming resurgent in the field of foreign policy. Prior to this time, Congress had been criticized for allowing the the President as Commander-in-Chief to repel military force without congressional approval. This acquiescence helped to "open up a broad opportunity for the President to evade the rights of Congress in connection with the declaration of war."[96] Now, in the aftermath of the War Powers Resolution, americanists view its enactment as representing an "important political shift in the country as a whole and within its highest legislative body in particular."[97]

Americanists carefully trace the development of the war powers controversy created by the Constitution, which provides the President with authority as Commander-in-Chief to conduct war while giving Congress the authority to declare war as well as determine whether there was just cause for such a declaration. The accumulation of executive power in the war powers field is also described. Americanists trace how the originally recognized right of the President to repel sudden attacks on the United States without Congressional approval was unilaterally extended by Presidents to include protection of American citizens and property, troops stationed abroad and even foreign policy and national security interests generally.

Soviet scholars also trace the long legislative gestation of the War Powers Resolution from 1970-1973, which originated in the House as a simple requirement for a Presidential report to Congress before sending troops abroad, and culminated in a final text of the Resolution which required specific Congressional approval of any commitment of troops into conflict no more than 60-90 days after their initial deployment by the President. The role of key Senate and House leaders in the development of the Resolution is detailed, including Rep. Zablocki and Senator Jacob Javits (R-NY), John Stennis (D-Miss.), Thomas Eagleton (D-Mo.), and others. Amerikanistika contemporary with the passage of the Resolution called it "an additional push toward continuing to struggle for strengthening (Congressional) influence in determining the nation's foreign and military policy," and "almost the equivalent of a constitutional amendment in importance."[98]

Subsequently, some of the enthusiasm among americanists for the significance of the War Powers Resolution has died down. It is pointed out, for example, that "the executive branch is attempting to free itself even of those formal limitations for presidential conducting of undeclared wars which the law imposes upon him," and that the Resolution "allows fairly broad presidential use of armed force, without a congressional declaration of war."[99] When Congress and the President reached agreement in 1983 on the invocation of the terms of the War Powers Resolution to allow U.S. Marines to remain in Lebanon for 18 months as part of a multinational peacekeeping force in support of the Amin Gemayel government, americanists were disappointed that the agreement represented "capitulation with insignificant and even nonexistent concessions by the President."[100] Some Soviet scholars saw hope that although Congress supported the President's decision to send troops into Lebanon, it enforced the War Powers Resolution and strengthened its prerogatives and legal position. Most, however, saw the Lebanon crisis as "the first serious test of the effectiveness of this law, and it did not pass the test."[101]

Americanists have also analyzed the importance of treaties and executive agreements and Congress' role in their formulation and implementation. The use of executive agreements as a means of conducting foreign policy without the constitutional procedure for two-thirds approval in the Senate required for treaties has attracted considerable attention.

For example, these agreements have been viewed as having "strengthened the President's foreign policy powers by imparting to him functions which in their content may in certain cases go beyond the limits allowed by the Constitution."[102] Americanists trace the historical evolution of the increasing use of such agreements because of the often protracted Senate delays in the consideration of treaties, and the various types of such agreements (those concluded with or without Congressional consultation and/or approval and those concluded pursuant to broad legislative grants of authority to the President). The scope and subject matter of agreements are also thoroughly analyzed by Soviet scholars. In particular, americanists take great pains to point out that executive agreements, from the standpoint of international law, have the same legal effect as do treaties. However, concern for this maxim of international law, which is consistent with the traditional interpretation of the identically-binding nature of treaties and international agreements under international law, may also reflect apprehension that Congressional activism might seek to undo a plethora of U.S.-Soviet agreements across a broad spectrum of issues. Most of these agreements were concluded as executive agreements without formal Congressional approval.

Congressional efforts to require legislative approval of executive agreements, efforts which came from the conservative right in the 1950s and the liberal left in the 1970s have been identified. The major effort by the Senate in the late 1960s to identify the scope of the executive agreements never approved or even notified to Congress is detailed. Finally, the subsequent enactment of the 1972 Case-Zablocki Act (named for Senator Clifford Case (R-NJ) and Rep. Zablocki) which required Congressional notification of all executive agreements 60 days after their conclusion is approvingly described in amerikanitika as "the first successful congressional action aimed at the restoration of its foreign policy prerogatives."[103]

Analysis of Amerikanistika on Constitutional Responsibilities Concerning War Powers, Treaties, and Executive Agreements and Their Effect on Foreign Policy

Amerikanistika on war powers, treaties, and executive agreements and the effects of joint executive-legislative reponsibilities in these areas is straightforward and non-polemical. No one can deny that the enactment of the War Powers Resolution in 1973, particularly over the veto of President Nixon, represented and still represents one of the clearest manifestations of renewed legislative activism in foreign policy. The tracing of the legislative history of the Resolution is remarkably accurate, both in terms of the key institutional actors and the course of deliberations in the House, Senate, and House-Senate conference. There is also no question, as americanists have pointed out, that the public pressure emanating from the undeclared and unpopular Vietnam war was a catalyst for its original consideration and enactment. It should be noted, however, that americanists fail to analyze the crucial political compromise the Resolution represented between legislators who opposed the Vietnam War and those that still supported a U.S. commitment. Because both could agree that undeclared wars without congressional approval should not be repeated, the Resolution thus had bipartisan, cross-factional appeal.

Diminished enthusiasm of americanists for the Resolution since its passage is shared by some American scholars. The failure of successive Presidents to consult with Congress before U.S. forces have been committed into hostilities or imminent involvement in hostilities is clear. Presidents have also singularly refused to report under the section of the legislation which triggers legislative approval of commitments of troops beyond a 60-90 day period. Reports of U.S. actions have been superficial and have been phrased in terms of "taking note of the War Powers Resolution" rather than pursuant to the relevant section. This approach avoids legislative review and Congressional approval of long-term troop commitments.

Finally, when the War Powers Resolution was triggered in the case of the U.S. troop commitment in Lebanon, it was agreed to by Congress (as is permitted under the provisions of the Resolution) in exchange for an 18-month authorization of the presence in Lebanon which the President desperately wanted. In his signing statement on the Lebanon War Powers Resolution, the President disassociated himself from the provision triggering legislative approval, because, in his view, it was inconsistent with his constitutional reponsibility as Commander-in-Chief. To americanists, this demonstrated that Congress had gotten meaningless concessions for agreeing to a commitment of troops in Lebanon and that the War Powers Resolution had failed its first major test.

However, supporters of the War Powers Resolution have argued that while Presidential implementation of the Resolution has been spotty, its very existence as well as executive branch procedures to comply with its terms, has had a deterrent effect on the willingness of Presidents to use military force to advance foreign policy objectives. One Soviet scholar, in a distinct minority among his colleagues, acknowledged this to me when he succinctly stated that not every law needs to be implemented fully to be effective. Supporters of the Resolution also argue that since enactment of the Resolution, nearly all use of force by the President relevant to the Resolution's terms have been politically popular (e.g. the rescue of the Mayaguez from Cambodia, the effort to free the American hostages in Iran, or the response to Libyan attacks on U.S. forces in the Mediterranean). They have also been concluded well within the 60-90 day period before legislative approval would be required, "making demands for compliance seem trivial and nitpicking."[104] In the Lebanon case where the U.S. presence was an extended one, and the President clearly did not want the Resolution to be implemented, Congress prevailed. The President's signature on war powers legislation "speaks for itself and represents a grudging but richer acceptance of the reality of the Resolution that previously had not existed in the executive branch."[105]

Moreover, the 18-month authorization in Lebanon granted to the President limited the functions and numbers of U.S. troops, fully affirmed the right of Congress to remove the troops at any time and required further congressional approval for any substantial expansion of U.S. military activities. Thus, the legislation applying the War Powers Resolution to Lebanon gave Congress far greater control of U.S. military operations than it would have had if it simply let the President conduct the Lebanon operation without congressional approval. Furthermore, for those who opposed the measure, the Lebanon War Powers Resolution provided a properly ordered legislative platform for opposition to the continued presence of United States troops in Lebanon. This opposition did in fact take place, providing evidence for the minority of americanists that saw the Resolution's implementation in the Lebanon case as a future expansion of the legislative prerogative in the war powers area.

With respect to executive agreements, Soviet scholars are undeniably correct that the numbers of executive agreements have grown tremendously during the postwar period and their use in lieu of treaties requiring Senate approval is also quite evident. A 1984 Library of Congress study found that since 1939, the number of executive agreements increased by more than tenfold and more than 90% of the international agreements concluded were executive agreements.[106]

The discussion of types of executive agreements, as well as the history of legislative efforts to regulate their use is also accurate. Such efforts began in the 1950s when the Senate sought a constitutional amendment giving Congress the power to approve all executive agreements other than treaties. In 1969 the Senate passed the National Commitments Resolution expressing the sense of the Senate that a U.S. national commitment should result "only from affirmative action taken by the executive and legislative branches of the United States Government by means of a treaty, statute, or concurrent resolution of both houses of Congress specifically providing for such commitment." In 1972, the Case-Zablocki Act was enacted into law and has been subsequently amended to clarify and expand what constitutes an executive agreement. Further efforts to allow a legislative veto of executive agreements failed.

Prior to passage of the Case-Zablocki Act, the americanist argument, that executive agreements had become extraconstitutional if not unconstitutional also reflects a body of thought among international legal scholars that such agreements violate the spirit of the Constitution which sought to make the implementation of treaties more difficult than legislation. On the other hand, the somewhat contradictory argument among some americanists that from the standpoint of international law executive agreements and treaties are equally binding is also accurate.

Overall Assessment of Amerikanistika on Process and Procedural Issues

This chapter has revealed some interesting insights and theoretical implications concerning Soviet foreign policy. On balance, amerikanistika on Congress concerning process and procedural issues in U.S. foreign policy demonstrates political awareness, ideological pragmatism, and intellectual quality. This evaluation generally holds for amerikanistika on all five of the process and procedural issues discussed in this chapter.

However, on three issues, the separation of powers, the two-party system, and pressure groups, other tendencies are present. For example, in some cases actions taken by the Congress are evaluated in terms of their negative or positive effects on the Soviet Union, thereby reducing the ability to examine phenomena more fully. There also appears to be conceptual difficulties in understanding the genuine significance of the separation of powers and the two party system in evaluating foreign policy outcomes. To further develop these conclusions, the following chapter will shift its focus to an analysis of case studies, by individual or groups of americanists engaged in studying Congress' role in contemporary foreign policy issues.

Notes

1. For further information on the internal political struggle to establish political science as a separate social science discipline in the Soviet Union, see Malcolm, pp. 5-12.

2. Oded Eran, *The Mezhdunarodniki*, (Ramat Gan, Israel: Turtledove Publishing, 1979), pp. 31-59, and United States International Communication Agency, *Soviet Research Institutes Project*, 3 vols. by Blair A. Ruble, Research Report No. R-5-81, (February 1981) 1: 396-397.

3. V. Lan, *Klassy i partii v SShA: Ocherki po ekonomicheskoi i politicheskoi istorii SShA*, Moscow: 1937, cited in Richard M. Mills, "One Theory in Search of Reality: The Development of United States Studies in the Soviet Union," *Political Science Quarterly* LXXXVII, (March 1972): 66.

4. Mills, p. 69.

5. Malcolm, pp. 7-8.

6. Ibid., p. 120.

7. Schwartz, p. 57.

8. Paula Stern, *Water's Edge: Domestic Politics and the Making of American Foreign Policy*, (Westport, Conn: Greenwood Press, 1979), p. 209. This book is without a doubt the finest and most definitive scholarly work on history of the Jackson-Vanik amendment.

9. See Malcolm's chapter 4 footnotes, pp. 192-199, particularly footnote 4.

10. Iu. I. Nyporko, *Constitutional Interrelationships between the President and the U.S. Congress in the Area of Foreign Policy*, May, 1980, FBIS, L-9112, p. 8.

11. Iu. A. Ivanov, "Congress: Labyrinths of Power and Foreign Policy-Making," trans. Joint Publications Research Service, *USSR Report, USA: Economics, Politics, Ideology*, 71548, (June 1978): 101.

12. S.B. Cherverikov, *Kto i kak delayet politiku SShA?* (Moscow: Mezhdunarodnye otnosheniia, 1974), pp. 20-21.

13. Ivanov, p. 100.

14. For example, Nyporko writes: "it should be noted that the intensified conflict between legislative and executive power in the sixties was connected also with the intesified disorder in the ruling circles of the nation which arose in connection with the expensive venture in Vietnam . . . In foreign policy, the President, naturally, strives toward the 'maximum possible'—to ensure support from both parties for himself since the issue is in the interests of the entire nation." (Nyporko, pp. 81-82). For another adherent to the idea of executive dominance in foreign policy, see A.A. Mishin, *Gosudarstvennoe pravo SShA* (Moscow: Nauka, 1976).

15. V.A. Savel'ev, "The President and Congress in an Election Year," trans. Joint Publications Research Service, *USSR Report, USA: Economics, Politics, Ideology* 80-011 (August 1984): 1-14.

16. T.N. Iudina, "'Congress Factor' in U.S. Foreign Policy in the 1970s," trans. Joint Publications Research Service, *USSR Report, USA: Economics, Politics, Ideology* 7118 (April 1978): 56-61.

17. V.A. Savel'ev, *SShA: senat i politika* (Moscow: Mysl', 1976), pp. 167-168.

18. E.I. Popova, *Amerikanskii senat i vneshniaia politika 1969-1974* (Moscow: Nauka, 1978); also see A.K. Kislov and N.V. Osipova "Obsuzhdenie Sinaiskogo soglasheniia," *SShA: Ekonomika, politika, ideologiia* (December 1975): 75; N.I. Pakhomov, "Trezvyi

podkhod," *SShA: Ekonomika, politika, ideologiia* (April 1976): 66-69; and Savel'ev, *Senat i politika*, pp. 135-142.

19. Iu A. Ivanov, "The Honeymoon and After (Congress and the President in 1981,)" trans. Joint Publications Research Service, *USSR Report, USA: Economics, Politics, Ideology* 80743, (February 1982): 68.

20. V.A. Savel'ev "Sluzhebnyi apparat kongressa," *SShA: Ekonomika, politika, ideologiia* (March 1976): 122-127. Also see "Informatsionno Analiticheskii sluzhbi Kongressa" *SShA: Ekonomika, politika, ideologiia* (April, 1987): 112-115.

21. V.A. Savel'ev, "Zakonodatel'noe veto," *SShA: Ekonomika, politika, ideologiia* (March 1979): 119-125.

22. Iudina, p. 63.

23. Ibid., p. 64.

24. G.A. Arbatov, director of ISKAN, quoted in Malcolm, p. 138.

25. Malcolm, p. 148.

26. See for example, Cecil V. Crabb, Jr. and Pat M. Holt, *Invitation to Struggle: Congress, the President, and Foreign Policy* (Washington: Congressional Quarterly Press, 1980), pp. 37-56.

27. Ibid., p. 53.

28. Thomas E. Cronin, "A Resurgent Congress and the Imperial Presidency," in *Perspectives on American Foreign Policy*, eds. Charles W. Kegley and Eugene R. Wittkopf (New York: St. Martin's Press, 1983), p. 326.

29. I.M. Destler, "Trade Consensus, SALT Stalemate: Congress and Foreign Policy in the 1970s," in *The New Congress*, eds. Thomas E. Mann and Norman J. Ornstein (Washington: American Enterprise Institute, 1981), p. 355.

30. Crabb and Holt, p. 208.

31. The so-called Chadha decision in 1983 by the Supreme Court ruled that legislative resolutions, which seek to deny individual uses of authority granted to the President in enacted legislation, violate the presentment clause of the Constitution. This decision, according to a Library of Congress researcher, has swept away "an instrument of legislative oversight that has been applied over the past 50 years to virtually every field of governmental concern including foreign affairs and war powers." The court ignored the reality that many individual laws would never have become laws without the compromise mechanism of the legislative veto, which enabled the President broad exercises of legislatively-conferred authority while giving Congress the right to object to individual exercises of that authority. For further information see U.S. Congress, House, Committee on Foreign Affairs, *The U.S. Supreme Court Decision Concerning the Legislative Veto*, Hearings. 98th Cong., 1st Sess., 1983; for a Soviet perspective on the Chadha decision see A.A. Mishin, "Legal Relations Between the President and the Congress," trans. Joint Publications Research Service, *USSR Report, USA: Economics, Politics, Ideology* 84-012 (February 1982): 53-57.

32. G.A. Trofimenko, "Too Many Negotiators," *The New York Times*, 13 July 1979.

33. For analysis of the 1978, 1980, 1982, and 1986 elections see V.P. Zolotukhin and V.A. Linnik, "Congress After the Elections" trans. Joint Publications Research Service, *USSR Report, USA: Economics, Politics, Ideology* 73015 (February 1979): 65-70: E.M. Silaeva "The Congress After the Elections," trans. Joint Publications Research Service, *USSR Report, USA: Economics, Politics, Ideology* 77507 (January 1981): 34-46; V.O. Pechatanov, "Midterm Elections: Results and Prospects," trans. Joint Publications Research Service, *USSR Report, USA: Economics, Politics, Ideology* 83559 (January 1983): 21-30, and E.M. Verem'eva, "Kongress i belyii dom," *SShA: Ekonomika, politika, ideologiia* (October 1987): 74-78.

34. V.A. Savel'ev and E.M. Silaeva, "New House and Senate Leaders," trans. Joint Publications Research Service, *USSR Report, USA: Economics, Politics, Ideology* 69244 (March 1977): 66-79.

35. Iu. A. Ivanov, "Trudnye problemy kongressa," *SShA: Ekonomika, politika, ideologiia* (April 1987): 69, 73.

36. For Lugar, Iu. K. Abramov, "Richard Lugar - predsedatel' Komiteta po innostrannym delam senat SShA," *SShA: Ekonomika, politika, ideologiia* (April 1985): 111-112; for Church, V.A. Savel'ev, "Frenk Cherch - predsedatel' senatskoi kommissii po inostrannym delam," *SShA: Ekonomika, politika, ideologiia* (April 1979): 115-119; for Percy, Byrd, Cranston, Baker, and Stevens, Yu. A. Ivanov, E.M. Silayeva, and T.Z. Dzhaparidze, "Peremeny v kongresse," *SShA: Ekonomika, politika, ideologiia* (May 1981): 78-83; and for Dole, Iu. K. Abramov, "Robert Dole, New Republican Senate Majority Leader," trans. Joint Publications Research Service, *USSR Report, USA: Economics, Politics, Ideology* 85-006 (March 1985): 77-79.

37. Mishin, *Gosudarstvennoe pravo,* p 81; also I.V. Lebedev, "'Split Government Again,'" trans. Joint Publications Research Service, *USSR Report, USA: Economics, Politics, Ideology* 58418 (February 1973): 28-33.

38. Chetverikov, pp. 20-21, also see Iudina, pp. 56-57.

39. See for example, V.S. Guseva, "The 96th Congress and Domestic and Foreign Policy Issues," trans. Joint Publications Research Service, *USSR Report, USA: Economics, Politics, Ideology* 70707 (January 1978): 68-71, and V.A. Savel'ev, "The President and Congress in an Election Year," pp. 7-13.

40. N.N. Sokov, "On the Road to the Elections: The Search for an Alternative Foreign Policy," trans. Joint Publications Research Service, *USSR Report, USA: Economics, Politics, Ideology* 84-001 (November 1983): 59.

41. Ivanov, "Congress: Labyrinths," p. 10.

42. Ibid.

43. Ibid.

44. Ibid., p. 113.

45. Nyporko, p. 77.

46. Savel'ev, "The President and the Congress in an Election Year," p. 1.

47. Barbara Sinclair, *Majority Leadership in the U.S. House* (Baltimore: The Johns Hopkins Press, 1983), p. 38.

48. For more information see Sinclair, pp. 215-224; from a Soviet source see Iu. A. Ivanov, "Congress and the U.S. Intervention in Lebanon," trans. Joint Publications Research Service, *USSR Report, USA: Economics, Politics, Ideology* 85-003 (December 1984): 60-61.

49. Richard E. Neustadt, *Presidential Power: The Politics of Leadership from FDR to Carter* (New York: John Wiley & Sons, 1980), p. 65.

50. Destler, p. 345.

51. Cronin, pp. 335-336.

52. See for example, Ivanov, "Congress: Labyrinths," pp. 104-110, and I.N. Mosin, "Krizis amerikanskykh programm 'Pomoshchi,'" *SShA: Ekonomika, politika, ideologiia* (July 1975): 15-26.

53. Ivanov, "Congress: Labyrinths," p. 104.

54. Ibid., p. 105.

55. V.A. Savel'ev, "Foreign Policy and Congress," trans. Joint Publications Research Service, *USSR Report, USA: Economics, Politics, Ideology* 1/6761 (December 1976): 56.

56. A.A. Kokoshin, *SShA: za fasadom global'noi politiki* (Moscow: Politizdat, 1981), p. 215.

57. Ivanov, "Congress: Labyrinths," pp. 106-107.

58. Popova, pp. 17-18.

59. Savel'ev, "The President and Congress in an Election Year," p. 7.

60. Ivanov, "Congress: Labyrinths," p. 107.

61. Ibid.

62. Ibid., p. 108.

63. Savel'ev, "Foreign Policy and Congress," p. 57.

64. Popova, pp. 26-27.

65. Ivanov, "Congress: Labyrinths," p. 109.

66. Malcolm, p. 136.

67. Crabb and Holt, p. 191.

68. Ibid., p. 215.

69. R. Douglas Arnold has argued that Members of Congress join the House Armed Services Committee for two reasons: because of an interest in defense policy and in obtaining benefits of the defense budget for their district. Members of the Committee include a disproportionate number of Congressmen who have defense installations in their districts, while those attracted to the Committee for policy reasons seem less satisfied with their ability to influence the direction of defense policy. On balance, turnover is low, with only Rules, Ways and Means, Appropriations, and Foreign Affairs Committees having lower turnovers. For further information, see R. Douglas Arnold, *Congress and the Bureaucracy: A Theory of Influence* (New Haven: Yale University Press, 1979), pp. 125-128.

70. For the Soviet perspective, see Savel'ev, "Foreign Policy and Congress," p. 49, Iudina, pp. 57-59, S.B. Chetverikov, "Organizational Problems of Foreign Policy," trans. Joint Publications Research Service, *USSR Report, USA: Economics, Politics, Ideology* 62874 (August 1974): 33-41; and V.S. Zorin, "200 letie i 'konstitutionii krizis,'" *SShA: Ekonomika, politika, ideologiia,* (July 1976): 24-26. For the American perspective, see Crabb and Holt, pp. 33-218, Destler, pp. 329-359, and Cronin, pp. 320-343.

71. Popova, pp. 19-20, Ershova, pp. 42-43.

72. Zorin, pp. 25-26.

73. Chetverikov, "Organizational Problems," p. 35.

74. Iudina, p. 57.

75. S.N. Kondrashev, "The President's Fist and Unavoidable Compromises," trans. Foreign Broadcast Information Service *Daily Report* 5 June 1985, p. A1.

76. Ibid.

77. Current Senate Minority Leader Dole, for example, is portrayed as favoring the lifting of the partial grain embargo due to "agrarian circles in his state." For further information, see Abramov, "Robert Dole," p. 78.

78. Savel'ev, "The President and Congress in an Election Year," p. 1.

79. Ivanov, "Congress: Labyrinths," p. 108.

80. Ibid., p. 102.

81. Kokoshin, p. 249.

82. Ibid., p. 129. For a useful summary of amerikanistika on the "military-industrial complex" see Schwartz, pp. 66-73.

83. V.A. Kremeniuk, "Presidentskie vybory i blizhnii vostok," *SShA: Ekonomika, politika, ideologiia,* (January 1973): 71-77; also E.M. Primakov, "Pruzhiny Blizhevostochnoi politiki, SShA," *SShA: Ekonomika, politika, ideologiia,* (November 1976): 3-15.

84. Ivanov, "Congress: Labyrinths," p. 103.

85. N.V. Osipova, "The Senate and the Package Deal," trans. Joint Publications Research Service, *USSR Report, USA: Economics, Politics, Ideology* 72348 (October 1978): 111.

86. Iu. V. Kazakov, "Congress and U.S. Subversive Policy in East Europe," trans. Foreign Broadcast Information Service *Daily Report,* 21 October 1981, pp. 6-7; and Ivanov, "Congress: Labyrinths," p. 103.

87. Ibid.

88. A.A. Sergunin, "Presidential Lobbying under Ronald Reagan: Patterns and Methods of Influencing Congress," trans. Joint Publications Research Service, *USSR Report, USA: Economics, Politics, Ideology* 84-005 (February 1984): 64.

89. David R. Mayhew, *Congress and the Electoral Connection,* New Haven: Yale University Press, 1974, p. 28.

90. Senators considering the Panama Canal Treaties were deluged with mail opposing the Treaties. According to Crabb and Holt: "letters and postcards poured in, at one point in ratios as great as 300/1 against the treaties . . . The Conservative Caucus, one of the most active opposition groups, had a voter pledge program with the goal of getting commitments from 10,000 voters in each state that would 'never vote for any person who votes for the treaties.'" (Crabb and Holt, p. 73.)

91. For a useful summary of the activities of liberal pro-arms control lobbying groups, as well as their conservative counterparts, see Margaret Ann Latus, "Assessing Ideological PACs: From Outrage to Understanding," in *Money and Politics in the United States: Financing Elections in the 1980s,* ed. Michael J. Malbin (Washington: American Enterprise Institute, 1974), pp. 142-171.

92. Ibid., p. 95.

93. The 'don't offend' principle in the case of Jackson-Vanik is described by Crabb and Holt as follows: "Said one senator, in explaining the number of cosponsors of the Jackson amendment to the Trade Act of 1974, relative to Jewish emigration from the Soviet Union, 'There is no political advantage in not signing. If you do sign, you don't offend anyone. If you don't sign, you might offend some Jews in your state.'" (Crabb and Holt, p. 95.)

94. Congress, House, Committee on Foreign Affairs, *U.S. Relations with the Countries of Central and Eastern Europe,* by Francis Miko of the Foreign Affairs and National Defense Division, Congressional Research Service, Library of Congress (Washington, D.C.: Government Printing Office, 1979), p. 3.

95. Ibid., p. 4.

96. A.S. Nikiforov, "Legal Peculiarities of Presidential Authority," trans. Joint Publications Research Service, *USSR Report, USA: Economics, Politics, Ideology* 56958 (August 1972): 31.

97. D.N. Konovalov and V.A. Savel'ev, "Action to Limit Presidential War Powers," trans. Joint Publications Research Service, *USSR Report, USA: Economics, Politics, Ideology* 61346 (February 1974): 108.

98. Ibid., p. 115.

99. Nyporko, pp. 104-105.

100. Ivanov, "Congress and U.S. Intervention in Lebanon," p. 62.

101. Ibid., p. 65.

102. Nikiforov, p. 30.

103. Iudina, p. 58.

104. Dante B. Fascell, "The Crucial Importance of the War Powers Resolution," *Miami Herald,* 31 March 1986.

105. Clement J. Zablocki, "War Powers Resolution: Its Past Record and Future Promise," *Loyola of Los Angeles Review,* 17, (March 1984): 595.

106. U.S. Congress, Senate, Committee on Foreign Relations, *Treaties and Other International Agreements: The Role of the United States Senate,* by Ellen Collier of the Congressional Research Service, Library of Congress (Washington, D.C.: Government Printing Office, 1984), p. 39.

3

Soviet Case Studies on Congress and U.S. Foreign Policy

Amerikanistika concerning Congressional involvement in specific foreign policy issues is not as extensive as the effort devoted to the enduring process and procedural issues discussed in Chapter 2. Nonetheless, individual americanists or groups of americanists have produced a number of what could be called case studies of Congress' actions on specific issue areas. The five issues analyzed in this chapter are by no means exhaustive of americanist case studies on Congress' role in foreign policy. They do represent, however, a cross-section of the issues which are of high salience to Soviet foreign policymakers. As in the previous chapter, americanist perspectives will be provided followed by an analysis utilizing American sources on the same issues.

Chapter 3 deals with five contemporary foreign policy issues in which Congress has had an active interest and, importantly, a considerable impact on the formulation of U.S. foreign policy. The issues are: (1) U.S. relations with Western Europe; (2) U.S. relations with Eastern Europe; (3) U.S.-Soviet trade; (4) U.S. arms sales to the Middle East; and (5) Congressional attitudes regarding defense and arms control. As in the previous chapter, americanist perspectives will be followed by an analysis utilizing American sources on the same issues.

Amerikanistika on Contemporary Issues:
Congress and U.S. Relations with Western Europe

Americanist Perspective

Soviet scholarship has examined several key aspects of Congressional involvement in U.S.-West European relations. Because of Western Europe's importance as one of the main regional actors in contemporary international relations, one Soviet writer stresses that conflicts between the executive and legislative branches on U.S. policy toward Western Europe "have sometimes been severely exacerbated by their different approaches to foreign policy issues in general and to relations with West European countries in particular."[1]

Congress is generally viewed favorably with respect to its involvement in U.S.-Western European relations. For example, Representative Lee H. Hamilton (D-Ind.), Chairman of the Europe and Middle East Subcommittee on the House Foreign Affairs Committee, receives attention for his comments during a July 1982 Committee hearing that President Reagan's attempts to make light of U.S.-West European differences at press conferences masked serious strains in relations. Hamilton was also quoted as having clearly established "obvious differences in appraisals of mutual relations by American and West European leaders."[2]

Furthermore, several Congressional actions in the 1980's concerning U.S.-West European relations are cited to demonstrate executive-legislative differences and emphasize the influence of the "peace movement" on the Congress. Specifically, Senator Charles Percy (R-Ill.), former chairman of the Senate Foreign Relations Committee is cited for his advice in March 1983 to President Reagan to revise the so-called "zero-option" arms control proposal at the Geneva negotiations on intermediate-range nuclear forces (INF); although one americanist notes with chagrin that Percy's revisions did not include an accounting of British and French INF systems.

Congressional resistance to the scope and size of funding requests for the Pershing II, the focal point of U.S.-NATO INF modernization has also been detailed. Again, however, it is noted that eventually intense Administration lobbying by then Secretary of Defense Caspar W. Weinberger and NATO Supreme Allied Commander Bernard Rogers produced results, and funding for the Pershing II program was increased.

Also analyzed approvingly is Congress' independent-mindedness on U.S. policy with respect to Greece and Turkey. Rather precise understanding of Congress' insistence on a 7-10 ratio of military assistance to Greece and Turkey, respectively, is demonstrated as is the unsuccessful lobbying efforts of then Assistant Secretary of Defense Richard Perle to shift this aid ratio in favor of Turkey.[3] The relatively greater reluctance of the Congress to criticize the current Socialist government in Greece and Prime Minister Andreas Papandreou for its rhetorical anti-American pronouncements and its willingness to consider closing U.S. military bases in the near future are accurately described in Soviet foreign policy analysis. The fact that Congress refused to reduce aid to Greece despite the more anti-American posture of the Greek government is emphasized. Congress is said to have been cautious to use foreign assistance funding levels for Greece as a means to express disapproval of Greek actions.

Congressional skepticism about the Reagan Administration's failed effort to stop the Soviet gas pipeline to Western Europe is also highlighted in Soviet analysis. Congress is seen as "seriously disturbed by the rift between the United States and its West European allies as a result of Washington's attempts to stop, or at least slow down, the construction of the gasline."[4] Congressional sources are described as outraged by the administration's rude and biased treatment of the allies when "without any kind of consultations with allies, they instituted unprecedented sanctions against West European companies producing equipment for the pipeline on American licenses."[5] Interestingly, Congress is viewed as working with the allies in eventually reversing American policy on the pipeline because many Members were disturbed that a fundamental worsening of U.S.-West European relations would result if the pipeline sanctions continued.

The efforts of the House Foreign Affairs Committee to vitiate the Executive Order mandating pipeline sanctions are cited as one such example of Congress' efforts to reverse American policy on the pipeline. Soviet analysis points out that the effort was spearheaded by Rep. Robert H. Michel (R-Ill.), the House Republican leader. In this instance, at least, Congress is seen as a sober, sophisticated equilibrium force in U.S.-West European relations despite the fact that such actions frustrated the longstanding Soviet foreign policy objective of encouraging political division between the United States and Western Europe. The tendency in other Soviet writings to view Congress favorably only when it took positions seen as favorable to Moscow is muted in this instance.

At the same time, Congress is subjected to some criticism for its efforts to influence U.S.-West European relations. Interest in reducing U.S. troop presence in Europe is seen as having evolved from the efforts in the early 1970s when liberal members of Congress sought to reduce what they regarded to be an excessive American military presence to contemporary efforts aimed at pressuring NATO allies to spend more on conventional defense. Several funding cuts for programs designed to implement NATO cooperative defense efforts are cited, as is the refusal to allow certain European high-grade steel imports for military purposes. These efforts are seen as the result of the pressure of domestic steel interests.

Finally, the protectionist sentiment in Congress is referred to disapprovingly. Insistence by some Members of Congress on full enforcement of anti-dumping legislation, import quotas, and reduction of European Community agricultural subsidies are cited as part of the "United States determination to defend the interests of its monopolies."[6]

In general, with respect to U.S.-West European relations, Congress is seen as "gradually realizing that Ronald Reagan is imposing his own interpretation of foreign policy problems on the country and is ignoring the views of the highest legislative body."[7] This leads to the modification or denial of Administration funding requests to implement its West European policy. Nonetheless, the Soviet case study takes pains to point out that Congress' approach to U.S. policy in Western Europe "cannot be defined precisely . . . and the composition of the Congress is heterogeneous, with its members influenced by a number of political and economic considerations in its decisionmaking."[8]

Analysis of Amerikanistika on Congress
and U.S.-West European Relations

This Soviet case study on Congress and its role in U.S. policy in Western Europe is on balance quite thorough. Clearly, in the early 1980's, most notably in 1982, a growing number of Members, particularly Democrats, came to the conclusion that the Reagan Administration's approach to Western security issues was producing serious disquiet and deep resentment in Western Europe, not only among left wing opposition groups but conservative governments in power. Moderate Democrats such as Rep. Hamilton could not quarrel with the growing congressional arguments that in the eyes of our NATO allies, the administration's emphasis on increasing strategic forces independent of arms control negotiations, "does not strengthen world stability, but only constitutes another step in a continuing arms race with the Soviet Union . . . that imposes increased risks to European security."[9] This growing perception of alienation between the Administration and Western Europe concerning the appropriate Western security posture was in part responsible for Congressional pressure on the Reagan Administration to resume stalled arms control negotiations as well as to revise the original U.S. positions at those negotiations.

However, viewed in retrospect, the americanist interpretation and analysis of Congress' initial resistance to funding for the Pershing II missile is incorrect. Undoubtedly this analysis, which was contemporaneous with the major Soviet effort to prevent Pershing deployments in Europe, was intended to complement that effort by showing evidence of Congressional resistance on arms control grounds. In fact, the early actions taken by the Congress to slow funding were based almost exclusively on budgetary considerations. The funding requests for Pershing IIs were excessive. Congress sought to cut those funds in order to apply the savings to other defense programs or domestic programs believed to be underfunded by the Reagan Administration. The clearest evidence of this motivation lay in the fact that efforts to delete funding for arms control reasons or because of political opposition to the Pershing II in Western Europe were soundly defeated in Congress.

Soviet analysis on Congressional attitudes regarding foreign assistance to Greece and Turkey is indeed fascinating. The informal 7-10 ratio on military assistance to the two countries and the singularly unsuccessful efforts by several Administrations to change the ratio in favor of Turkey are strikingly accurate. The ratio continues to be an inelegant but highly effective legislative device to stave off Greek-American political organizations who would like to substantially cut or eliminate military assistance to Turkey and successive Administrations who would like to increase it. An americanist citation from an American newspaper column to the effect that altering the 7-10 ratio was like playing in a minefield, accurately describes the Congressional politics of funding foreign assistance for Greece and Turkey. When members of Congress are told by executive branch witnessess that such a ratio is arbitrary, they sometimes even candidly respond that there is an unmistakable political rationale to such a ratio.[10]

Nonetheless, americanist analysis clearly overreaches when it seeks to link Congressional support for Greece to support for Prime Minister Papandreou's criticism of Reagan Administration foreign policy and his implied threats to close American military bases in Greece. In fact, the Subcommittee on Europe and the Middle East of the House Foreign Affairs Committee, which has strongly supported the 7-10 ratio in the past, unanimously concluded in 1985 that "the continuation of anti-American and anti-NATO behavior could undermine the historical goodwill between our two countries and hurt Greek and American interests in the Eastern Mediterranean."[11]

The description of the Congress' response to the gas pipeline controversy is also essentially accurate. There is little question that the decision by President Reagan to extend U.S. sanctions on oil and gas equipment to include sales of such equipment by European subsidiaries of U.S. companies produced serious Congressional concerns. Concern came from those worried about the effects of still another exercise of U.S. foreign policy linkage to trade which would inevitably erode the image of U.S. business and government as a reliable supplier. Still others complained about the "potential damage that unilateral action might have on the alliance."[12] The specific reference by Soviet scholars to House efforts to overturn the pipeline sanctions is also interesting, particularly the recognition that Rep. Michel was under constituent pressure to get the sanctions lifted because pipeline-related equipment was produced in his district. Thus, the Soviet case study accurately recognizes that Michel, who was in a tough reelection fight in 1982, had to pursue legislative relief efforts for purely political reasons despite their contradiction with existing administration policy.

Additionally, the Soviet case study correctly surmises that the pipeline sanctions bill in the House of Representatives was essentially designed to send a clear signal to the Administration that the political damage to U.S.-West European relations clearly outweighed any supposed punitive effects on the Soviet Union for its actions in Poland. The November, 1982 revocation of the sanctions was in part due to growing Congressional opposition to the pipeline sanctions, as symbolized by the House action, as well as strong, united West European resistance to this policy.

Soviet analysis of Congress' efforts to reduce the physical and budgetary scope of the U.S. defense contribution in Europe is somewhat shallow. While it can be argued that liberal members of Congress are no longer taking the lead in seeking to reduce U.S. commitments in Europe, it is nevertheless too simplistic to argue that the conservative components of the coalition are simply out to "pressure and blackmail U.S. allies."

In fact, as American analysts have pointed out, a number of concerns have produced "a renewed willingness among Members to consider coercive legislation as a way of influencing allied defense efforts."[13] The failure of the NATO allies to meet the established 1978 goal of increasing real defense spending growth by 3% annually, and major political resistance to the Pershing II and ground-launched cruise missile deployments in Western Europe accounts for some of this willingness. Growing concerns in Congress about "burdensharing" can also be explained by divergent U.S. and Western European approaches to relations with the Soviet Union, ranging from questions of how to respond to the Soviet invasion of Afghanistan and the impositon of martial law in Poland, to the gas pipeline controversy and increasing budgetary pressures on the Congress as a result of growing budget deficits. Resistance to defense cooperation efforts such as host-nation support and the lifting of restrictions on imports of specialty metals to increase European defense sales to the United States also stem from the above concerns as well as constituent pressures to "buy American."

Americanist analysis also does not point out that coercive burdensharing amendments, including the effort sponsored in 1984 by Senators Sam Nunn (D-Ga.) and William Roth (R-Del.), have uniformly failed to become law. Contributing to defeat such amendments have been concerns about the political cohesion of the alliance, the effects of manpower ceilings on NATO force planning, and the effects of a perceived American deemphasis on the defense of Europe for Western European commitments to defense. Opponents of such amendments have also pointed out the negative effects of unilateral troop reductions on conventional arms control negotiations in Vienna and have argued that Congress in the final analysis should not bear the political responsibility for a major shift in American defense policy.

While Congress will always press for greater burdensharing from the NATO allies, its willingness to enforce its wishes by legislated troop cuts seems lacking. Soviet analysis fails to recognize both the varied political reasons for supporting more burdensharing and for rejecting coercive amendments to produce it by legislative fiat.

Finally, the analysis of the effects of economic difficulties in U.S. relations in Western Europe and Congress' role in U.S.-West European trade issues is intriguing. A virtually liberal free trade philosophy is espoused in the condemnation of Congress' support for domestic constituencies and commodities. The Soviet case study is able to accurately identify controversies concerning imports of European Community steel, and the use of EC agricultural subsidies to promote exports and reduce American imports to European markets.[14]

However, American sources correctly point to a lack of Congressional unity on trade issues. While some Members of Congress support aggressive enforcement of existing international agreements such as the General Agreements on Tariffs and Trade and favor retaliatory measures if these agreements fail to correct perceived inequities, other Members believe such measures are self-defeating and not only cost U.S. taxpayers money but also benefit a few favored industries. Some Members demand vigorous pursuit of relief provisions in anti-dumping legislation as a means of temporary protection while certain industries restructure their technology and employment practices. Still other Members tend to oppose temporary protectionist measures on economic grounds believing that restrictions are never temporary and do not deal with structural economic problems that are the root causes of economic difficulties in some industries. Thus, Congressional attitudes on U.S. approaches to trade with Western Europe are divided and cannot simply be defined, as Soviet analysis does, as "defending the interests of monopolies."

On balance, the americanist case study on Congress' role in U.S. policy toward Western Europe acknowledges differing legislative perspectives. Indeed, it is hard to criticize the conclusion that "Congress' approach to U.S. policy in Western Europe cannot be defined precisely" and that its responses are "heterogeneous" and "influenced by a number of political and economic considerations." The identification of constituent politics (for example, the 7-10 ratio on military aid to Greece and Turkey, Rep. Michel's efforts on the gas pipeline) and the portrayal of Congress as a responsible critic of Administration policy seeking to advance goals generally shared by the Congress and the Administration (the gas pipeline, harmonious U.S.-West European relations, preserving close ties with both Greece and Turkey) suggest an ability to perceive realistically differences between the Executive branch and the Congress on how U.S. policy should be conducted.

Congress and U.S. Relations with Eastern Europe

Americanist Perspective

Unlike the relatively sympathetic and sophisticated portrayal of Congress' role in U.S. policy toward Western Europe, americanist analysis of Congress' role in U.S. policy in Eastern Europe is uniformly negative, simplistic, and vitriolic.

Congressional support for the U.S. policy of "differentiation"[15] with respect to Eastern Europe is attacked by Soviet scholarship as an effort "aimed basically at splitting the socialist community and setting the states of the region against each other and against the Soviet Union."[16] Promoting improved relations with individual East European countries on a country-by-country basis, not merely as a byproduct of detente with the Soviet Union, is seen as part of the framework of the global confrontation with the Soviet Union. Even the encouragement of internal political evolution more amenable to liberal democracy is seen as "creeping counterrevolution."

Congressional criticism of human rights violations in Eastern Europe, and the human rights performance of Warsaw Pact states with respect to the Helsinki Final Act is viewed as a result of the fact that "many congressmen and senators had directly stepped up their subversive activity and acts of ideological sabotage against the socialist countries."[17] The Commission on Security and Cooperation in Europe, also known as the Helsinki Commission, a joint executive-legislative commission set up to monitor compliance by signatories to the Helsinki Final Act, is referred to as "notorious." Individual efforts to maintain U.S. government contacts with opposition intellectuals and church leaders, which have been advocated by many Members of Congress, are also labeled subversive.

Amerikanistika regarding Congress' reaction to the situation in Poland is equally polemical. From the Soviet perspective, Poland's political crisis during the 1979-1981 period was aggravated by Congress as a result of a "provocative campaign around the events in Poland aimed at giving support to antisocialist forces in that country and encouraging their subversive activity."[18] Congressional support for the AFL-CIO's contacts with the Polish labor union Solidarity is seen as "rendering support to the subversive activity of the AFL-CIO leadership . . . (who) have already shown themselves to be direct stooges or accomplices of the CIA."[19]

Resolutions passed by Congress on the situation in Poland are seen by Soviet scholarship as couched in overtly anti-Polish and anti-Soviet terms and are aimed at using a "distorted interpretation of the policy of the Soviet Union and the other Warsaw Pact states to attempt to drive a wedge into their fraternal relations with socialist Poland."[20]

Even modest Congressional efforts which are aimed at resolving Poland's political and economic problems are seen as having sinister ulterior motives. For example, Senator Edward Kennedy's (D-Mass.) comments about resolving Poland's crisis exclusively by peaceful means are viewed as an effort to "strengthen U.S. influence—only by more flexible methods . . . and more effective use of financial and economic levers."[21] Representative Les Aspin's (D-Wis.) proposal that Western bank loans to Poland be linked to economic and political reforms, including recognition of Solidarity was regarded as part of a "broad arsenal of political and economic methods of influence to extend the influence of the reactionary, antisocilaist forces which have entrenched themselves in the Solidarity trade union association."[22]

Finally, Congressional support for Radio Free Europe (RFE), Radio Liberty (RL) and the Voice of America (VOA) is described as increasing ideological pressure from these organizations which are regarded as "blatantly subversive," and which assume "wide and manifestly scandalous powers as disseminators of shabby misinformation and lies."[23]

Analysis of Amerikanistika on Congress
and U.S.-East European Relations

The exceptionally low quality of amerikanistika on Congress' role in influencing U.S. policy toward Eastern Europe ignores a number of differing Congressional perspectives which can be identified regarding appropriate U.S. policy in the region. Political observers in the U.S. have identified at least four different perspectives including: (1) the view of Eastern Europe as a buffer between the Soviet Union and Western Europe and thus an area where confrontation must be avoided; (2) the view that political and economic policies in Eastern Europe can have a "spillover effect" that will enhance the prospects for U.S.-Soviet detente and political and economic reform in the Soviet Union; (3) that Eastern Europe will always remain tightly dominated by the Soviet Union and a staging area for Soviet military aggression against Western Europe; and (4) that Eastern Europe is an important region in its own right whose countries should be dealt with according to the nature of their economic, social and foreign policies.[24]

Moreover, in light of the obvious Soviet military, political, and economic presence in Eastern Europe, U.S. policy has always sought to avoid making Eastern Europe a source of major East-West confrontation. Even the Reagan Administration has acknowledged this fact, pointing out that "we need to be realisitic about the practical limits of our direct influence in Eastern Europe."[25]

U.S. policy in Eastern Europe, largely supported by the Congress, has stressed differentiation. The principal tenets of this policy are (1) the best way to advance U.S. interests in the region is through recognition of the diversity of the region and; (2) the degree of willingness of East European states to develop distinctive and productive relations with the United States, notwithstanding the reality of Soviet hegemony in the region, should be recognized. Indeed, U.S. policy has established specific criteria by which East European states are differentiated. These criteria have included the adoption of more independent foreign policies, increased political and economic exchanges with the West, improved emigration and human rights performance and economic liberalization. However, it is difficult to see how, as Soviet specialists charge, these criteria represent "global confrontation" or "setting states of the region against each other and against the Soviet Union."

Undoubtedly, Soviet analysis is also troubled by official U.S. policy towards Eastern Europe which refuses to recognize any permanent division in Europe, and any exclusive Soviet interest in Eastern Europe. Yet no discernible political group in Congress, even the most conservative, would reject the argument that the United States can only improve conditions and relations in Eastern Europe through peaceful engagement. Thus, Congress' approach to Eastern Europe does not appear to translate into the creation of a "zone of unease for the Soviet Union."

Congressional concerns about human rights performance in Eastern Europe are indeed extensive and continuing. However, americanist analysis ignores the impact of East European-American ethnic groups as one reason for such interest. Furthermore, the intense rivalry by both major political parties for the votes of several million ethnic East Europeans does not receive heavy emphasis.[26] The possibility that traditional American democratic concerns about individual freedom and national self-determination might also play a role in Congressional concerns is similarly ignored.

Activism by Congress on human rights now directly influences U.S. policy toward Eastern Europe. Both the House Foreign Affairs and Senate Foreign Relations Committees, as well as the Helsinki Commission, have conducted ongoing reviews of Eastern European human rights performance. Granting or withholding trade benefits, export control legislation, funding for RFE, RL, and VOA, and non-binding resolutions expressing Congressional views on political changes in Eastern Europe (such as the imposition of martial law in Poland) are all examples of direct Congressional involvement in the formulation and implementation of U.S. policy.

However, to dismiss human rights concerns as "subversive activity" or "ideological sabotage" ignores the detailed discussions which occur in Congress over the effective limits of pressing human rights concerns, how economic incentives might contribute to improved human rights performance, and the potential of trade, cultural and educational exchanges in modifying

Soviet and East European attitudes about human rights. Furthermore, the extension of trade benefits to Hungary, Romania and, until 1981, Poland, despite poor human rights records, indicates a certain pragmatism on this issue that is totally ignored by Soviet scholars. Amerikanistika on Congress and its role in shaping U.S. policy towards Eastern Europe seems to proceed from the premise that any dialogue or discussion about human rights in Eastern Europe constitutes a direct challenge to Soviet foreign policy interests in the region.

Americanist discussions about Congress' role in U.S. policy toward Poland borders on the hysterical. It is true that rhetorical expressions in Congress regarding the imposition of martial law and Soviet involvement in Poland have been intense. Nonetheless, it appears that any contact with Solidarity or opposition political figures, or suggesting any approach that ties the lifting of U.S. economic sanctions imposed after martial law to political liberalization and economic reform is inadmissible as "undermining socialist Poland" or "extending the influence of reactionary, antisocialist forces." While it is accurate to say that a majority in Congress supported the continued suspension of most-favored nation trade status to Poland in response to the martial law decision, in-depth discussions of the advisability of continuing economic sanctions against Poland occurred in Congress, and influential House Members spoke against their continuation. The sanctions were eventually lifted by the Reagan Administration.

Unlike the Soviet case study on Congress' role in U.S. policy toward Western Europe, a crude, polemical, ideologically-rigid style with a bipolar worldview is evident concerning analysis on Congress and U.S. policy toward Eastern Europe. Serious discussion of Congress' attitudes and actions is almost entirely missing. Symptomatic of this trend are sweeping rejections of any legitimate Congressional involvement in Eastern Europe. Rational discussion is replaced by simplistic nostrums. An excellent example of this is the conclusion of one americanist that the differences of opinion among U.S. legislators on matters of U.S.-East European policy are not fundamental and "the essential purpose of all these approaches is to weaken the socialist community as much as possible."[27]

One is indeed struck by the stark differences in depth and quality of analysis in Soviet writings on Congress and its influence on U.S. policy on Western and Eastern Europe respectively. While the reasons may be speculative, several come to mind.

First, Soviet policy toward Western Europe has long involved an effort to weaken political, economic, and military ties between the United States and Western Europe. Soviet diplomacy and its implementation by the Soviet leadership have sought to stress common historical and political experiences with the countries of Western Europe and has clearly made pan-European proposals, particularly on security questions, a cardinal principle in dealing with West European leaders. The ritualistic calls for the dissolution of NATO and the Warsaw Pact, the original effort to prevent the United States from participating in the Conference on Security and Cooperation in Europe, the intense effort to prevent the deployment of U.S.-owned, European-based intermediate nuclear weapons, and the more recent efforts to build a conventional arms control regime based on the concept of "Atlantic to the Urals" all exemplify this basic Soviet policy approach to Western Europe. Given the importance attached to this Soviet foreign policy objective it may well be that the Soviet leadership is demanding of americanists clearcut analysis of U.S. policy in Western Europe, including Congress' role in that policy, as well as the points of policy contention between the Congress and the executive branch. Thus, the type of analysis we have seen with respect to Congress and U.S. policy in Western Europe may reflect a leadership requirement for sophisticated, thoughtful analysis that helps outline courses of action and policy options being evaluated at the highest levels of the Soviet political system.

By contrast, while Soviet foreign policy has sought a recession of close U.S.-West European ties, it has sought to prevent a similar recession with respect to Soviet military, political, and economic ties with Eastern Europe. The limits of toleration concerning political diversity in Eastern Europe are clearly drawn. Continued membership of all Eastern European nations (except Yugoslavia) in the Warsaw Pact, tighter economic cooperation and coordination within the Council of Mutual Economic Assistance, and the maintenance of political systems which are dominated by ruling communist parties leave relatively little room for U.S. influence of a fundamental or lasting nature. Given the sensitivity and importance of Eastern Europe to Soviet foreign policy and national security objectives, there seems little opportunity or incentive for a sober, sophisticated analysis of U.S. policy in the region, particularly when that policy is perceived as contributing to political instability, as in the case of Poland. Eastern Europe may well be a subject so critical to Soviet policy objectives that it is simply too sensitive for americanists to make rational, cool analysis of U.S. policy and Congress' role in the making and conduct of that policy.

Finally, perhaps as a result of differing policy objectives and needs with respect to Western and Eastern Europe, the quality of scholars permitted to write on these respective subjects may vary as well. As we have seen in this chapter and the preceeding chapter, amerikanistika is uneven in quality from subject to subject and within individual subject matters. Since the range of tolerated discussion clearly varies with respect to Congress' role in U.S. policy in Western and Eastern Europe, the type of scholars providing analysis in these two areas may clearly vary as well.

Congress and U.S.-Soviet Trade

Americanist Perspective

While not approaching the dogmatic, vitriolic tone of analysis of the previous section, Soviet analysis not surprisingly has a low regard for Congress' role in U.S. trade policy toward the Soviet Union. In fact, congressional actions have been characterized as interjecting a largely negative element in the development of U.S.-Soviet trade.

In particular, the Jackson-Vanik amendment has come under severe criticism as "one of the first serious blows against detente," "an unceremonious attempt to politicize trade," and "flagrant interference in Soviet internal affairs."[28] The lack of Congressional interest in revising the legislation is seen in one case study as support for the concept of "linking the normalization of trade with the domestic policy of socialist states," which is "aimed at undermining the socialist countries from within and weakening the unity of the socialist community."[29]

Nonetheless, a Soviet analyst in this case study on Congress and U.S.-Soviet trade does, however, recognize some positive aspects of Congress' influence on trade policy, particularly when legislative concerns about the domestic effects of economic sanctions against the Soviet Union are voiced. Thus, the Soviet americanist is quick to point out that when sanctions injured U.S. farming interests and undermined U.S. trade reliability, Congress was instrumental in removing the partial grain embargo in 1981, and passing legislation which restricted the use of embargoes on agricultural commodities and would provide compensation to farmers for losses ensuing from embargoes. Amerikanistika also notes with approval Congressional pressure for the eventual conclusion in October, 1983 of a Long-Term Grain Agreement with the Soviet Union, despite initial resistance by the Reagan Administration to negotiate such an agreement after the imposition of martial law in Poland in December 1981.

Congress' response to the West European gas pipeline is viewed as mixed. A House resolution advising against U.S. participation and proposing alternative sources of energy be found for Western European participants because of concerns about undue dependence on Soviet energy was regarded as hostile. Congress' attitude changed shortly thereafter as constituent economic concerns about the effect of U.S. export controls on the pipeline against Western European subsidiaries of U.S. firms began to be felt. A subsequent House attempt was led by the House Republican leader Michel, who had two firms in his district affected by the controls, to remove the controls mandated by executive order.

The long process of revising U.S. export laws during 1983-1985 also attracted the interest of Soviet scholarship, particularly Congressional efforts to strengthen the principle of "contract sanctity" against efforts by the executive branch to impose foreign policy export controls that often interrupt existing contracts with foreign customers, including the Soviet Union. However, the author of the americanist case study is not impressed by the results of the recently enacted Export Administration Act, which dealt with a wide range of trade issues including contract sanctity. It is argued that while members of Congress questioned the effectiveness of trade sanctions, the majority in both the House and the Senate were unwilling to take away all Presidential power to impose such sanctions. Furthermore, it is argued that "not one of the proposals submitted for inclusion in the new export legislation can allay the fears about the reliability of American companies as trade partners."[30] Cited as evidence for this judgment is the fact that both the House and the Senate versions of the Export Administration Act allowed Presidential waivers of provisions mandating fulfillment of existing contracts when export controls are imposed for foreign policy purposes.

Americanist analysis is even more critical of national security export controls. While the House of Representatives was cited for its efforts to relax such controls, the Senate bill was attacked because it envisaged the curtailment of trade with the Soviet Union and Eastern Europe and declared "the U.S. right of the unilateral oversight of the observance by West European firms of restrictions stipulated in the American export regulation act."[31] The strengthened role for the Defense Department in regulating exports for their high-technology content and strengthening the multilateral Coordinating Committee (COCOM) in order to limit high technology exports to the Soviet Union and Eastern Europe has also been roundly criticized.

While Congress does not receive high marks in the area of U.S.-Soviet trade, the discussion of Congress' role on this foreign policy issue seems far more subtly nuanced and sophisticated than the discussion on Congress' role regarding U.S. policy in Eastern Europe. Class analysis is largely absent and strong disagreement between different factions in Congress are described. Congress is even given credit, in isolated instances such as the gas pipeline and the grain embargo, for having a pragmatic attitude towards U.S.-Soviet trade. Nonetheless, in the final analysis, it is argued that real progress in the normalization of American-Soviet trade relations on the basis of "equality, mutual advantage, and a total lack of discrimination is still being impeded by negative tendencies in the highest legislative body."[32]

*Analysis of Amerikanistika on Congress
and U.S.-Soviet Trade*

The stinging effects of the Jackson-Vanik amendment, which ironically did so much to increase the intensity and quality of amerikanstika on Congress and U.S. foreign policy, also colors the americanist attitude on U.S.-Soviet trade. The amendment is always the first topic of discussion and is always cast in profoundly negative terms. Aside from this, one cannot quarrel with the political judgment evident in amerikanistika that its repeal or significant modification is clearly not in the political cards. At this juncture, no significant element in either the Reagan Administration or the Congress is contemplating action to change the requirements of Jackson-Vanik. Significant Jewish-American organizations, alarmed at periodic stoppages of Jewish emigration from the Soviet Union, have privately considered possible modifications but for the time being have decided against supporting such changes in Congress.

The americanist in the U.S.-Soviet trade case study seems better able to perceive a more positive Congressional role in other aspects of Congressional actions concerning U.S.-Soviet trade. Congress did play a major role in the demise of the partial grain embargo imposed by President Carter after the

Soviet invasion of Afghanistan. Grain exports have been and remain the largest commodity in U.S.-Soviet trade and "for many Members of Congress, particularly those from grain-growing regions, grain sales are seen as a very high priority issue in U.S.-Soviet relations."[33] Recurring U.S. grain surpluses and trade deficits also add political momentum to the promotion of U.S. grain exports to the Soviet Union.

Farm interests also played the key role in the process of lifting the embargo. A Senate effort in 1980, led by Senator Robert Dole (R-Kans.), to deny funds for the implementation of the embargo was eventually defeated in the House and dropped in conference. In the interim, then-candidate Ronald Reagan pledged to lift the embargo and did so in April 1981, after he became President. Congress' efforts to demonstrate that other nations would circumvent the embargo and that it would have more impact on American farmers than on the Soviet Union were successful. Soviet analysis is also correct in pointing out that legislative protections against future grain embargoes, including compensation for farmers, were enacted. Congressional resolutions in support of negotiations for a Long-Term Grain Agreement were an important element in overcoming initial Reagan Administration resistance to beginning such negotiations.[34]

As we have already seen, Soviet political analysis on the gas pipeline controversy is basically accurate. Initial Congressional support for the pipeline sanctions quickly evaporated under constituent pressures and the intense Western European opposition. The House effort to vitiate the sanctions has already been discussed in detail.

The analysis of Congressional consideration of the Export Administration Act is less impressive. Congress, contrary to americanist analysis, was highly sensitive about the effect of past executive impositions of foreign policy controls on the credibility of U.S. businesses to be "reliable suppliers." The enacted version of the Export Administration Act contained contract sanctity provisions protecting all U.S. export contracts from disruption from future foreign policy export controls except in the case of a "breach of the peace" and in declared national emergencies. Furthermore, U.S. restrictions on export items freely available abroad were dropped and agricultural exports contracts were protected from foreign policy controls. While pure contract sanctity from Executive controls was not approved, the compensation required of the U.S. government for private concerns affected by the cancellation of contracts made the use of such controls in the future highly problematic and politically unlikely. Thus, the export promotion motivation in U.S.-Soviet trade was advanced, at least with respect to foreign policy export controls.

Soviet analysis of national security controls fails to address the motivation for such controls. The illegal obtaining of technology that has military applications by the Soviet Union is well-documented in the United States. In late 1981, a U.S. Customs Service enforcement effort, dubbed Operation Exodus, produced numerous examples of illegal Soviet diversions of legitimate shipments of sensitive technology items through third countries and onto the Soviet Union. A celebrated case involved a digital high-speed computer scheduled to be delivered to South Africa that was seized in the Federal Republic of Germany and Sweden. Other diverted parts of the computer were believed applicable for missile targeting, at faster than real time, or the time it takes for a missile to hit its target; the simulation of terrain-following radar for cruise missiles and flight paths of intercontinental ballistic missiles; command and control for targeting anti-aircraft batteries of guns and missiles; and the design and manufacture of very high-speed integrated circuits. Against this backdrop, conservative members of Congress had credibility in pressing for tighter licensing requirements and for Defense Department management of high-technology exports.

Despite increased publicity about illegal Soviet exports of U.S. sensitive technology, Members were also confronted with the argument from U.S. businesses that because of the availability of many items from a variety of sources, export controls should be liberalized rather than tightened. It was this balancing of export and national security considerations which confronted the Congress, not, as the Soviet americanist has argued, "curtailment of trade with socialist countries."

Furthermore, contrary to Soviet analysis in amerikanistika, what emerged from Congressional consideration was not a major increase in authority for the Defense Department to review exports. No increased authority for the Defense Department to review licenses for non-Communist countries was granted while DOD's role in regulating exports to Communist countries was merely reaffirmed. The ability to regulate high-technology exports to Western Europe to prevent Soviet diversion was strengthened, but this did not imply any increased DOD role. In this way, export and national security concerns were balanced.

In the final analysis, amerikanistika appears to have great difficulty acknowledging positive Congressional actions in U.S.-Soviet trade unless they appear to directly benefit the Soviet Union. Concerns about human rights or technology diversion are apparently still too sensitive for open discussion concerning Congress' role in U.S.-Soviet trade. There is a heavy stress on Soviet benefit as a barometer of the value of Congress' actions and an analytical strain that appears to favor only a U.S.-Soviet trade pattern which unilaterally strengthens Soviet national security interests.

Congress and U.S. Arms Sales to the Middle East

Americanist Perspective

Americanist contributions on Congress' role in influencing U.S. arms sales to the Middle East appear to capture the variety of perspectives, concerns, and political motivations which have shaped Congress' involvement in these matters. For example, the traditionally strong support for Israel in Congress is juxtaposed against a concern to support moderate Arab states as well in order to have a "balanced" U.S. foreign policy in the region.

Strong support for Israel in Congress is usually expressed in Soviet analysis through such terms as the "pro-Israeli coalition" or the "Zionist lobby." It is argued such a lobby seeks to influence Congress because "Tel Aviv looks with extreme suspicion on the expansion of U.S. ties with Saudi Arabia, fearing that it might replace Israel as the privileged ally of American imperialism in the Middle East."[35] The activities of AIPAC are also described in some detail and that organization is credited with obtaining the support of 75-80% of the Senate and 60% of the House. By contrast, the Arab lobbying effort under the auspices of the National Association of Arab Americans (NAAA) is not seen as being able to "compete 'on equal terms' with the pro-Israeli lobby."[36]

A Soviet case study on U.S. arms sales to the Middle East also identifies the steady stream of Middle East leaders who visit the Congress, particularly during times of pending or imminent arms sales proposals. A 1978 article on the fighter aircraft sales proposed by the Carter Administration to Israel, Egypt and Saudi Arabia described visits to the United States by Prime Minister Menachem Begin, Foreign Minister Moshe Dayan, and several members of the Saudi royal family. The Begin visit, which sought to persaude the Carter Administration not to sell F-15 fighter aircraft to Saudi Arabia was described as a "propaganda tour against the proposals of the American President," while Saudi visitors "persistently stressed the anticommunist nature of the Saudi Arabia regime and the 'needs' of its defense."

This Soviet case study also describes the primary arguments used in support of major U.S. arms sales to the Middle East.[37] It is stressed that among conservatives the threat of increased Soviet involvement or domestic instability exacerbated by the presence of states sympathetic to aspects of Soviet foreign policy is a major reason for supporting arms sales. Another argument cited is the extension of U.S. military power through force deployment arrangements that may ensue from certain arms sales. The sense that strong support for Israel must be coupled with a strong commitment to friendly Arab states is a third. Fourth, a pragmatic argument that prospective arms purchasers will go elsewhere, perhaps to the Soviet Union, and that U.S. influence is maximized if sales are made is also frequently stated. Finally, Soviet analysis points out that, particularly with respect to Saudi Arabia, financial considerations including increased exports and the stability of the world economy are often invoked by members supporting arms sales.

Also identified are the primary arguments used in Congress against major arms sales in the Middle East, particularly to Arab states.[38] One frequent argument among opponents of major arms sales to the Middle East is that such sales, particularly in large numbers and of a sophisticated nature, threaten the balance of military forces in the region against Israel. Soviet scholars cite the argument of opponents that the major threats to Arab states come from their economic backwardness which leads to domestic instability and arms sales do not address this problem. Opponents also refute the notion that moderate Arab states will become radicalized or anti-American if arms sales are not approved, pointing to their intrinsically more important economic relations with the United States that are not affected by arms sales. Also described are opponents' claims that the effects of arming both Israel and the Arab states in the region produces a new spiral in the conventional arms race in the Middle East.

Americanist analysis also describes procedural and political coalitions which help determine the outcome of Congressional consideration of arms sales. For example, future promises of additional weapons to Israel will sometimes enable pending sales to Arab countries to go forward. Letters of assurance regarding the safety and security of weapons sold to Arab states and that they will not be used against Israel are often sent to Congress from the Secretary of Defense or the President. Soviet scholars also identify the importance of gaining support of the Democratic and Republican leadership in both Houses of Congress as well as the moderate-liberal bloc of votes as keys to gaining approval of major arms sales.

Analysis of Amerikanistika on Congress and U.S. Arms Sales to the Middle East

One finds amerikanistika on the subject of Congress' consideration of U.S. arms sales to the Middle East to be impressive. While there is often resort to the practice of quoting American sources without comment, this practice in this case enables a sophisticated analysis of the myriad of legislative perspectives on U.S. arms sales to the Middle East.

Despite its overall quality, there are some aspects of americanist analysis that are questionable. For example, pressure from pro-Israel lobbying groups like AIPAC has usually been stronger in the House than the Senate, the reverse of americanist calculations. For example, in 1981 the House of Representatives rejected the sale of AWACS aircraft to Saudi Arabia and the Senate subsequently approved the sale. The major political reason the House did not vote on the 1978 arms package to Egypt, Israel, and Saudi Arabia was at the request of the Carter Administration, which believed, accurately, that it had a better chance of success in the Senate than in the House in avoiding rejection of the sale.

Several other points are missing from Soviet analysis. First, Soviet analysis does not recognize the importance of the process of 30-day prior notification and review by Congress in ensuring legislative consideration of major arms sales. Most participants in both the legislative and executive branches agree that if such a review period did not exist, consultations regarding controversial arms sales would certainly not reach their current level of intensity.

Second, the ability of Congress to reject sales is more important for its threat value than its actual use. Thus, while Congress has never rejected a major arms sale, the threat of such action has been used to force administrations to consult with Congress, leading to modifications of the original scope and terms of the sale in many instances. The Hawk missile sale to Jordan in 1975, the Maverick and Sidewinder missile sales to Saudi Arabia in 1986, the F-5 and F-15 aircraft sales to Egypt and Saudi Arabia in 1978 and a subsequent sale of F-15s and associated equipment to Saudi Arabia in 1987 are all examples of such modifications. Thus, the threat of rejection insures legislative involvement and americanist analysis has failed to recognize this.

Amerikanistika also neglects the institutional advantages the President has over Congress in the debate about controversial arms sales to the Middle East. The use of appeals to the public, arguments about negative effects on bilateral relations with the proposed recipient (relations which are conducted first and foremost by the executive branch) and the usual lack of consensus in Congress about the proper course of action beyond simple rejection are all procedural and political realities which diminish legislative power in the consideration of arms sales.

Nonetheless, the overall quality of amerikanistika on Congress and U.S. arms sales to the Middle East is quite good. The identification of powerful lobbying groups like AIPAC, the importance of visits by foreign dignitaries, the generally accurate portrayal of the major arguments for and against major sales, and the description of assurances and modifications used by the executive branch to gain Congressional approval of arms sales suggest an informed, pragmatic approach to the issues involved.

Congress and U.S. Defense and Arms Control Policy

Americanist Perspective

Americanists have mixed reviews of Congressional action in the field of defense and arms control. While Congress is often attacked, as it was in the early 1980s, for not adopting legislation to improve U.S.-Soviet relations and reduce international tensions, it is also recognized as representing "negative attitudes toward the uncontrolled buildup of nuclear arms and the dangerous escalation of Soviet-American friction."[39]

Soviet scholars never hesitate to point to increasing defense budgets as an "opportunity to continue escalating the arms race and build up U.S. military presence in various parts of the world in order to stifle national liberation movements and undermine the positions of socialism."[40] The Reagan Administration in particular is seen as opposed to meaningful arms control efforts and as engaging in "maneuvers and accompanying its policy of forcible pressure with rhetoric about a desire for 'dialogue' and better relations with the USSR,"[41] to get its defense programs appropriated.

In particular, this perception of a cynical Reagan Administration successfully contronting a somewhat gullible or incompetent Congress on defense and arms control matters permeates amerikanistika on legislative consideration of the MX missile. The 1983-1984 effort, spearheaded by Rep. Aspin, to support the recommendations of the Scowcroft Commission report on strategic forces is seen in this light. The central recommendation of the report, which in essence called for continued funding for the MX missile in exchange for revisions in the U.S. position at the Strategic Arms Reduction Talks (START), including a proposal for a "builddown" in nuclear weapons, was dismissed out of hand by americanists. They regarded the builddown proposal as a "reduction then buildup" and completely acceptable to the Reagan Administration, which saw the builddown as good political strategy but not a viable arms control concept in any event. Conservatives who supported the builddown approach were regarded as using the proposal to garner enough votes to defeat other more far-reaching arms control proposals, including the nuclear freeze.

Nonetheless, the contentious, protracted debate over MX funding is acknowledged to have produced at least tactical defeats for the Reagan Administration. The original decision to build 100 missiles in concentrated configurations, aimed at producing survivability by inducing physical conditions under which incoming missiles would destroy each other (the so-called Dense Pack basing mode) was defeated by the House in late 1982 leading to the ultimate success of the Scowcroft Commission recommendations. This early and temporary defeat for the MX was viewed by americanists as the result of "heightened activity of the advocates of constructive talks, reasonable compromises, and consideration for the security interests of both sides."[42] The continuing reluctance to fund the full 100 MX missiles and the possibility that only 50 will ever be built was seen as evidence that political opposition to the Reagan Administration's arms control policy was growing.

Soviet scholarship also devotes considerable attention to the consideration of proposals for a U.S.-Soviet nuclear freeze that were considered in Congress in 1982 and 1983. Generally heightened perceptions about growing possibilities of nuclear war, freeze referendums approved in 8 states and numerous local areas and freeze political organizations were identified as the main reasons the freeze "aroused the rapt interest of the general public and the legislators."[43] The success of the freeze movement in local referendums was described as a triumph for popular democratic forces, the likes of which had not been seen since the Vietnam War.

Soviet scholars accurately describe the evolution of nuclear freeze proposals in the House, their eventual acceptance by the House Foreign Affairs Committee and House floor consideration of resolutions calling for a mutual and verifiable freeze on and reductions in nuclear weapons. In this instance, as in the case of the MX analysis, americanists see the results of Congressional action as essentially minimal and largely ineffective in halting the "militarism" of the Reagan Administration.

The House outcome on the nuclear freeze resolution in 1982 was the approval by the narrow margin of 204-202 of a Republican substitute to the Foreign Affairs Committee version calling for a freeze at substantially reduced levels of nuclear weapons. The wording of the substitute was nearly identical to an Administration-supported resolution in the Senate sponsored by Senators Jackson and John Warner (R-Va.) which assumed that Soviet nuclear superiority required a U.S. strategic modernization if a freeze at reduced levels were to occur. Thus, Soviet writers viewed the Jackson-Warner proposal as continuing the Reagan Adminstration's military modernization program.

The House outcome in 1983 was also criticized, particularly in light of the 1982 elections which americanists rightly argued had produced a more liberal House (the Democrats captured a net gain of 26 seats). The Foreign Affairs Committee version was eventually approved on the House floor but not before numerous amendments were adopted and a 42-hour Republican-led filibuster was conducted. Confusion among proponents about the weapons systems included or excluded by a bilateral freeze gave opponents a chance to gain political momentum. The non-binding nature of the resolution, assurances that strategic modernization could proceed before a freeze agreement was completed and that reductions would have to proceed within a reasonable period after a freeze agreement were all agreed to as amendments on the House floor. Americanists argued that "countless compromises divested (the freeze) of much of its original meaning."[44]

Americanists rightly point out that the Senate, because it was controlled by the Republicans at the time of the nuclear freeze debate in Congress, was far less active on the freeze issue. The freeze resolution supported by the freeze movement and sponsored by Senators Kennedy and Mark Hatfield (R-Ore.) was rejected twice by the Foreign Relations Committee and twice on the Senate floor in the form of nongermane amendments to pending legislation raising the national debt ceiling. A resolution sponsored by Committee chairman Percy, which proposed a mutual observance of the SALT I and SALT II agreements but support of the Administration's START negotiating position, was never considered on the Senate floor.

While americanists do argue that House passage of the freeze resolution "acknowledged the existence of an approximate balance in nuclear potential and the possibility of controlling a nuclear freeze,"[45] they express disappointment at the fact that, after the submission of the Scowcroft Commission report, some supporters of the freeze in the House and Senate agreed to support the administration proposals for nuclear weapons programs in exchange for a modification in the administration's arms control negotiating position in Geneva. The decision to fund the MX under the Scowcroft Commission guidelines was regarded as a serious setback to proponents of progress in the strategic nuclear arms control.

As the arms control debate between the Congress and the executive branch intensified in the mid-1980s, Soviet americanists devoted considerable coverage to disagreements over the making and conduct of defense policy. One americanist, while recognizing the significance of the enactment of an amendment to the Defense Department authorization bill banning funds for fiscal year 1986 for the Administration's anti-satellite (ASAT) weapons program, argued that "the congressionally approved act does not envisage the cessation of work on the ASAT program and even allocates $15 million more than the Administration requested for the creation of the system."[46] Another americanist rejected this judgment, seeing the grudging acceptance of the ASAT amendment as "Congress' affirmation of its financial and other prerogatives to correct administration policy."[47]

In August 1986, critics of the Reagan Administration's defense and arms control policy, who had argued that a six-year trillion dollar defense modernization program had failed to produce any progress in reaching arms control agreements, passed in the House of Representatives a series of extraordinary amendments to the Defense Department authorization bill for fiscal year 1987. In addition to extending the ASAT ban for another fiscal year, the House passed amendments: (1) to prohibit funds for nuclear tests above one kiloton if the Soviet Union refrained from such tests; (2) to prohibit funds for any weapons deployments that would exceed the numerical weapons sublimits of the SALT II agreement provided the Soviet Union did not exceed those sublimits; (3) a 40% reduction of the Administration's budget request for the Strategic Defense Initiative (SDI), the President's proposed research program designed to explore the feasibility of developing a strategic defense system to protect U.S. offensive nuclear systems and; (4) a denial of production funds for the production of binary chemical weapons. The Administration bitterly opposed all five of these amendments arguing that their implementation in the case of the nuclear testing amendment could not be verified and that the other proposals undercut the President's ability to negotiate arms control agreements with the Soviet Union because arms control policy was being rigidly set by the Congress.

Soviet americanists hailed the adoption of these amendments as evidence that the Congress was responding to American public opinion and rejecting the Reagan Administration's "obstructionist, anti-Soviet, and chauvinistic" arms control policies."[48] But as the amendments were considered in a House-Senate conference on the DOD authorization bill (the Republican-controlled Senate had not included any of these amendments in their version of the bill), americanists became disillusioned with Congress' eventual compromise on these issues. When President Reagan and General Secretary Gorbachev agreed to have a summit meeting in Reykjavik in October, 1986, congressional supporters of the amendments, particularly those in the House leadership, were put in the politically impossible position of appearing to hamstring the President's policy options at the Reykjavik summit. While retaining the ASAT ban, the House-Senate conference decided to make the nuclear testing and SALT II provisions non-binding policy statements, to restore most of the SDI funding cut, and to begin production of chemical weapons after a 17-year hiatus imposed by the Congress. One americanist saw this political retreat on the arms control amendments as reaffirming "a traditional rule of the American political game: Congress has to support the President when he faces an opponent in the international arena."[49] Another americanist was more charitable seeing the effort as a whole as "the result of disagreements over long-range priorities and the desire of certain forces in the ruling class to exert legislative pressure on the White House to force it to take a more serious and responsible approach to arms control and Soviet-American relations."[50]

In general, Soviet scholars see the Reagan Administration as having "to make a vigorous effort to surmount the pressure of arms limitation,"[51] felt in Congress. By changing political tactics and making certain compromises, the Administration was able to obtain funding for the major aspects of its defense program. Still, americanists argue that the struggle over arms control policy in Congress continues and that Congress is "playing the role of a restraining factor, forcing the administration to sometimes soften its rhetoric and make foreign policy concessions."[52] Americanists have identified serious concerns about nuclear war manifested in freeze referendums and greater arms control concern and organization at the grass roots levels which in turn has forced greater sensitivity in Congress about the need to factor arms control considerations into defense spending decisions. In turn, Congress has also exerted greater pressure on the executive branch for progress in arms control. In the final analysis, however, despite the judgment that Congress is a "mirror of U.S. politics" and a "political barometer of the changing mood in American society,"[53] americanists argue that the administration has for the most part retained sufficient congressional support to continue its defense modernization program with few impediments.

Analysis of Amerikanistika on Congress and U.S. Defense and Arms Control Policy

Amerikanistika on Congress' role in U.S. defense and arms control policy demonstrates an ability for thorough and reasonably accurate analysis. The 1980s witnessed an unprecedented legislative involvement in arms control matters as a result of popular support for a nuclear freeze, the controversy over the MX missile and other issues. While perhaps excessively critical of the Reagan Administration, and excessively pessimistic of Congress' ability to influence and modify Administration arms control policy, americanist attitudes about Congress' actions on defense and arms control paralleled non-Soviet sources who argue that "the assertion of congressional influence . . . reflected the lack of progress of the Reagan Administration in the area of arms control."[54]

The general perception that the Administration has scant interest in arms control beyond demonstrating sufficient flexibility to get its defense programs through Congress is by no means held only by Soviet americanists. Large numbers of American defense experts and Members of Congress share this perception as well. The effort headed by Representative Aspin to bring changes in Administration policy in exchange for support for the MX missile is the prime example of how, in the view of some, the Administration has implemented this strategy to achieve its weapons objectives with only tactical concessions that Members had hoped would be more significant.

The MX missile debate has been the most prolonged and contentious of any arms control issue considered by the Congress in the 1980s, and a full discussion is not possible here.[55] While it is now evident that at least some missiles will be deployed, it is wrong to suggest no arms control price was extracted. On the issue of land-based missiles, the Administration was forced to raise its proposed ceiling while retaining a low overall warhead limit, thus creating conditions for a lesser number of MX missiles (because they contained 10 warheads each) and a greater number of single warhead mobile missiles. These mobile missiles have been favored by the Aspin group as more stabilizing because of their reduced ability (compared to the MX) to destroy Soviet missiles and greater ability to survive because of their mobility. The incorporation of the builddown idea which envisioned destroying greater numbers of warheads as lesser numbers of new warheads were deployed was also forced on the Administration.

Moreover, the Aspin group, and their counterparts in the Senate, Senators Nunn, William Cohen (R-Me.) and Percy, sought to bring about "the creation of a durable strategic consensus embracing both weapons modernization and arms control which would transcend arguments between liberals and conservatives and which would last from one administration to the next."[56] The Scowcroft Commission report sought to achieve this consensus by adopting an approach designed to integrate military force building and arms control negotiations in a way that would reduce the first-strike capability on both sides through deployment limits on types of weapons that enhance that capability. The intensity with which the House and Senate groups negotiated changes in the Administration's START position before they supported MX funding is ignored by americanists. Also ignored is the fact that the President of the United States was forced to accept grudgingly a direct congressional role in the making of arms control policy.

There is indeed much to criticize about the results of the legislative foray into the formulation of arms control policy. No agreement has been reached at Geneva, while at the same time the MX has been deployed, although the fact that the Soviet Union walked out of both the START and INF talks for a period of slightly over a year from late 1983 to early 1985 is not mentioned in amerikanistika. There is also no question that the "builddown" idea itself was supported by some because it contained the same sort of useful simplicity that the nuclear freeze did and could be used in the public relations battle against the freeze. It could also be argued convincingly that the vagueness of the builddown concept (it originally started as a 2-1 warhead reduction and had blossomed into several permutations during legislative-executive negotiations on revising the START proposal) allowed the Administration to trivialize its concession on the builddown "by simply making it the mechanism for carrying out whatever reduction level would be negotiated in a full START agreement."[57]

Finally, the development of a single-warhead mobile missile, the cherished goal of the Aspin group, received a major rebuff by the Administration in its most recent negotiating proposal in November 1985 which called for the banning of new mobile missiles. Conservative legislators and their allies in the Administration are also contemplating the elimination of the mobile missile on budgetary grounds.

Nonetheless, legislative activism on defense and arms control policy issues in recent years was unprecedented, as americanists appear to acknowledge. The rejection of the MX basing mode in 1982, the arms control compromises needed for its continued funding in 1983, its near defeat in 1984, and the realization even among the MX's most ardent supporters that only 50, not 100, MX missiles will ever be built confirms the judgment of americanists that Congress is a restraining factor on the Administration's defense policy. It also seems to demonstrate the point made by Soviet scholars that concessions on arms control have been demanded as a Congressional price for supporting weapons systems.

Soviet analysis on the nuclear freeze debate in Congress is remarkably accurate. The argument that Congress took up the issue of a nuclear freeze because of mounting public pressure arising out of increased fears of nuclear war as manifested in various state and local referenda must be acknowledged.[58] The legislative history of nuclear freeze resolutions in 1982 and 1983 is also adequately described, particularly the critical debate between those who sought a freeze once U.S.-Soviet strategic forces had been reduced to equal levels (a position supported by the Administration, because it constituted an endorsement of their strategic modernization program) and those who believed U.S.-Soviet forces were basically equal and therefore sought an immediate, mutual, and verifiable freeze. Also strikingly accurate was the reporting of the confusion of the meaning of the freeze among its supporters which enabled a Republican filibuster and scores of amendments to be added which removed much of the political momentum from the resolution. The much-amended character of the freeze resolution cushioned the political blow to the Administration when the resolution eventually passed.

Americanists are also correct in describing the keen disappointment among arms control advocates when numerous Congressional supporters of the nuclear freeze resolution supported funding for the MX after submission of the Scowcroft Commission report. In fact, many arms control advocates would accept this passage from one Soviet scholar:

> The congressmen who voted for the MX included many who had supported the nuclear freeze less than a month before. This seemingly more than strange contradiction is actually the best proof of the Congress' real position, its willingness to verbally support the highest principles, especially if they are popular with the electorate and are worded in general and unbinding terms. When it comes to specific arms programs, however, the majority of congressmen easily forget these principles and consistently support the buildup and modernization of armed forces.[59]

Finally, americanist criticism and skepticism about the series of arms control amendments passed by Congress in 1985 and particularly in 1986 is not well-founded. The adoption of and then enactment into law of an amendment prohibiting production and deployment of an ASAT system represented a major defeat for the administration. For its supporters, the ASAT amendment was the first mutual arms control restraint imposed on the United States and the Soviet Union since the beginning of the Reagan Administration although the subsequent conclusion of an INF agreement eventually belied that argument. Supporters have also pointed out that the ASAT deployment ban (since extended for another year in 1987) has prevented both sides from pursuing weapons that could effectively blind the other side (ASAT systems could deny satellite intelligence information about nuclear and conventional weapons deployments), thereby increasing the risk of accidental war and shortening decision time about the use of military force.

The fact that the Reagan Administration was forced to accept this prohibition for three consecutive years in order to preserve congressional support for other elements of its defense modernization program attests to the growing political influence of Congress in the making and conduct of U.S. arms control policy. The americanist argument that some additional research monies for the ASAT program were approved obscures the achievement of the ASAT deployment ban. It was also eventually proved to be inaccurate because the Reagan Administration appears to have abandoned the ASAT program and has not requested any additional budget funds. It appears that nothing short of total repudiation of the entire Reagan Administration defense modernization program, a very unlikely development, will impress some americanists in their evaluation of Congress' arms control activity.

With respect to the americanist analysis of the package of arms control amendments in 1986, it is quite true that members of Congress are quite reluctant to be put in a position of limiting by legislation the President's ability to negotiate arms control agreements with the Soviet Union. As an institution the Congress cannot conduct such negotiations. But what is most important about the 1986 amendments was that never before had either house of Congress passed such a far-reaching set of amendments that were clearly antithetical to the arms control policy of a sitting President. The coalition that passed these amendments in the House included some centrist Republicans and even conservative Democrats who had previously never supported arms control limitations on the Reagan Administration's defense modernization program. The fact that such members supported such amendments in 1986 is testament both to the growing arms control sensitivity among members of Congress and the general feeling that the Administration would have to be pushed politically to achieve progress in arms control.

Whether the Administration's subsequent conclusion of an INF agreement with the Soviet Union represented an acknowledgement of stonger congressional demands for arms control progress remains to be seen. What can be said is that unlike in 1986 when the prospects of the Reykjavik summit produced a major political retreat by critics of the Reagan Administration arms control policy, it did not stop the Congress in 1987 from passing, this time in both the House and the Senate, another series of arms control amendments similar to those passed in 1986. And unlike 1986, the prospect of the Washington summit did not deter Congress from making cuts in the SDI budget and enacting into law with grudging Administration acceptance, binding limitations on further excessions of the SALT II numerical weapons sublimits and on maintaining the limitations in the U.S.-Soviet Anti-Ballistic Missile (ABM) Treaty on testing and development of space-based defense systems despite executive branch efforts to end such limitations for the purposes of the SDI program. In many ways, Congress' influence on U.S. defense and arms control policy is at an all-time high.

In conclusion, amerikanistika on Congress and its role in U.S. defense and arms control policy reflects a nuanced, sophisticated albeit sometimes excessively critical understanding of the issues. One cannot quarrel with the relationship between the "pressure of arms limitation in Congress and the Administration's need to deal with it to get weapons systems approved."[60] Greater public interest in arms control, exemplified by the nuclear freeze debate and more recent comprehensive efforts to develop an alternative arms control policy, is also apparent. One is intrigued by the americanist portrayal of Congress as a "political barometer of the changing mood in American society." This judgment, which appears to acknowledge Congress as at least in some ways representative of the wishes of the American people is remarkable for a group of scholars professing to be Marxist-Leninist in their orientation. Yet it is a theme which is struck repeatedly by americanists both in their written work and in interviews conducted for this study. The apparent gap between activism and actual results has been decried by non-Soviet sources as well as Soviet scholars and reflects the tension created by the twin legislative motivation of support for an adequate defense and arms control agreements that reduce the risk of nuclear war.

Overall Assessment of Amerikanistika
on Contemporary Issues

Chapter 3 has helped to enrich the conclusions of the previous chapter and its theoretical implications. Amerikanistika on contemporary issues, like efforts on process and procedural issues, demonstrates qualities of political awareness, ideological pragmatism, and intellectual power, particularly with respect to the discussions on Congress' role in U.S. policy toward Western Europe, U.S. arms sales to the Middle East, and defense and arms control policy. Nonetheless, some reservations must be stated. On one issue examined in this chapter, Congress and U.S. policy toward Eastern Europe, a dogmatic, unitary worldview seems to be present. Furthermore, with respect to Congress' actions in U.S.-Soviet trade, the tendency to assess actions with clear reference to the salutory or negative effects on the Soviet Union is apparent.

This chapter and the previous one have provided a comprehensive recitation and analysis of a broad cross-section of amerikanistika on Congress and foreign policy. While its quality has been uneven at times, more often than not americanists have produced a level of scholarship qualitatively comparable to American efforts on similar subjects and the trends described on many issues have been accurate.

As the next chapter will explore in detail, americanists, operating in the Marxist-Leninist tradition of the unity of theory and practice, as well as scholarship and politics, are expected to analyze aspects of international relations like Congress' role in U.S. foreign policy, not in the abstract, but as a means of making concrete recommendations that contribute to more effective formulation and implementation of Soviet foreign policy. If this is true, the last two chapters have amply demonstrated that americanists have produced a rich vein of material for which Soviet foreign policymakers can assess the "Congress factor" in U.S. foreign policy.

But what do Soviet decisionmakers at the Politburo and Central Committee Secretariat level do with this information? If the information has been digested, how has it shaped leadership attitudes toward Congress and foreign policy? What other sources of information are available to shape those attitudes? What are the manifestations of those attitudes? The answers to these questions, much like the study of amerikanistika, have profound theoretical as well as practical implications for the study of Soviet foreign policy.

Notes

1. V.S. Mikheev, "Congress and the 'Atlantic Partnership'" *SSHA* no. 2, February 1984, in USSR Report, USA, JPRS 84-005, p. 44.

2. Ibid., p. 45.

3. Mikheev writes: "The ratio of U.S. military aid to Greece and Turkey in recent years has been 7-10, allegedly to secure a balance of power in the region . . . Assistant Secretary of Defense for International Security Policy R. Perle, telephoned and visited prominent Members of Congress from both parties in an attempt to surmount the opposition of the influential Greek lobby (Mikheev, p. 49.).

4. Ibid., p. 50.

5. Ibid.

6. Ibid., p. 51.

7. Ibid.

8. Ibid., p. 52.

9. U.S. Congress, House, Committee on Foreign Affairs, *Overview of Nuclear Arms Control and Defense Strategy in NATO*, Hearings before the Subcommittees on International Security and Scientific Affairs and on Europe and the Middle East. 97th Cong., 2nd sess., 1982, p. 1.

10. See for example, the statement of Rep. Hamilton in U.S. Congress, House, Committee on Foreign Affairs, *Foreign Assistance Legislation for Fiscal Years 1986-1987, Part 3*, Hearings and Markup before the Subcommittee on Europe and the Middle East, 99th Cong., 1st sess., 1985, p. 33.

11. Ibid., p. XXXI.

12. U.S. Congress, House, Committee on Foreign Affairs, *Congress and Foreign Policy, 1982*, by the Foreign Affairs and National Defense Division, Congressional Research Service, Library of Congress (Washington, D.C.: Government Printing Office, 1983), p. 109.

13. U.S. Congress, House, Committee on Foreign Affairs, *Congress and Foreign Policy, 1984*, by the Foreign Policy and National Defense Division, Congressional Research Service, Library of Congress (Washington, D.C.: Government Printing Office, 1985), p. 139.

14. For more on Congressional sentiments in favor of protectionist legislation against member states of the European Community see *Congress and Foreign Policy, 1982*, p. 98 and pp. 105-106; also see U.S. Congress, House, Committee on Foreign Affairs, *The United States and Europe: Focus on the Expanding Agenda for the 1980s*, Report of the Twenty-First and Twenty-Second Meetings of Members of Congress and of the European Parliament, 98th Cong., 1st sess., 1983, pp. 14-35, 61-82, and U.S. Congress, House, Committee on Foreign Affairs, *The Active Agenda: Outstanding*

Issues in U.S.-E.C. Relations, Report of the Twenty-Fourth and Twenty-Fifth Meetings of Members of Congress and of the European Parliament, 99th Cong., 1st sess., 1985.

15. The policy of differentiation is a longstanding U.S. foreign policy guideline toward Eastern European countries which seeks to provide economic and political incentives to those countries which demonstrate a modicum of independence from the Soviet Union in their foreign policies or engage in modest forms of political liberalization in their domestic policies. The Reagan Administration's formulation of differentiation involves several criteria including the adoption of distinct and more independent foreign policies, greater political and economic exchange with the non-Communist world, greater tolerance of emigration, greater respect for human rights, encouragement of a more flexible climate for political expression and economic change, and experimentation with economic decentralization. For further information, see U.S. Congress, House, Committee on Foreign Affairs, *U.S. Policy Towards Eastern Europe, 1985,* Hearings before the Subcommittee on Europe and the Middle East, 99th Cong., 2nd sess., 1986, pp. 7-27.

16. Iu. V. Kazakov, p. 2. For a similar analysis see S.I. Bol'shakov, "Congress and U.S. East European Policy," trans. Joint Publications Research Service, *USSR Report, USA: Economics, Politics, Ideology* 74022 (June 1979): 106-113.

17. Kazakov, p. 4.

18. Ibid., p. 5.

19. Ibid.

20. Ibid.

21. Ibid., p. 6.

22. Ibid.

23. Ibid., p. 7.

24. For further discussion of these varying Congressional perspectives on Eastern Europe, see *U.S. Relations with the Countries of Central and Eastern Europe,* pp. 1-10.

25. *U.S. Policy Toward Eastern Europe, 1985,* p. 10.

26. For a discussion of this competition for political support of East European-Americans, see *U.S. Relations with the Countries of Central and Eastern Europe,* pp. 3-4.

27. Kazakov, p. 7.

28. Prokudin, p. 54.

29. Ibid., p. 55.

30. Ibid., p. 59.

31. Ibid., p. 60.

32. Ibid. p. 61.

33. U.S. House of Representatives, Committee on Foreign Affairs, *Congress and Foreign Policy, 1983,* Washington: Government Printing Office, 1984, p. 73.

34. In March and April, 1983, a number of resolutions were introduced in Congress urging the President to open negotiations with the Soviet Union on a Long-Term Grain Agreement. On April 22, 1983, President Reagan lifted his ban on such negotiations, a ban that had been imposed after the declaration of martial law in Poland in December, 1981. For further information, see *Congress and Foreign Policy, 1983,* pp. 73-74.

35. Osipova, p. 104.

36. Ibid., p. 105.

37. For a summary of the arguments cited in this case study and used by Members of Congress in support of specific arms sales to the Middle East, see Osipova, pp. 106-108.

38. For a summary of the arguments cited in this case study and used by Members of Congress against specific arms sales to the Middle East, see Osipova, pp. 108-111.

39. N.B. Tatarinova and V.L. Chernov, "The 97th Congress and Soviet-American Relations," trans. Joint Publications Research Service, *USSR Report, USA: Economics, Politics, Ideology* 83788 (March 1983): 57. Also see E.N. Ershova, "Congress and the Issue of the Nuclear Freeze," trans. Joint Publications Research Service, *USSR Report, USA: Economics, Politics, Ideology* 85-013 (October 1985): 42.

40. Tatarinova and Chernov, p. 57.

41. V.I. Batiuk, "98th Congress: Debates on Armaments," trans. Joint Publications Research Service, *USSR Report, USA: Economics, Politics, Ideology* 85-002 (November 1984): 41.

42. Tatarinova and Chernov, p. 61.

43. Ershova, p. 42.

44. Ibid., p. 46.

45. Ibid.

46. Iu. A. Ivanov, "Samaia dolgaia sessia," *SShA: ekonomika, politika, ideologiia,* (April 1986):77.

47. V.A. Savel'ev, "U.S. Approaches to Dialogue with the USSR," trans. Joint Publications Research Service, *USSR Report, USA: Economics, Politics, Ideology* 87-002, (November 1986):10.

48. Ivanov, "Trudnye problemy . . . ," pp. 74-75.

49. Ibid., p. 75.

50. Savel'ev, "U.S. Approaches to Dialogue . . . ," p. 10.

51. Ershova, p. 49.

52. Ibid.

53. Tatarinova and Chernov, p. 58.

54. *Congress and Foreign Policy, 1983,* p. 86.

55. For a thorough discussion of the MX debate in Congress, see *Congress and Foreign Policy, 1983,* pp. 86-108, and *Congress and Foreign Policy, 1984,* pp. 48-68.

56. *Congress and Foreign Policy, 1983,* p. 105.

57. Ibid., p. 106.

58. Congressional Research Service specialists clearly acknowledge that the "impetus for the congressional nuclear weapons freeze initiatives came largely from a grassroots movement which grew dramatically during 1982. Beginning in New England, the movement to freeze the arms race spread across the country to such a broad spectrum of the population that it has been described as the 'broadest based movement since civil rights.'" (*Congress and Foreign Policy, 1982,* p. 12.)

59. Ershova, p. 47.

60. Batiuk, p. 41.

4

Soviet "Congress-Watchers": The Soviet Academic Community

It is evident from the previous two chapters that a wide range of information is available to the Soviet leadership on Congress' role in U.S. foreign policy. If we are to define the term "leadership" to be those members of the Politburo and Central Committee Secretariat who have major impact on the making and conduct of Soviet foreign policy, it is clear, as we shall see, that the organization, functions, and channels of information by which amerikanistika is made available helps to insure that access to americanist analysis is readily available to the Soviet leadership.

Functions and Organization of Amerikanistika on Congress and Foreign Policy

Generally speaking, amerikanistika on the subject of Congress' role in U.S. foreign policy comes to the Soviet leadership from the social science institutes of the USSR Academy of Sciences. The information produced at the institutes is filtered to the Politburo through the Central Committee bureaucratic structure. Four institutes in particular predominate writing on Congress and foreign policy: The Institute of the USA and Canada (ISKAN) in particular, and to a lesser degree the Institute of the World Economy and International Relations (IMEMO), the Institute of State and Law (IGPAN), and the Institute of World History.

Americanists are a part of a wider group of individuals that have come to be called the "mezhdunarodniki," the Russian monicker for experts on foreign countries and international relations. The mezhdunarodniki, which includes americanists, serve the essential function, of utilizing specialized knowledge to provide information on foreign affairs to the Soviet leadership. According to one scholar, serving the leadership takes three forms: (1) the training of qualified executive bureaucratic personnel in the Central Committee apparatus, the All-Union ministries and administrations, the various Academies of Sciences, the universities, and the editorial boards of the printed and electronic mass media; (2) the application of specialized knowledge and expertise in the making of decisions; and (3) the legitimation of the official policy line by providing it with the scientific and scholarly imprimatur.[1]

The three types of service to Soviet decisionmakers produce several effects on the work product of americanists. For example, scholarship conforms to the principle of "konkretnost" or concreteness, which means research must advance and be responsive to current policy requirements. The Marxist conception of the unity of theory and practice also demands that "theory must provide mankind with adequate information to guide its activity in the real world; in return, practical action should test the validity of the theory and contribute to its further elaboration."[2] Americanists therefore must submit to the firmly entrenched principle in Soviet scholarship that science produce policy-relevant studies that can be used by policymakers in the Soviet political system.

In addition, the legitimation function performed by americanists results in their employment by the Soviet political system as media commentators both at home and abroad. Not only scholarly writing but "simple journalism, publicistic work, commenting on current policies, therefore remains . . . an integral part of scholarly duties."[3] The frequent appearance on American and Soviet television of americanists Georgii Arbatov and Valentin Zorin, both of whom have written on Congress' role in U.S. foreign policy, demonstrate a tangible manifestation of this legitimation function.

In this regard, Soviet journalists covering U.S.-Soviet relations must also be considered americanists. Soviet journalists share the same career patterns as those of Academy scholars and often serve a stint at Academy institutes like ISKAN and IMEMO. Soviet journalists covering foreign policy receive the same type of academic training as do their counterparts in the Academy. Most are graduates of Moscow State University (Russian acronym MGIMO) or the Ministry of Foreign Affairs' Institute of International Relations (Russian acronym IMO). Once assigned to foreign policy coverage, journalists usually remain international reporters and do not shift back to domestic reporting. The career profiles of Soviet journalists often reflect the attributes of the postwar generation of Soviet elites: better educated, well-travelled and less traumatized by social upheavals like the industrialization and Great Purges of the 1930's and the devastating effects of World War II.

One finds this pattern evident in the career profiles of two well-known Soviet journalists on Congress' role in foreign policy: Stanislav Kondrashev and Valentin Zorin. Kondrashev graduated from MGIMO and began his career with *Izvestiia* in 1951. After serving abroad in Cairo from 1957-1961, he became *Izvestiia's* New York correspondent from 1961-1968 and its bureau chief in Washington from 1971-1976. He then became deputy editor-in-chief and then a political observer. He has written extensively on American politics, and covered numerous elections and party conventions.

Zorin is also a MGIMO graduate. Since the mid-1950s he has conducted roundtable discussions on international affairs on Soviet radio and television. He has been a correspondent for both TASS and Radio Moscow, and a political observer for *Pravda* and *Izvestiia*. He has contributed numerous articles to ISKAN's monthly journal as well as serving on its editorial board. He also has written on and covered various aspects of American politics.

As examples of shared career patterns between Soviet journalists and academicians, we can examine the biographies of the directors of ISKAN and IMEMO, Arbatov and Evgenii Primakov. In both cases, these americanists spent considerable time in the field of journalism. Arbatov, after graduating from MGIMO in 1949, spent eleven years working with a number of journals and periodicals including the mass circulation periodical *Novoe Vremia*. Primakov worked for nine years (1953-1962) for the State Committee for Radio and Television and subsequently for eight years (1962-1970) as deputy editor of *Pravda* in the newspaper's Department of Asian and African Countries.

Thus, the distinction between journalist and americanist is indeed an artificial one. Many Soviet academicians have been both, evidence of the requirement placed on academicians to not only perform policy-relevant research but also engage in legitimation functions with respect to the making and conduct of Soviet foreign policy.

Participation of americanists in decisionmaking is expected to be on the basis of observing current events and "the demand that theory be adjusted to policies and not vice-versa and that scholars be in charge of ideological elasticity."[4] The shift in Soviet attitudes from support for Congress in the early 1970s in its struggle against an executive branch seen as concentrating state power in service of monopoly capital, to support for the President in the late 1970s against a Congress susceptible to the pressures of the powerful military-industrial complex and the Zionist lobby, illustrates this type of ideological elasticity.

To perform their duties, access is required to foreign literature and sources. ISKAN is believed to subscribe to several hundred U.S. and Canadian journals and newspapers, although access is restricted and parcelled out on a need-to-know basis. Daily news reports from Western sources are compiled on a classified basis by the official Soviet news agency TASS for use by designated personnel. To augment published sources, ISKAN and IMEMO personnel host visiting congressional delegations, serve tours in the Soviet Embassy in Washington, and travel to the U.S. under scientific scholarships. These additional opportunities to gain first-hand information on Congress' role in foreign policy are extremely valuable to an americanist, and anyone in contact with americanists who have visited the Congress finds them to be avid assimilators and collectors of information.

This collection process helps serve decisionmakers in two ways: (1) it provides, deepens, and updates information already gathered, and (2) it makes americanists "faithful observers and reporters."[5] In one sense, it is "no accident" that amerikanistika on some issues involving Congress' role in foreign policy is consistent with American views on those issues because amerikanistika is heavily derived from American sources.[6] As a result, Soviet scholars "see the United States largely through American eyes . . . what passes through this prism is in turn sent through the Marxist-Leninist prism."[7]

The importance to the Soviet leadership of specialized knowledge on foreign policy questions has led them to place great emphasis on improving social science research, including the subject of this study. While insisting on konkretnost, the leadership has permitted study of fundamental processes central to the study of current problems.

Thus, as we have seen in the previous two chapters, analysis of topical contemporary issues (e.g. congressional actions concerning arms control) has been complemented by studies of a longer-term, process-oriented nature (the role of pressure groups, bipartisanship or the lack of it, the use of the organization of Congress to delay or modify legislation.) Without a full understanding of the process-oriented issues, an understanding of "current problems" would not be possible, and the leadership has apparently granted the americanists the freedom to explore these issues.

Moreover, while americanists on Congress and foreign policy maintain a Marxist-Leninist outlook and analytical framework, concepts borrowed from "bourgeois" political science such as pressure groups, bipartisanship, the legislative veto, and others are common. Soviet americanists must by the very nature of their work evaluate the validity of such "subjective" concepts and to some degree implicitly acknowledge their usefulness in understanding Congress' foreign policy actions.

This limited type of academic freedom has been accompanied by more pragmatic incentives. Material rewards, special titles, access to special distribution shops and cultural events, opportunities for extracurricular lecturing and writing, and the ultimate prize, foreign travel, are all used to attract the brightest as well as the well-connected.[8] Privileged status and material incentives makes competition to become an americanist very keen. Attesting to this competition is the fact that the sons and daughters of Politburo members have been among those who have become americanists. In fact, the son of former Foreign Minister Andrei Gromyko, Anatolii, now director of the Africa Institute of the USSR Academy of Sciences, wrote one of the earliest books on the operations of the Congress over 30 years ago.

All told, there are approximately 10-15 Soviet scholars who devote fulltime study to the Congress and perhaps another 50 who will contribute articles and books in part or in full dealing with the Congress' role in the American political process and U.S. foreign policy. A small number of graduate students, estimated by Soviet scholars to be about 5-10, are engaged in doctoral research on the Congress.

Of the institutes of the Academy of Sciences that write extensively on the subject of Congress' role in foreign policy, the largest share of activity is concentrated at ISKAN. ISKAN has developed a rather developed sense of konkretnost with a reputation for research and writing intended to be utilized by a number of Party and government institutions. Arbatov, ISKAN's director, has written on aspects of Congress' role in foreign policy. He has accompanied official delegations of the USSR Supreme Soviet that visited the Congress in 1978 and 1985, and has participated in reciprocal visits by Members of Congress to Moscow in 1978, 1983, 1985 and 1987. He has also met with other Congressional delegations that have visited the Soviet Union.

Arbatov is considered a moderate on issues affecting U.S.-Soviet relations. He supports peaceful coexistence, arms control negotiations and has taken reformist positions concerning the establishment of political science as a separate discipline in the Soviet Union. He has also spoken against "left sectarianism," "dogmatism," and "vulgar Marxism." Western scholars concur in the argument that "Arbatov was undoubtedly chosen to head the institute because he was personally committed to a pragmatic and open approach to Soviet-American relations."[9]

Arbatov is currently chairman of the Academy's Scientific Council on Economic, Political and Ideological Problems of the USA. Councils of this type have "responsibility for research, planning, and coordination not only within the Academy of Sciences system but also in higher educational institutions and Ministry research establishments throughout the Soviet Union."[10] Western scholars have regarded the Scientific Councils' coordinating role as exaggerated. In fact, the creation of these Councils in 1974 appears to have been "supportive of the institutes in their unrelenting attempts to extend control and authority over as wide an area as possible."[11]

Nonetheless, the Council under Arbatov's direction has organized conferences of experts on issues, and Soviet scholars interviewed for this study confirm that such conferences involve discussions of Congress' role in U.S. foreign policy. Subject matter of Council-sponsored conferences touching on Congress' role in foreign policy have included Soviet-American Relations and the Problems of European Security, and New Forms of Economic Cooperation and Soviet American Relations. The Council on Economic, Political and Ideological Problems of the USA has several sector heads, including a foreign policy section headed by senior ISKAN staffer Genrikh Trofimenko, and economic and disarmament sections headed by senior IMEMO staffers A.V. Anikin and O.N. Bykov respectively.

ISKAN staffers, particularly at less senior levels, are usually graduates of MGU or MGIMO. Aside from Moscow-based centers, faculty of universities in Tomsk, Novasibirsk, Kiev, and Leningrad also include members with knowledge of Congress' foreign policy role. MGU has set up an ongoing "Problem Laboratory on Amerikanistika" which has has already done a "substantial amount of work on the history and current state of the party system, and an annual *Problemy Amerikanistika* has appeared since 1978, containing material on history, economics, social, political, literary, and other topics."[12] A new handbook on the United States, the first since the wartime period, including basic information on various aspects of U.S. economic, social, and political life is due to appear in the near future.

Members of MGU and MGIMO are usually present at Scientific Council meetings or conferences of experts and it is common for ISKAN staffers to have spent a part of their careers in MGIMO and MGU. For example, nearly a quarter of ISKAN's staff have been stationed at the Soviet Embassy in Washington or the Soviet United Nations mission in New York. Thus, cross-cutting links between americanists develop and as one scholar has correctly argued, it would be "mistaken to conceive of particular centres of American studies as unified bodies of opinion identified with particular styles of interpretation."[13]

Nonetheless, in terms of manpower and number of publications on Congress' role in foreign policy, it is ISKAN that is most prominent. With a staff of about 350, it is second in size only to IMEMO among foreign policy institutes in the Academy. Three departments of ISKAN have scholars who write on Congress' role in foreign policy: Foreign Policy; Domestic Policy; and Political-Military. Other Soviet scholars who write on Congress and foreign policy are scattered throughout ISKAN in unidentified departments and sections.[14] Two department heads, Trofimenko and Andrei Kokoshin, have written on Congress and foreign policy.

ISKAN's journal, *SShA: Ekonomika, politika, ideologiia*, is published monthly and often contains full length articles or shorter book reviews on various aspects of Congress' role in foreign policy. The journal has both academic and propagndistic functions in that it not only rationalizes existing foreign policy positions but also conducts analytic research on a variety of issues confronting Soviet foreign policy. ISKAN's journal is augmented by full-length monographs on legislative involvement in foreign policy written by ISKAN staffers.

Another influential institution on the study of Congress and foreign policy is IMEMO. While IMEMO is a much larger institution as a whole with about 700 staff, americanists are concentrated in two departments: U.S. Economy and International Relations, and Internal Political and Social Problems of the Developed Capitalist Countries.

Nonetheless, americanists at IMEMO are well-placed and believed to be influential. Bykov is Deputy Director of IMEMO and is the most visible of IMEMO's staffers in dealing with Members of Congress. I.D. Ivanov, another deputy director of IMEMO, maintains an active interest in the Congress, particularly on questions of foreign trade. Bykov is a sector head of the Scientific Council headed by Arbatov. The last three directors of IMEMO, N.N. Inozemtsev, A.N. Iakovlev, and E.M. Primakov, all have met with Congressional delegations.

The history of IMEMO as a foreign policy research institution is beyond the purview of this study.[15] Nonetheless, IMEMO's role as the primary center of Soviet foreign policy studies before World War II, its subsequent demise during the immediate postwar period as Stalin closed the Soviet political system behind a cold war edifice and generally discredited international studies, and its resuscitation as a major foreign policy center after the 20th Party Congress have helped IMEMO to be politically visible and influential. Inozemtsev and Primakov, for example, were believed to be close to Brezhnev. Although Iakovlev is no longer at IMEMO, he is regarded as a close confidant of Gorbachev and was one of the four advisors who sat in on the meetings with President Reagan at the Geneva, Reykjavik, and Washington summits.

IMEMO's two departments dealing with Congress and foreign policy, among other issues, are believed to contain about 65 staff, although considerably fewer devote much time to this subject. The institute's journal, *Mirovaia Ekonomika i Mezhdunarodnye Otnosheniia*, is published monthly with some related material on Congress and foreign policy appearing occasionally. It is also publishes an international yearbook on the politics and economics of international relations.

Another of the major Academy institutes that produces writing on Congress and foreign policy is IGPAN. IGPAN, established in December, 1922, has "remained the Soviet Union's most prestigious and important scientific establishment conducting research on governmental, legal and political affairs."[16] While primarily active in domestic law, and the writing of domestic legislation, two departments, Comparative Law and International Law, headed by V.A. Tumanov and N.A. Ushakov, organize conferences, publish articles, and initiate joint research with IMEMO and ISKAN on politics in "bourgeois" nations. IGPAN as a whole has a staff of about 260; staff of the above mentioned department is unknown. IGPAN's journal *Sovetskoe Gosurdarstvo i Pravo*, is published monthly with periodic articles on Congress and foreign policy.

IGPAN, unlike IMEMO and ISKAN, have stressed, not surprisingly, the legal-institutional approach to the study of Congress and foreign policy. Its focus is clearly partial to studies of Congress' formal role in the U.S. foreign policy mechanism while leaving to ISKAN actual studies of Congress' foreign policy involvement. It was involved in the reaction in the 1960s against the establishment of political science as a discipline, as well as the use of "subjectivist bourgeois terms" in the study of foreign political systems. This trend, in turn, has tended to produce more orthodox analysis of Congress' role in foreign policy, with greater emphasis on "the crisis of capitalism" and less acknowledgement of Congress as a separate actor in U.S. foreign policy. IGPAN scholars favor an analytical approach which sees the executive branch as clearly preeminent in the making and conduct of foreign policy and views Congressional oversight and legislation as having marginal impact on foreign policy direction.

The Institute of World History, orginally founded in 1926 as part of a larger historical institute, also has a rich academic history. Since 1968 the Institute has functioned separately from the Institute of History of the USSR. Formerly, the two institutes were merged as a single Institute of History.

The Institute of World History's Department of Modern and Contemporary History of the Countries of the Americas has provided numerous studies on the history of the American political system, the two-party system and other process and procedural issues. Institute scholars also have done quantitative studies on voting records of members of Congress on key domestic and foreign policy issues.

The Institute sponsors scholarly conferences with historians from other countries including the United States. It also maintains an active graduate program and publishes periodic articles on subject matters dealing in part with Congress' role in U.S. foreign policy. Institute scholars also contribute articles to *Problemy Amerikanistika.*

Influence of Americanists on the Soviet Leadership

A crucial question about Soviet scholarship and scholars on Congress and foreign policy is to what degree the information they produce is received and assimilated by the Soviet leadership and how it influences leadership perceptions. Opinion on this point appears to be divided between emigre accounts which tend to downplay, even belittle the influence of foreign policy institutes in the Academy, and Western academic accounts which tend to verify the institutes' ability to influence the leadership.

For example, one former ISKAN staffer who defected from the Soviet Union in 1979, argues that ISKAN's influence on leadership decisionmaking is negligible. According to this defector, ISKAN's main purposes are twofold: providing comfortable jobs for the progeny of the ruling class and to provide a way to get as much as possible—politically and materially—out of the policy of detente."[17] Thus, it is argued that ISKAN basically satisfies only the third of the major functions of americanists discussed earlier, namely the legitimizing, propaganda function.

According to this view, ISKAN studies as well as those of other Academy of Sciences institutes, are totally disregarded by the Party bureaucracy and leadership. Documents sent to the Central Committee apparatus "from all the rival academic institutions find their way straight into the wastepaper basket."[18]

Arkady Shevchenko, the highest ranking Soviet diplomat ever to defect to the West, basically shares this perspective. Despite the widespread Western perception that Arbatov was a close confidant and advisor to Brezhnev on U.S. foreign policy, Shevchenko argues that Arbatov was never seen in then Soviet Foreign Minister Gromyko's office, and that his moderate opinions on U.S.-Soviet relations were encouraged by the leadership as a means of fostering the myth of ISKAN's independence as a quasi-academic think-tank. Visits by Arbatov and other ISKAN staffers to the United States are believed by Shevchenko to be information-gathering, propaganda and legitimation exercises, as well as disinformation campaigns used by the KGB and the Central Committee's International Department.

Furthermore, Shevchenko stresses that ISKAN is essentially excluded from participation in the making of Soviet policy toward the United States. He points out that "no one in the institute is really consulted by the Foreign Ministry or given access to its proposals to the Politburo on Soviet-American relations."[19] Thus, while Arbatov has always been very visible on American and Soviet television defending existing Soviet foreign policy positions on a variety of issues, Shevchenko argues that Arbatov is not privy to policy details, or Politburo decisionmaking. He is seen as clearly less influential than former Soviet Ambassador to the U.S. Anatolii Dobrynin.

According to Shevchenko, Arbatov primarily serves as a gatherer of informal "background" information gleaned from influential Members of

Congress or the executive branch and their staffs. Many such officials "were taken in by his seeming objectivity and independence, his calculated liberalism, and his purported influence with the Soviet leadership."[20] Thus, like other defectors, Shevchenko confines ISKAN's functions to propaganda, intelligence gathering, and legitimation of regime policies.

Other sources, particularly Western scholars, see americanists as much more influential in affecting leadership perceptions on U.S. foreign policy, including Congress' role in its making and conduct. For example, Soviet scholars have privately told me during my visit to the Soviet Union in 1987 that former IMEMO director Inozemtsev and Arbatov were personally called by Brezhnev, his top foreign policy staff assitant A.M. Aleksandrov-Agentov, and former director of the Central Committee International Department Boris Ponomarev. Interviews conducted for this study also confirm that IMEMO director Primakov has close personal and professional ties to Gorbachev and Iakovlev and that Arbatov has been given access to Gorbachev as well. While reports of these contacts admittedly come from IMEMO and ISKAN staffers, americanists generally believe their work has had an impact on the Soviet leadership, particularly in softening totalitarian images.

Particularly since Gorbachev became General Secretary and Dobrynin was named head of the International Department, Academy of Sciences scholars believe their research is being widely read, by both the Central Committee Secretariat and Politburo members, and that Dobrynin in particular serves a special role in increasing leadership competence and understanding of Congress' role in U.S. foreign policy. Thus, Soviet scholars heatedly contest the view that their research is irrelevant and see themselves as indirectly influencing the conduct of Soviet foreign policy.

Analysis of career patterns also tends to confirm that links between the Institutes and the Soviet leadership are continuing. Gorbachev's top foreign policy assistant, A.S. Cherniaev, was formerly at the International Department as deputy chief for North America. Since the Department is one of the main Soviet political institutions that have sustained contact with ISKAN, Arbatov and Cherniaev have had numerous dealings. Similarly, V.V. Zagladin, first deputy director of the International Department, has had extensive contact with both IMEMO and ISKAN, and has participated, together with Arbatov, in past parliamentary exchanges with Members of Congress. The new head of the International Department, Dobrynin, has of course had extensive contact with Arbatov, although as will be detailed in a later chapter, there is evidence that this contact has not been cordial.

There is also evidence that the training and advising functions of americanists, totally dismissed by Shevchenko, are in fact quite impressive. As mentioned earlier, one-fifth of ISKAN's staff has at one time or another served as Soviet diplomats in the United States and it strains credulity to believe they are sent there only on propaganda missions. In fact, service at ISKAN, MGU, and MGIMO are quite typical experiences in the career pattern of a Soviet diplomat. Shevchenko himself served as a part-time senior researcher at ISKAN, although he tends to diminish its significance to his career advancement.

Other evidence that the institutes are very involved in advising the Soviet leadership also appears to be highly credible. Parliamentary exchange visits to the United States usually carry a high political profile, and are headed up by full or candidate members of the Politburo. Americanists, including the directors of ISKAN and IMEMO, have always been a part of these delegations. There is also a rich history of patron-client relationships between highly-influential political institutions and the social science institutes of the Academy of Sciences. In fact, one scholar argues that "Soviet leaders confront a veritable smorgasbord of academic ideas and information about the U.S. from which they must choose what they need or want."[21] Also not to be discounted is the effect of the service of leadership sons and daughters at ISKAN and other Academy institutes. These familial links provide information and advice on the U.S. to top Soviet policymakers.

In fact, Western scholars tend to argue that if anything, information reaching the Soviet leadership from the americanists has been excessive rather than scarce or irrelevant. Central Committee departments, particularly the International Department, can request information from Academy institutes. Meetings between americanists and the Central Committee International Department are believed to be frequent. Interview research conducted for this study, as well as other sources, tend to confirm that Institute members are apparently called into meetings of the Central Committee Secretariat and the Politburo, and are asked to provide information, given instructions, or asked to formulate proposals to deal with particular foreign policy issues.[22] As such, research institutes provide an important link in the International Department's efforts to inform Soviet leaders as well as formulate foreign policy proposals for the consideration of the Secretariat and Politburo. Classified studies, information reports, and full-length analytical studies are regularly requested by the International Department, the Committee for State Security (KGB) and the Ministry of Foreign Affairs (MFA).

Moreover, a whole range of officials in the Central Commitee apparatus and government ministries can request specialized reports from the Academy institutes. As a result, while many scholars sought patron leaders who would adopt them as spokesmen, "many leaders constantly watched the academic world for scholars of competence and stature who could be harnessed to their political wagon."[23] As a result, americanists often become "'court experts' of the very top leaders, belonging ad personam to the foreign policy milieu of the leadership."[24]

As such, decisions about foreign policy issues, including the question of Congress' role in U.S. foreign policy, could suffer not from a lack of americanists input but from too much input. The pattern of personal relationships with leadership figures can result in the use of academics for power political purposes. Irrational accumulation of information may also make it difficult to choose a particular course of actions as leaders are bombarded with briefing papers and analytical studies. By Soviet definition, this constitutes a disservice to the political leadership.

However, particularly since the tenure of Party General Secretary Leonid Brezhnev, various foreign policy oriented party or government administrations, "have supported the creation of new institutes, the transformation of teaching institutions into research operations, and the expansion of research projects of existing regional institutes."[25] Research institutes have become a weapon of bureaucratic infighting. Another important factor has been that because of the privileged status that comes with being an americanist, "many academics have been trying to enter and reach the top of this privileged elite," and those scholars already in the elite have become interested in "enlarging their research empires . . . in order to be recognized by leaders as useful politically and to obtain scarce benefits."[26] Finally, since it appears budgetary allocations for the Academy institutes are linked to output of reports, monographs, intelligence analyses, etc., institutes engage in self-promotion through a proliferation of research products. This type of behavior "has been highly appreciated and probably nicely rewarded by the Party authorities."[27]

Western scholars have also identified a significant role for americanists in "long-range forecasting about social, economic, and scientific problems of concern to Soviet leaders" and "presenting different points of view on subjects which are deemed fit for controlled debate and disagreement."[28] One example of this process is the attempt to forecast the future direction of U.S. foreign policy based on economic trends and input-output models which have been undertaken at ISKAN.[29]

The institutes will also occasionally generate different views on U.S. foreign policy (reflecting at least in part the views of their Party or government patrons), serve as articulators of innovative ideas or changes in policy not yet embraced by the leadership as well as reflect their own personal predilections about the nature of U.S.-Soviet relations. While americanists do not openly challenge current foreign policy direction they do "clash over specific issues, over tactics to be followed in attaining the best results for the Soviet Union, and in their evaluations of the 'lessons of the past' as these may be applicable to new situations."[30]

Americanists often fulfill this role as innovators of policy in international conferences with American scholars and representatives of the Congress in order to "advance on an unofficial and experimental basis, new ideas (which in retrospect appear to have reflected internal discussions) in order to test the reactions of a select foreign audience."[31] This practice of launching policy trial balloons can also fulfill advisory as well as propaganda functions for new policy proposals.

The above discussion demonstrates clearly that the debate on whether americanists are influential in shaping Soviet leadership attitudes on the United States, including Congress' role in U.S. foreign policy, is rich in detail but still unresolved. Emigre accounts tend to downplay, even disregard, the influence of Academy institutes in the making and conduct of Soviet foreign policy, including the assessment of Congress' role in American foreign policy. Moreover, it will always be difficult to evaluate how much of the voluminous americanist work product actually receives the attention of the Soviet leadership. In some instances where the influence of such information could be considerable, it appears the information is not being utilized.

For example, Chapter 3 has extensively reviewed americanist analysis of Congress' role in U.S. defense and arms control policy, including americanist descriptions of the effort in 1986 in the House to enact a variety of far-reaching arms control limitations on the Reagan Administration's defense modernization program. As the fall of 1986 approached and these amendments were being considered in the House-Senate conference on the DOD authorization bill, the Administration and the Republican-controlled Senate leadership were opposed to their inclusion in the final DOD authorization bill that would be considered by both Houses of Congress after the House-Senate conference had reached agreement. The Democratic-controlled leadership of the House sought their inclusion in the final bill. In early October, in the middle of House-Senate conference meetings on the DOD authorization bill came the particularly jarring news that General Secretary Gorbachev had offered to meet President Reagan in Reykjavik and President Reagan had accepted.

Politically speaking, supporters of the arms control amendments had the rug pulled from under them by the Gorbachev initiative. There was simply no way politically that the amendments' supporters could in the atmosphere of the impending Reykjavik summit sustain political support for a position clearly opposed by the Administration. Since americanists had to be clearly aware of this, and the Soviet Union had adopted positions on these arms control issues that were similar in many respects to the position the House had taken, why did Gorbachev decide to propose a summit at this particular time instead of waiting for the executive-legislative confrontation to play out? What does the timing suggest for the level of americanist influence on the making and conduct of Soviet relations with the United States?

Americanists interviewed for this study had varying responses to these critical questions. One americanist pointed out that their role in serving the Soviet leadership was purely informational and educational and that while the details of congressional consideration of the DOD bill were communicated to the Central Committee International Department, which then had the option of presenting it to the Politburo, direct policy advice from americanists on how to proceed was not provided.

Another americanist told me that in his view the result of the House-Senate conference would not have been appreciably different even without the Gorbachev initiative. Given the Congress' inability to stop the MX missile and the largely diluted result of the nuclear freeze resolutions, the Soviet leadership must have calculated that a direct Reagan-Gorbachev summit would accomplish more than waiting for the Congress to impose arms control restraints on the President. In the view of this scholar, the Soviet leadership and Dobrynin in particular had concluded that Congress was simply too complex and ambivalent an institution on critical foreign policy questions. One could not calibrate Soviet policy options on a possible legislative outcome. As such, this americanist believed Dobrynin counseled Gorbachev to transcend both the Congress and the foreign policy/ national security bureaucracy in the executive branch and deal directly with the President.

As such, the way in which americanist analysis on congressional actions on key foreign policy issues is utilized by the Soviet leadership is indeed problematic to evaluate. Nonetheless, an increasingly convincing body of evidence suggests americanist influence could be extensive. This body of evidence draws on personal relationships between Soviet scholars and leaders, the increasing number of Soviet diplomats who serve part of their careers at Academy institutes, and the regular participation of americanists in highly-influential parliamentary exchanges with the U.S. Congress and during congressional visits to the Soviet Union. Further evidence of americanist influence can be inferred from the presence of Soviet leadership progeny at Academy institutes, the establishment and intensification of a myriad of patron-client relationships between academy institutes and Soviet leaders and influential Party and government institutions, and the use of americanists as channels for policy discussion and innovation. From this evidence, a credible case can be made that americanists perform training and advisory functions, not only propaganda and legitimation functions, and that such training and advising is important to the making and conduct of Soviet foreign policy.

Notes

1. For a full discussion of the types and functions of mezhdunarodniki research, see Eran, pp. 135-161, 257-279.

2. Ibid., p. 137.

3. Ibid., p. 134.

4. Ibid.

5. U.S., International Communications Agency, *Soviet Americanists*, by Steven A. Grant, Research Report no. R-1-80, February 15, 1980, p. 9.

6. For an example of this type of amerikanistika, see Osipova, pp. 106-111.

7. *Soviet Americanists*, p. 15.

8. Malcolm estimates that about forty Soviet scholars visit the United States every year, with almost half of them for periods of three months or longer. As for the well-connected, the late General Secretary Yuri Andropov's son, former Foreign Minister Andrei Gromyko's son, former Council of Ministers chairman Aleksei Kosygin's daugther to name only a few, have been or are americanists. For further information, see Malcolm, p. 16, and Grant, p. 7.

9. Morton Schwartz, "The Americanists," *Across the Board* 16 (August 1979): 59.

10. Malcolm, pp. 13-14.

11. Eran, p. 264. For more on this point, see Malcolm, p. 14.

12. Malcolm, p. 15.

13. Ibid., p. 14.

14. For a comprehensive listing of americanists by institutional affiliation, see Steven A. Grant, *Soviet Americanists: A Supplement*, Research Report, Office of Research, United States Information Agency, August, 1982,; for an organizational chart on ISKAN, see Jeffrey T. Richelson, *Sword and Shield: Soviet Intelligence and Security Apparatus* (Cambridge, Mass.: Ballinger Publishing Co., 1986), p. 61.

15. See Eran, pp. 31-59 for a useful institutional history of IMEMO.

16. *Soviet Research Institute Project*, 1:440.

17. Nora Beloff, "Escape from Boredom: A Defector's Story," *The Atlantic Monthly*, (November 1980), p. 44.

18. Ibid., p. 45.

19. Arkady N. Shevchenko, *Breaking with Moscow* (New York: Ballantine Books, 1985), p. 280.

20. Ibid.

21. *Soviet Americanists*, p. 16.

22. For more on this point, see Ned Temko, "It's Not a Democracy, But Many Soviets Have a Say," *Christian Science Monitor*, 24 February 1982.

23. Eran, p. 155.

24. Ibid.

25. Ibid., p. 259.

26. Ibid.

27. Ibid., p. 260.

28. Richard S. Soll, Arthur A. Zuehlke, Jr., and Richard B. Foster, *The Role of Social Science Research Institutes in Formulation and Execution of Soviet Foreign Policy* (Arlington, Va.: SRI International, March, 1976), p. 73.

29. For more on such forecasting efforts and their methodological problems see Soll et al., pp. 85-88.

30. Ibid., p. 90.

31. Ibid., p. 93.

5

Soviet Party and Government Interactions with Congress

Information on the role of Congress in U.S. foreign policy does not come to Soviet leaders only from the Soviet academic community. In addition to Soviet academia, three alternate sources of information are particularly relevant: 1) the MFA and in particular the Soviet Embassy in Washington and the Central Committee International Department; 2) the KGB; and 3) direct exposure through parliamentary exchanges and Congressional visits to the Soviet Union.

The Ministry of Foreign Affairs, the
Central Committee Apparatus, and the Soviet Embassy

The MFA is regarded by most observers as the principal Soviet political institution which handles the day-to-day conduct and operations of U.S.-Soviet relations. Shevchenko, for example, sees the MFA as preeminent among Soviet foreign policy institutions, particularly concerning matters involving U.S.-Soviet relations. He argues that under Gromyko, the Ministry reported directly to the Politburo, not the Central Committee International Department, that the Ministry initiated as well as carried out Politburo instructions, and unlike the Central Committee, had its own code service. It decided what Politburo members received cables, how many they received, and gave instructions to ambassadors without Politburo approval. As such, Shevchenko argues "the ministry has a strong hand in deciding what matters should be reported to the Politburo for consideration and is in a position to exert considerable influence upon the decision-making process."[1]

This is not to say, however, that the Central Committee party apparatus is not active in U.S.-Soviet relations. Several departments are relevant. The International Department, it is believed by some, sets the foreign policy agenda for the Central Committee Secretariat and the Politburo. The Foreign Cadres Department approves personnel selections and shifts. The International Information Department and the Propaganda Department control the dissemination of Soviet foreign policy positions and the heads of both those departments were among the four principal advisors to Gorbachev at the

Reagan-Gorbachev summit in November, 1985. With the exception of the Foreign Cadres Department, well-known americanists can be found in all of the above Central Commitee departments.

Particularly since Dobrynin became its head, the Department has added a number of very notable americanists and arms control experts including Georgii Kornienko, who was a former First Deputy Foreign Minister and is now First Deputy Head of the Department, Vitalii Churkin, a former diplomat at the Soviet Embassy in Washington who made an unprecedented appearance before a Congressional committee on the Chernobyl nuclear accident, and Lt. Gen. Viktor Starodubov, a former member of the Soviet SALT II delegation and now a section chief for arms control within the Department. The expansion of the Department's staff, and the appointment of the experienced americanist Dobrynin as its head, suggests an effort by Gorbachev to bring greater Party control of U.S.-Soviet relations, particularly in the area of policy formulation.

Nonetheless, the MFA, particularly under the long tenure of Gromyko, and to a large degree under current Foreign Minister Eduard Shevardnadze, has made U.S.-Soviet relations its special preserve. First Deputy Foreign Minister Aleksandr Bessmertnykh, is a trained americanist with wide experience. Bessmertnykh, along with Shevardnadze, was part of the official Soviet delegation at the Washington summit, while only Dobrynin represented the First Department. The issues affecting U.S.-Soviet relations receive continuing attention in the Ministry's Collegium. The MFA's USA and Canada Department contains the cream of the Soviet diplomatic crop. Moreover, unlike American foreign service officers, Soviet diplomats specialize in a particular country or geographic region and "their careers show a pattern of assignments alternating between diplomatic appointments to the country or area of their expertise and service in Moscow in the corresponding Ministry desk or department."[2] Thus, Soviet diplomats specializing in American affairs can expect a long, uninterrupted service in their area of expertise.

The USA and Canada Department is generally filled with the so-called third generation of Soviet diplomats, including "younger men who entered the Ministry since the mid-1950s and who have benefited from the rigorous training programs of the IMO (Institute of International Relations) and the Diplomatic Academy."[3] This generation of diplomats benefited from service in the growing number of foreign policy institutions that developed in the Khrushchev and Brezhnev eras as well as greater exposure and travel to the United States. Some American scholars see this generation of diplomats as having strikingly different attitudes than the second generation 'Molotov diplomats' of whom Gromyko is the personification.

While differences between the generations can easily be exaggerated (Gromyko, after all, was one of the major architects of detente), one scholar describes the third generation as seeing the world "in more differentiated terms and (they) are more likely to find local explanations for an event rather than blame it on the machinations of the imperialists."[4] This younger group of diplomats tends to be strong supporters of detente and fears that "xenophobia and cold war relations with the West are associated with reaction at home—with a fundamentalist, ultranationalist mentality that bodes no good for them personally or for the values to which they adhere."[5]

With respect to the issue of Congress' role in foreign policy, the Soviet Embassy in Washington has the most sustained and continuing exposure. As a practical matter, because Congressional travel to the Soviet Union requires visas, groups travelling to the Soviet Union find their first and often most sustained point of contact with the Soviet Embassy. The Embassy is also the repository of letters by Members of Congress to the Soviet leadership on a variety of issues, most notably human rights issues.

By contrast to the Embassy's expansive KGB operations for general information-gathering purposes, its contacts with Members and staff for purposes of travel to the Soviet Union are consistently handled by a small group of Soviet diplomats at the high levels of First Secretary, Counselor, and Minister-Counselor. According to House and Senate staff interviewed for this study, after a steady series of contacts between staff and these officials to work out schedule and travel arrangements for a visiting Congressional delegation, a courtesy call will be arranged with the Ambassador to 'seal the deal.' On other occasions, Members become actively involved in scheduling questions from the outset, dealing only with the Ambassador until they are satisfied they will get the meetings that they want in the Soviet Union.

When members of the USSR Supreme Soviet visit the United States, contact between this same select group of Soviet diplomats and the Congress is even more intense. Since these delegations are usually headed by full or candidate members of the Politburo, the Embassy is under enormous political and protocol pressure to ensure that the delegation's logistical needs are attended to and that meetings with Congressional leadership are arranged. Thus, the involvement at the Minister-Counselor and Ambassador level becomes more frequent.

In an interesting revelation of the possible 'pecking order' in Soviet foreign policy, one House staffer who worked closely with the Supreme Soviet delegation visit headed by Politburo member Vladimir Shcherbitskii in 1985, felt that Embassy diplomats gave the greatest deference and attention to high-ranking diplomats from the USA Department. While Shcherbitskii received the proper protocol deference, his lack of activity in issues affecting U.S.-Soviet relations apparently did not require a great deal of political deference. Furthermore, ISKAN director Arbatov, who was a member of the delegation, was seen as an annoyance to the Embassy, perhaps because of his network of American contacts outside Embassy control. The differences in treatment must also stem at least in part from the fact that the future career advancement of Soviet diplomats stems in part from good relations with high-level Foreign Ministry officials in Moscow who were accompanying the delegation.

Soviet diplomats who deal directly with Congress appear to have a general understanding of its role in foreign policy. One House staffer interviewed pointed out that Embassy representatives often have positive or negative reactions to the inclusion of individual Members of Congress on a congressional delegation but never attempt to interfere or offer comments on delegation selection. Not all Members of Congress are recognizable to Embassy diplomats but key figures in the leadership or on foreign policy committees appear to be.

Because Congressional delegations invariably ask to see Politburo members, including the General Secretary as well as the Foreign Minister, Soviet diplomats are also concerned about the weightiness and seriousness of the delegation and what issues will be discussed during the visit. Finally, since Congressional delegations universally dedicate at least part of their business to an investigation of Soviet human rights abuses through visits with dissidents and refuseniks, and present unresolved emigration cases to the Soviet leadership for their resolution, the amount of emphasis on human rights can play a role in whether visas are granted, or at what level meetings will be scheduled.

Since the decision about visa approval seems to come in part from Embassy recommendations, concerns by Soviet diplomats about how human rights issues will be raised by Congressional delegations are in part a form of institutional self-defense. It appears that the Embassy has a clearcut need to demonstrate to the MFA, the Central Committee bureaucracy, and the Politburo, that meetings between Members of Congress and high-level officials of those institutions advance Soviet foreign policy objectives and help to improve U.S.-Soviet relations.

Regardless of Embassy recommendations, delegations visiting the Soviet Union often discover that their schedule is basically uncertain when they arrive. Assurances about a meeting with the General Secretary may be given in advance without providing a specific date, but other meetings are arranged while in country. Some House staffers who have 'advanced' trips to the Soviet Union believe that such trips prove more useful than dealing only with the Embassy. At times the Embassy itself is not told of critical details in a delegation's schedule. Follow-up meetings with Foreign Ministry, Supreme Soviet, and Party officials can contribute to the success of a delegation's visit.

House and Senate staff interviewed for this study are divided on the influence of the Embassy's recommendations with respect to the level and scope of meetings that a visiting Congressional delegation will receive. While all agree Embassy recommendations, particularly when the Ambassador has been active in preparatory negotiations with Members, are important, at least one participant interviewed regarded such recommendations as not decisive. Decisions about meetings with the Soviet leadership were seen as a collective decision made by the MFA and the Central Committee International Department, with the concurrence of the General Secretary himself. Since the accession of Dobrynin to the head of the International Department, that Department is being given credit for an increasingly high profile in determining the level and the scope of treatment given congressional delegations. Dobrynin, for example, is thought responsible for arranging for Speaker Wright's delegation to meet with an unprecedented five Politburo members during a 1987 visit. In January, 1988 when the Supreme Soviet was reluctant to invite Rep. Tom Lantos' (D-Calif.) delegation to visit, but the Ministry of Foreign Affairs and the Soviet embassy in Washington were urging such an invitation, the International Department is believed to have persuaded the Supreme Soviet to extend an invitation to the delegation.

A fairly sophisticated understanding of Congress' role in foreign policy can be postulated by the Embassy and MFA consideration and processing of official visits to the Soviet Union. From the author's own experience and interview research, there are three distinct categories of treatment for Congressional delegations.

The first and best treatment comes when a delegation is invited to visit by either one or both houses of the Supreme Soviet. The invitation can come from the Foreign Affairs Commissions of the Council of the Union or the Council of Nationalities (the protocol equivalent of the House Foreign Affairs Committee and the Senate Foreign Relations Commitee) or from the chairmen of the Councils (the protocol equivalents of the Speaker of the House and Senate Majority Leader). The chairmen of the two Foreign Affairs Commissions are usually high-ranking Party officials. For example, Gorbachev was chairman of the Council of the Union's Foreign Affairs Commission in the early 1980s before he became General Secretary. The Union's Commission is now headed by Egor Ligachev, believed to be the second most powerful member of the Politburo. Until the 27th Party Congress in February, 1986, the Council of Nationalities' Foreign Affairs Commission was headed by Ponomarev, and it is now headed by Dobrynin.

Congressional delegations invited to the Soviet Union by the Supreme Soviet are often given all the trappings of a state visit. They stay in the best government guest house, are whisked through airport controls by limousine and bus, and are given formal, sometimes lavish receptions in the Kremlin. Plenary sessions are set up with a select group of high-ranking Supreme Soviet members including a number of Central Committee members, and other foreign policy and national security experts from the Academy institutes, the Ministry of Foreign Affairs, and the Ministry of Defense. Meetings are also usually arranged if possible with the Party General Secretary and the Foreign Minister.

Visits by the House and Senate leadership invariably include this type of treatment, as exemplified by the visits led by former Speaker O'Neill, Senators Byrd and Strom Thurmond (R-S.C.) in 1985, and Speaker Wright in 1987. Wright, in fact, received extraordinary treatment, seeing five Politburo members in separate meetings. Other foreign policy leadership figures such as Rep. Dante B. Fascell (D-Fla.), chairman of the House Foreign Affairs Committee, have been accorded visits with Politburo members.

A second level of treatment can be described as warm but less distinguished. This type of congressional delegation is received well, but is not visiting pursuant to an official invitation from the Supreme Soviet. It does not get the 'state visit' treatment: no formal luncheon or dinner in the Kremlin, its meetings with Supreme Soviet members are of less prestige and influence; no meetings are granted with the General Secretary; but usually it meets with high-levels of the Foreign Ministry (but not the Foreign Minister) or other ministries of interest to the delegation (Foreign Trade, Agriculture etc.); and it has meetings with senior officials of ISKAN and IMEMO.

An excellent example of this second level of treatment was the visit of a delegation headed by then Rep. Paul Simon (D-Ill.) in mid-1981. This delegation was the first to visit the Soviet Union after the invasion of Afghanistan in December, 1979. While both the American executive branch and Soviet officials were hoping the visit would be a success, the poor state of U.S.-Soviet relations existing at the time and the fact that the Simon delegation was interested in education rather than foreign policy issues resulted in reduced but polite forms of attention from the Soviet side. The Simon delegation met with a number of government and party institutions concerned with education issues and had only one foreign policy meeting, held at the Kremlin with ISKAN and IMEMO representatives.

The third level of treatment is for those delegations who are clearly not welcome. Delegations may not be welcome for a variety of reasons. In some instances, the time of a visit is unsuitable to the schedules or political priorities of high Party or MFA officials with whom the delegation has requested appointments. In other instances, the delegation may have an active human rights profile without, from the Soviet perspective, the compensating effects of influential Members of Congress on the delegation. Whatever the reason, the Embassy will fail to issue visas, or will grant visas only to some in an effort to force the delegation to stay home for reasons of political solidarity.

If the delegation remains adamant about going to the Soviet Union, and is travelling by U.S. military aircraft, the Foreign Ministry may grant visas only to the delegation but not to the aircraft crew or military escorts, creating fundamental logistical problems for the delegation. If a delegation still insists on visiting, and uses the rationale that it seeks consultations with the U.S. Embassy as a means of entering the country, the MFA will relent and grant visas but the delegation will receive minimally cordial treatment. No meetings with either high Party officials or the Foreign Ministry are arranged, and only lesser levels of Supreme Soviet officials as well as senior officials of ISKAN and IMEMO see the delegation.

Occasionally, to speed a delegation's departure, exorbitant hotel and meal charges will be levied to exhaust delegation per diem. Nonetheless, if a delegation is adamant in its intentions to come, the MFA will not risk an international incident by refusing to let the delegation visit the Soviet Union. Two delegations in 1983 and 1985 led by Rep. Lantos, a sharp critic of Soviet human rights abuses, are examples of this third and least deferential reception.

It is uncertain whether the third type of delegation will continue to be a possibility. In the fall of 1986, after the dispute over the Soviet arrest of

U.S. News and World Report Moscow correspondent Nicholas Daniloff, the Reagan Administration retaliated by reducing the number of Soviet diplomats permitted to be stationed in the United States to the exact number of U.S. diplomats stationed in the Soviet Union. The Soviet Union responded by eliminating all Soviet employees at the U.S. missions in the Soviet Union, crippling the embassy's logistical and representational capabilities, including those for servicing congressional delegations. As such, congressional delegations travelling to the Soviet Union can now expect only meager embassy support and must have Soviet sponsorship to assure a successful visit. Without such sponsorship, delegations are forced to deal with the Soviet travel agency Intourist to assure its logistical needs. Such an arrangement is problematic at best.

The hierarchy of treatment for and the processing of Congressional delegations reveals a number of important insights for the study of Soviet foreign policy. First, the existence of a hierarchy suggests a fairly sophisticated understanding of the organization and power structure in Congress since only high-ranking Members receive the best treatment and the Embassy, the MFA, and the Central Committee Party apparatus know who is high-ranking and influential. Second, concerns about weightiness, seriousness, and motivation of individual delegations reflect a twofold concern that the Embassy appear knowledgeable in its recommendations about whether a delegation should be permitted to visit (and who it should see) and that such a visit advance Soviet foreign policy objectives and improved U.S.-Soviet relations.

Finally, the fact that all delegations, whether welcome or not, whether invited or not, see ISKAN and IMEMO scholars confirms the propagandistic function of these institutions. It may also shed light, at least in part, on their relative lack of policy influence since MFA and Politburo meetings are arranged only for those delegations judged to be influential.

In addition to the processing of Congressional delegation visits to the Soviet Union, the Embassy maintains a steady flow of contact on foreign policy matters with Members of Congress in Washington. During his 24 years as Soviet Ambassador, Dobrynin played host in social gatherings to a wide range of Members of Congress, including its leadership. His reputation in Congress was one of a 'pro' and 'political insider,' a smooth, sophisticated defender of Soviet foreign policy objectives as well as a keen observer and gatherer of information.

Dobrynin was regarded by Members and their staffs in both the House and the Senate as keenly aware of the foreign policy committees and leaders of Congress. He knew whom to speak to, and on what issues. One House Member interviewed said Dobrynin always sought cordial, personal relationships with Members, calling them by their first names when he got to know them, and treating them as a Member's colleagues would, in an effort to build credibility and trust which he would utilize at some future point.

Dobrynin regularly arranged private dinners with influential Members of Congress. He was described as a 'model of discretion.' Two House staffers interviewed described contact with Dobrynin and influential Members as always social, not substantive. Business contacts usually dealt with finalizing details of Congressional delegation visits to the Soviet Union or paying courtesy calls on Members after their return to receive an informal 'debriefing.'

The former Soviet Ambassador also had frequent meetings with Members on human rights issues, particularly involving the presentation of emigration cases to Dobrynin for resolution by Soviet authorities. Dobrynin is said to have handled these requests for resolution perfunctorily but politely, and there seems little evidence to suggest he acted on them with any more than the usual diplomatic processing. In fact, the steady stream of letters to the Soviet leadership on human rights issues and emigration cases that were routed through the Embassy were seldom if ever answered. Dobrynin was described as regarding human rights issues as trivial to the pressing problems of U.S.-Soviet relations and saw would-be emigres and defectors as traitors to the Soviet political system.

Actual direct lobbying by the Embassy under Dobrynin was rare and certainly more the exception than the rule. During the Watergate scandal, fears that the impeachment of President Nixon would lead to an unraveling of detente reportedly led Dobrynin to lobby Members of Congress on behalf of the President. At the request of Senate Majority Leader Byrd in 1979, Dobrynin was asked to help influence the Soviet government to provide some gesture regarding the controversy over revelations of a Soviet troop brigade in Cuba. Byrd, at least, is believed to have thought the meeting produced positive results in cooling rhetoric on both sides and helping the Senate to get past the issue in its ultimately failed consideration of the SALT II Treaty.[6]

Finally, during the lengthy consideration in Congress concerning funding for the MX missile, Rep. Aspin and Senator Cohen asked for lunch with Dobrynin to elicit Soviet reaction to their proposals for a 2-1 U.S.-Soviet builddown of strategic nuclear weapons (in exchange for which the Reagan Administration received the support of Aspin and Cohen for MX missile production). After commenting that many in the Administration were not supporting the builddown concept, Dobrynin promised only that he would convey the arguments presented to the 'proper quarters in Moscow.'

Unlike many other foreign countries, the Soviet Union does not have a professional lobbying firm, registered with the Congress, representing its interests. With the few exceptions mentioned above, direct lobbying on specific issues invariably takes the grass roots form, through the use of Soviet-funded front organizations that attempt to infiltrate existing lobbying groups, particularly on disarmament issues.[7] Contacts by the Embassy with Members of Congress and staff appear to be designed more to gain valuable information in casual social gatherings on the congressional power structure, a legislator's perceptions on key issues, and their predictions about outcomes. The Embassy does not appear to try direct lobbying to change votes or apply political pressure.

This type of contact is coordinated with KGB operations and the work of ISKAN representatives in the Embassy or visiting ISKAN scholars and senior officials. Interestingly, while both ISKAN and the Embassy perform this information-gathering role, Dobrynin was believed to have deeply resented Arbatov as an invention of the American media who had no influence in Moscow. Dobrynin is also believed to have expressed anger at Arbatov's circle of American sources on U.S. foreign policy that were outside Embassy control as well as Arbatov's failure to coordinate his public appearances with the Embassy.

Thus, Dobrynin developed a keen understanding of Congress' role in foreign policy through his long years of experience and exposure as Soviet Ambassador. On the issue of U.S.-Soviet relations, he has been generally seen as supportive of improved and enduring relations with the United States, but he is also seen as an implementer not an initiator of policy. His reporting to Moscow was thought to be relatively shorn of cables designed to curry favor and often times apparently included American criticisms of Soviet policy. He provided a good quality of information on the issue of Congress' role in foreign policy, but according to Shevchenko, to avoid being accused of having become 'Americanized,' "even Dobrynin dared not produce an accurate analysis of the division of power in America between the executive and legislative branches . . . Most of that kind of reporting he let his aides prepare."[8]

Nonetheless, Shevchenko also stresses that "one of Dobrynin's important functions has been as an informed educator trying to correct the limited and distorted picture Soviet rulers have of America."[9] Dobrynin's direct contact with the Politburo is also seen by Shevchenko as augmenting amerikanistika on Congress and foreign policy.[10] Dobrynin has prepared annual reports to Moscow covering several hundred pages on, among other things, the political situation in the United States, the U.S. military posture, and the current condition and likely future direction of U.S.-Soviet relations. Congress' actions, given Dobrynin's keen attention to its role in foreign policy, presumably receives considerable attention in the annual report.

As head of the Central Committee International Department, Dobrynin has clearly demonstrated his thorough knowledge of the Congress, In addition to arranging meetings with five Politburo members for Speaker Wright's delegation in 1987, Dobrynin himself met with that delegation, expressing his pleasure that the delegation would have 'first-hand knowledge of our top people.' He told the delegation that a Supreme Soviet commission had been set up to deal with emigration cases and in a tone clearly calculated to address the importance members attached to the issue, said the Soviet leadership did not want to aggravate the problem, but rather get rid of it.

Since moving to Moscow, Dobrynin also serves as Chairman of the Foreign Affairs Commission of the upper house of the Supreme Soviet, the Council of Nationalities. From this position Dobrynin has revitalized the Supreme Soviet structure in its dealings with the Congress, using it not only to extend invitations to visit the Soviet Union, but also to pass resolutions paralleling congressional legislation on arms control issues that have been opposed by the Reagan Administration. For example, in June, 1986 after the House of Representatives had passed legislation calling on the President to continue to abide by the terms of the SALT II Treaty, legislation clearly opposed by the Reagan Administration, the Supreme Soviet passed a similar resolution expressing Soviet support for continued compliance with the treaty and calling for cooperation between the Supreme Soviet and the U.S. Congress on international security issues. A similar action was taken by the Supreme Soviet when the House, in defiance of the Administration, passed both in 1986 and 1987 legislation calling for a mutual U.S.-Soviet moratorium on nuclear tests above one kiloton. In addition to enriching Supreme Soviet-U.S. Congress ties through parallel legislation, Dobrynin has also dispatched teams of Central Committee experts to brief members of Congress on internal political developments in the Soviet Union, including the results of Central Committee plenums conducted to implement Gorbachev's economic reform initiatives.

In May, 1986, the Soviet Embassy received a new Ambassador, Iurii Dubinin, a career Soviet diplomat who had previously served as Ambassador to Spain and the United Nations, as a Soviet representative to the United Nations Educational, Scientific, and Cultural Organization, and in numerous positions in the First European Department of the Ministry of Foreign Affairs.

Dubinin was a career 'Europeanist,' and his selection as Ambassador after Dobrynin was named to head the Central Committee International Department earlier in 1986 came as a surprise to Western scholars of the Soviet foreign policy establishment and to U.S. foreign policymakers as well. Most observers had expected the first deputy head of the International Department, Vadim Zagladin, to be named to the U.S. ambassadorial post.

Dubinin spoke little English at the time of his accession to Ambassador, although he was exposed to U.S. policymakers as a member of the Soviet delegation to the original Conference on Security and Cooperation in Europe in Helsinki in 1975, and in a subsequent Helsinki review conference in Madrid from 1980-1983. Dubinin knew very little English before his Washington appointment but has subsequently quickly improved his English and has began to cultivate a wide circle of acquaintances in Congress.

A number of individuals interviewed for this study saw Dubinin as faithful to protocol details and the pleasantries of diplomacy, but also as a no-nonsense advocate of existing Soviet foreign policy positions. He is seen as less interested than Dobrynin was in behaving like an 'insider' or colleague in his meetings with Members of Congress, although he is seen as proper, not harsh, in presenting his arguments. Dubinin is also apparently less interested than Dobrynin was in presenting the appearance of being an influential spokesman or confidant of the Soviet leadership. It has even been speculated that Dubinin was sent to Washington to 'normalize' the role of the Soviet Ambassador to that of communicator and implementer of existing policy rather than cultivating the image, as Dobrynin had, of being a policymaker himself and the main source of information to the Soviet leadership on the political situation in the United States. Such a view is consistent with the argument that actual policymaking responsibilities for U.S.-Soviet relations have been shifted with Dobrynin to the Central Committee International Department.

Nonetheless, Dubinin by all accounts has intensified the Embassy's interactions with the Congress. The Soviet presence on Capitol Hill has intensified and Dubinin has on at least one occasion directly intervened with the USSR Supreme Soviet to issue an invitation, which the Supreme Soviet had been reluctant to do, for Rep. Lantos and his delegation to visit the Soviet Union. Dubinin is strongly in favor of increased Congressional travel to the Soviet Union. Over time, Dubinin can be expected to maintain and enrich the channels of information on the Congress' role in U.S. foreign policy.

To augment the work of the ambassador, embassy staff attend congressional hearings, and cultivate congressional staff by way of collecting reports, statistics, surveys, white papers etc., as well as other types of inside information on foreign policy issues with which the Congress is concerned. Since much of this activity is closely coordinated with KGB intelligence operations, it is that agency's role as a source of information on Congress and foreign policy to which we now turn.

The Committee for State Security

The KGB, as well as to a lesser degree Soviet military intelligence, the GRU, maintains an active presence in the Soviet Embassy in Washington. Both organizations have made a thorough effort to solicit and gather information about Congress' actions affecting U.S. foreign policy. Estimates of KGB/GRU presence in the Embassy are usually put at somewhere between 40-45 percent, with this presence serving the usual twin role of intelligence gathering and monitoring of embassy staff loyalty and performance. The KGB's presence in Washington gets generally high marks for its intelligence-gathering and policy analysis, although unlike other Soviet ambassadors, Dobrynin exercised greater control over KGB operations, and the KGB presence in Washington was much smaller than at the UN mission in New York.

The KGB conducts ongoing efforts to gather information from Members of Congress and their staffs, as well as from congressional support agencies including the Congressional Research Service of the Library of Congress, the General Accounting Office, the Office of Technology Assessment, and the Congressional Budget Office. Embassy officers holding positions as diplomats, journalists, trade representatives, and cultural affairs officers can be KGB officers. KGB officers operating under these 'covers' are instructed to cultivate associations with Members and staff for the purpose of developing confidential relationships. These relationships augment communications intelligence, performed by technical surveillance, that enables the Soviet Embassy to intercept telephone conversations in the Washington area and elsewhere.

Signal intelligence (SIGINT) is conducted at the Soviet Embassy in Washington and includes SIGINT coverage of the Congress. One scholar has pointed out that each of the Soviet government installations in the U.S. has the capability to "intercept and record on a daily basis, hundreds of thousands of telephone conversations that are transmitted by microwave."[11] Only a few Congressional offices are linked to the executive branch's system of secure telephones.

Particular telephone exchanges can be monitored and it can be assumed that the Senate's 224 and the House's 225 exchanges are included in such monitoring. Police and government limousine communications related to Congressional operations can be monitored as well. The new Soviet Embassy compound soon to be completed overlooks the Washington area and is thought to have significant signal intelligence capabilities.

To complement SIGINT capability, KGB officers in Washington are generally well-trained, capable of approaching Members and staff with a cordial, non-threatening manner. Since the foreign policy committees of the Congress conduct regular liaison with the Soviet Embassy in any event, particularly in arranging Congressional visits or delivering letters to the Soviet Embassy on human rights issues, KGB operatives are assured contact with the Congress as a result of the normal conduct of diplomacy. This normal contact can be built upon for purposes of intelligence gathering or even recruitment.

The process of professional and social contacts is usually conducted by KGB personnel for an extensive period of time without the suggestion of anything improper or illegal. In fact, the technique of informal relaxed contact with foreign government officials is standard practice for every intelligence service, including the CIA.

Nonetheless, FBI officials report a major increase in the amount and intensity of KGB activities with respect to the Congress. The relatively relaxed security, open public hearings, and large numbers of open publications and reports enable the KGB free access to a wealth of information.

The FBI estimates that 85-90% of Soviet intelligence collection from the Congress is open source materials readily available to the general public as well. Open source collection is used in recruitment, since Member and staff access to congressional documents is usually the entree for establishing a relationship between the KGB/GRU and congressional employees. Open source materials can provide directions for clandestine collection, "indicating the existence of plans, programs, organizations, or weapons systems (which) will provide new targets to clandestine collection activities."[12] Open source materials also provide ready analysis on a whole gamut of political, economic, and military matters.

The process of congressional testimony, and congressional access to classified information, sometimes of a very sensitive nature, makes Congress a lucrative target. The free-wheeling style of congressional oversight, and the massive amount of hearings and materials processed and published by Congress can lead, although to a lesser degree than in the executive branch, to leaks of information for political purposes. The sheer volume of congressional testimony, and the process of publication, can lead to unintended disclosures of information as well.

Thus, during the congressional hearings leading up to congressional approval of SALT I, classified characteristics of U.S. intelligence satellites were revealed inadvertently by an executive branch witness. Classified details of the accuracy of the MX missile, as well as characteristics of Soviet weapons systems became public when Pentagon officials reviewing Congressional hearing transcripts failed to remove this information from the unclassified versions of testimony published for general distribution.

Aside from advertent or inadvertent disclosures of information, the Congress produces voluminous hearings and reports on foreign policy and national security topics. The process of authorizing and appropriating funds for the Defense Department, State Department, and for foreign assistance involves thousands of pages of information. So do articles and debate published in the *Congressional Record* on a multitude of subjects affecting U.S. foreign policy and U.S.-Soviet relations. Finally, studies by Congressional support organizations like the General Accounting Office, the Congressional Budget Office, the Office of Technology Assessment, and the Congressional Research Service of the Library of Congress help to produce a powerfully rich vein of detailed information for Soviet intelligence collection. Thus, U.S. defense and foreign policy objectives, and specific military, economic, and political programs designed to implement those objectives are readily available to the Soviet Embassy.

In fact, the incredible amount of information available to the Soviet Embassy and its diplomatic and intelligence analysts may actually be debilitating to crafting effective Soviet foreign policy responses to what is known about a particular U.S. foreign policy strategy. The duplication and overlap of information as well as the time it takes to synthesize, digest, and analyze this information avalanche may actually increase the need for recruitment to sort out the value of information available. Furthermore, the enormous quantity of data is often redundant, contradictory, and often suspect, particularly with respect to its accuracy vis-a-vis classified information. Sorting out unsubstantiated rumors from accurate information is a tremendous analytical burden. Human intelligence (HUMINT) must therefore be used to complement information obtained from open sources.

The HUMINT process begins by obtaining the names of Members and staff active in foreign policy issues. Meetings over lunch in public restaurants is the most often used method at which a variety of issues are discussed, including those related to U.S.-Soviet relations. Personal evaluations of the status of relations generally, information and opinion about actions being taken in the Executive branch or the Congress that may affect relations, inside information about Members attitudes, etc. will be discussed at such private meetings. This process can take several years and may involve several changes in KGB personnel visiting a single Congressional staffer.

FBI officials regard an invitation to lunch as the single most reliable indicator about whether Embassy personnel are KGB operatives, since regular Soviet diplomats are not provided with the resources required for a continuing social relationship. KGB operatives gathering intelligence may be rather open in their activities and many Members and staff, regardless of party affiliation, have frequent contact with them.

For example, Rep. Guy Vander Jagt (R-Mich.), chairman of the Republican Congressional Campaign Committee, has had open contact with a Soviet Embassy official believed by U.S. intelligence authorities to be a KGB agent. Vander Jagt reportedly has had lunch with this official several times, has introduced him to other Members, and has had "lively debates about foreign policy and other issues."[13] Staff members often provide Embassy officials, including suspected KGB operatives, with hearings, reports, and other unclassified government documents. According to FBI sources, careful records are kept by KGB personnel of each person they approach. The major purpose of these contacts is to evaluate political strategy, discover what top policy-makers think, collect technical information, gain entree to well-placed officials, and ultimately, to recruit people to turn over classified documents.

This final objective, the recruitment stage, takes place only after a long period of professional and social contact. FBI officials have pointed out that targets of recruitment have invariably been staff rather than Members of Congress. A KGB operative may be able to glean information as to a person's job satisfaction, as well as personal finances. The operative may ask a Congressional staffer if he would write an article for a Soviet publication for which he would be paid. If he accepts, payment becomes either the basis for blackmail or a clearcut signal that the individual is willing to be recruited. The social aspect of the relationship then dissipates. The focus shifts to weekend meetings, and eventually no contact except through dropoffs of classified documents in secluded areas with instructions at the dropoff points for the next assignment.

As a whole, recruitment of Congressional staffers has been rather un-successful. FBI sources report that of the 43 espionage cases leading to conviction in the period 1979-1986, none were Congressional employees. Many Members and staff report contacts immediately to the FBI and some have even consented to serve as double agents, recruiting the KGB operatives who have contact with them. Vander Jagt, for example, always reports his contacts with the Soviet Embassy to the FBI, and the FBI is known to encourage contacts between Members and staff and the Embassy so long as they are subsequently reported. Such contacts when reported can often simplify FBI identification of Embassy employees. They also may provide the FBI with inside information about day-to-day Embassy operations, as well as a ready-made assessment of their effectiveness.

In addition, staff members are generally encouraged by their superiors to report their meetings with Embassy officers to the FBI in order to fill gaps, clarify ambiguities, and shed new light on Embassy intelligence operations. Reports of contacts are held in confidence and used only for counterintelligence purposes with safeguards against compromising an in-dividual Member or staff.

Nonetheless, enduring concerns remain about adequate consciousness among Members of Congress and their staffs concerning the handling of classified information, as well as ongoing interactions with representatives of the Soviet government. Classified documents in general do not receive the same level of protection as they do in executive branch agencies, and Congress is not bound by the safeguarding requirements in executive orders for classified information. According to a 1986 Senate study, there are no established standards in Congress for handling such information and "practices vary widely in terms of their handling of clearances and classified material."[14] The report also criticized the lack of checks on the handling of classified material and the relatively few secure telephone lines free from Soviet signal and communications intelligence capabilities.

The Senate study recommended a variety of steps to reduce Soviet intelligence penetration of Congress including (1) mandatory reporting to the FBI of meetings by Members and staff with suspected Soviet and other communist country intelligence agents; (2) heightened security education programs for Members and staff; (3) the creation of a central office in the Senate to develop and oversee standards and procedures on personnel and information security issues; (4) possible reduction in the number of Congressional employees receiving security clearances; and (5) establishing more secure modes of communication and the development of in-house capabilities for transcribing and reporting classified hearings.[15]

While there is little evidence to suggest KGB/GRU recruitment activities have been successful, a number of questionable cases have been publicly reported. For example, Kenneth Tollivar, an aide to former Senator James Eastland (D-Miss), reportedly supplied information to the KGB for several years but said he did so under FBI instructions.[16] Eastland, however, stated that the FBI insisted he dismiss Tollivar. Tollivar claims he resigned voluntarily in the summer of 1968. FBI sources reported that Tollivar became a double agent only after a major espionage investigation had been launched. Tollivar insists that he was never recruited but worked with the FBI from the beginning. The FBI denies this and FBI sources claim he was treated first as a KGB recruit and then became an FBI double agent. Tollivar was never prosecuted for any crime.

In the early 1980's, a staff aide for Senator Lowell Weicker (R-Conn.), John Rote, was reportedly investigated by the FBI for his ongoing meetings with a Soviet Embassy employee at which Rote delivered packages. Rote reportedly gave conflicting stories about his meetings, saying on some occasions that he gave the Embassy officer classified information and on other occasions that he did not and only gave the Embassy public documents. FBI agents were apparently convinced that confessions about leaking classified documents to the Embassy were 'posturing' and the product of an individual who was "clearly arrogant and probably immature."[17] Rote was never prosecuted.

In 1976, it was revealed that a young American political scientist, James Frederick Sattler, was recruited by East German intelligence while in Berlin in 1967. In exchange for $15,000, Sattler transmitted to the East Germans information and documents received from NATO as well as West German,

American, British, and French governments. Sattler received training in codes and ciphers, microphotography, radio and mail communications, clandestine meetings, and concealment devices. Sattler visited the German Democratic Republic (GDR) on several occasions, and during his last visit in November, 1975, he was advised by his GDR contacts to obtain a position with the U.S. government that enabled access to classified information. During this eight-year period, Sattler had published widely on international security issues and had gained a reputation for moderate-conservative views on the subject. He was under serious consideration by Rep. Paul Findley (R-Ill.) for a job as a minority staff consultant to the House Foreign Affairs Committee's Subcommittee on Europe and the Middle East. The FBI, which by then had obtained information that Sattler was an East German agent, alerted Findley of Sattler's activities. He was never hired and in exchange for information on his activities was never prosecuted.

In the early 1980's it was reported that a Soviet diplomat went to the General Accounting Office and asked for and received "a list of numbered reports on highly classifed military subjects—some of which hadn't been published—and later walked around the building unescorted."[18]

Finally, in 1980 it was revealed that David Barnett, a former CIA contract employee and staffer in the 1950s and 1960s, received over $90,000 from the KGB beginning in 1976 in exchanges for "telling the KGB about CIA operations and the identities of Soviet officials who had been targeted by the CIA for possible recruitment."[19] He was instructed to seek employment at, among other places, the House and Senate Select Committees on Intelligence. He was never hired.

KGB targeting of Congress is not confined to Washington. Delegations visiting the Soviet Union are generally told by the U.S. Embassy to assume their rooms are bugged with electronic devices and two-way mirrors. Delegation members are followed when they attempt to walk the streets unescorted. Rooms where delegations are staying may be searched and even military aircraft carrying delegations to the Soviet Union can be broken into in a search for classified information.

Delegations may even have compromising offers made to them. For example, in 1976, a personal staff member for Senator Jake Garn (R-Utah), then a member of the Senate Select Committee on Intelligence, reported that he twice dated a Soviet tour guide in Kiev who the FBI believes was a KGB agent assigned to recruit or blackmail him. The liaison ended when the staffer left the Soviet Union with Senator Garn. An American intelligence expert interviewed for this study has also argued that the KGB keeps files on Members and their wives as well as staff, seeking personal weaknesses and vulnerabilities that could be exploited, particularly when they are traveling in the Soviet Union.

KGB surveillance of visiting delegations is most concentrated when such delegations visit Soviet dissidents or refuseniks. These groups, in the perception of the KGB, are seen as a clear threat. Their opposition to the Soviet political system, and the desire of most of them to leave, represents a challenge to a system that claims to have established a superior form of socio-political organization. Congress has been one of the most supportive of all U.S. foreign policy institutions in continuing to press the Soviet Union through the use of economic sanctions and a steady stream of condemnatory resolutions for greater emigration and an end to harassment, imprisonment, and torture of dissidents and refuseniks.

Visiting delegations invariably pursue what is euphemistically called an 'alternate schedule' of meetings with Soviet dissidents and refuseniks at their apartments or in delegation hotel rooms. These meetings are often essential sources of information on the actual state of human rights conditions in the Soviet Union. As a result, these meetings are usually the subject of electronic surveillances, and delegations are followed. No effort is made to break up such meetings, although reprisals against individuals and their families who meet with Members and staff have been known to occur. Soviet authorities seem to have grudgingly accepted these meetings as a security price they are willing to pay to gain access to influential Members of Congress.

Given what is known about the structure and operations of the KGB and the GRU, several bureaucratic units appear to have responsibility for contact with and operations directed against Congress. Activities conducted by these units include (1) penetration of foreign intelligence and security services; (2) analyzing and disseminating political and other intelligece and providing analysis to the Politburo; (3) disinformation and active measures; (4) cover positions for KGB and GRU personnel; (5) developing and supplying technical tools (cameras, concealment devices, electronic equipment, etc.) for clandestine operations; (6) recruitment and internal surveillance of Americans while in the Soviet Union; (7) physical penetration of the U.S. Embassy, as well as other physical assets such as official military transport planes carrying Congressional delegations to the Soviet Union; (8) intercepting communications and electronic signals at U.S. Government facilities in the Soviet Union and the United States and securing Soviet communications between the U.S. and the Soviet Union; (9) publishing in classified form, the successes and failures of intelligence operations; (10) maintenance of operational files; and (11) providing information to Soviet military and political authorities on foreign weapons, nuclear weapons, deployments, alert rates, doctrine and targeting policy, foreign country arms sales, production and technical development, strategic resources, and vulnerabilities.[20]

In addition, two Central Committee departments with responsibility for ensuring Party control of the Soviet intelligence apparatus could well be involved concerning relations with the Congress. The Administrative Organs Department is responsible for approving promotions within the KGB. The General Department also appears to provide some intelligence analysis services for the Politburo with respect to important issues, "synthesizing KGB and GRU reports and placing the information in the broadest policy context."[21]

The foreign policy research institutes discussed earlier in this chapter also have analysts assigned to them who are believed to be KGB and GRU employees. The KGB maintains at ISKAN, IMEMO, and other foreign policy institutes a first department of officers that perform both personnel checks and security functions. This department "provides for an on-site channel between KGB headquarters and the directors of particular institutions, a channel via which KGB directions can be transmitted."[22] As an example of this channel, one of the Deputy Directors of ISKAN, Radomir Bogdanov, who supervises ISKAN's study of disarmament issues, is generally believed to have had a long association with the KGB.[23]

While KGB operations against visiting Congressional delegations are extensive, the most continuous activity takes place against Congress as an institution and is therefore concentrated in the Soviet Embassy in Washington. The Embassy represents the central core of Soviet intelligence operations in any given country. The KGB is well-organized to deal with the Congress through the Soviet Embassy.[24]

The chief of KGB operations is known as a Resident. He has a Deputy Resident and several staff elements, including political, economic, and intelligence sections. The Resident is responsible for all KGB personnel and directly responsible to KGB headquarters in Moscow. Under Dobrynin, the Resident was believed to be under greater control of the Ambassador than was the Resident in the Soviet UN mission, owing to Dobrynin's prestige, his closeness to Gromyko and the Politburo, and his own Party rank as a Member of the Central Committee. Liaison is close between the Resident and the Chief of the GRU in the Embassy to avoid duplication.

The Resident is also supported by a Technical Support Group which provides equipment and expertise to conduct surveillance, phone taps, bugs, and secret photography, and to prevent these activities from being directed against the Embassy. Recruitment and espionage sections attempt to obtain classified information from U.S. government sources. A Reports Officer prepares information obtained by agents for communication to Moscow and a Residence Secretary maintains classified materials, a secure communications area, and intelligence reports.

The GRU intelligence unit in the Embassy is smaller but performs recruitment and collection efforts on defense-related subjects. It also operates the communications intelligence facilities that are a familiar part of Soviet embassies and consulates. The GRU is clearly subordinate to the KGB in Embassy operations. For example, while the GRU is "required to clear all agent recruitment attempts with the KGB in advance so as to prevent competing approaches to the same individual, the KGB does not appear to be similarly obligated."[25]

The KGB's high priority targeting of congressional intentions and the availability of vast amounts of open source material generated by the Congress have led to understandable concerns about security and calls for restricting the activities of the Soviet Embassy in the halls of Congress and its office buildings. But beyond tightening procedures to protect classified information and the processing of Congressional publications, encouraging greater aware- ness of KGB operations among Members and staff, and encouraging intensification of FBI contact reports, Congress' critical oversight role with respect to defense and foreign policy will continue to generate voluminous open source material.

Moreover, meetings with Soviet embassy officials including possible intelligence agents is not a wholly predatory process providing for a one-way information flow to the Soviet Embassy. Such meetings can produce candid discussions of the direction of Soviet policy toward the United States. On many occassions, whether accidental or intended, Members and staff can learn as much about their Soviet interlocutors and their views of Soviet policy and internal development in the Soviet Union as the Soviets learn from their American counterparts.

While the products of congressional oversight are generated for a different purpose, there is no way to prevent them from reaching Soviet sources. Raising the costs and amount of time it takes the Embassy to formulate intelligence analysis and preventing deliberate or careless leaks of classified information is the best that can be accomplished since it is in the interest of both the Congress and the Soviet embassy to maintain ongoing, normal diplomatic contact and dialogue.

Other Direct Interactions

Party and government institutions also gather information on the Congress through direct negotiating fora where Members of Congress and their staffs actively participate. Two such fora are the periodic international review conferences on implementation of the 1975 agreements on security, economic and human rights issues, concluded by 35 nations at the Conference on Security and Cooperation in Europe (CSCE or the so-called Helsinki Final Act) and the House and Senate Observers Groups, established in 1985 to monitor the status of U.S.-Soviet arms control negotiations in Geneva.

The U.S. delegation to Helsinki Final Act review conferences in Belgrade in 1977-1978, Madrid in 1980-1983, and in Vienna presently, have included Members of Congress and staff from the Commission on Security and Cooperation in Europe, a joint legislative-executive entity established by the United States shortly after the signing of the Helsinki Final Act. The Commission is principally charged with monitoring progress on the human rights agreements of the Helsinki Final Act by signatory states, particularly the Soviet Union and East European countries.

The Commission is unique among Helsinki Final Act signatories in that no other state has created such a separate institution to review CSCE implementation. In addition to participating in review conferences mandated by the CSCE process, the Commission engages in ongoing research and publication of Warsaw Pact violations of human rights. It also compiles human rights cases and seeks their resolution through a variety of channels, including their submission to Soviet and East European leaders by visiting Congressional delegations. The Commission has helped to resolve hundreds of such cases, particularly in the area of family reunification.

The Commission's creation in 1976 as a separate human rights monitoring institution was originally opposed by the State Department on the grounds that the Department and the existing committees and subcommittees of Congress could adequately perform monitoring of the Helsinki Final Act. However, supporters of the Commission's creation disagreed, arguing that a special commission was needed to insure that the human rights provisions of the Helsinki Final Act would receive appropriate attention. The Ford Administration eventually accepted this argument and agreed to sign legislation creating the Commission into law in June, 1976.

For many years after its creation however, the executive branch resisted and attempted to minimize the role of the Commission in CSCE review conferences. The Soviet Union and Warsaw Pact states also refused to recognize the Commission as having legal standing with respect either to its participation in review conferences or to the conduct of oversight of CSCE implementation. Gradually however, first the executive branch and then Soviet and East European authorities began to accept grudgingly the role of the Commission staff in negotiations on communiques and other documents agreed to in CSCE review conferences. The executive branch has also revised its judgment about the value of the Commission, seeing its existence as tactically and politically advantageous in negotiating human rights issues with the Soviet Union. The Commission is now viewed by the executive branch as verifying to Soviet negotiators Congress' long-established activism on human rights issues, verification which is useful in dealing with the Soviet Union on the inevitably confrontational issue of human rights.

The Commission's Congressional members and staff have been in the thick of CSCE review conference activity, from developing strategy to chairing meetings, delivering speeches, preparing and negotiating final documents of review conferences, and providing administrative and logistical support to U.S. CSCE delegations. In this way, Soviet foreign policymakers have come to recognize the considerable foreign policymaking powers of the Congress, even in the area of directly participating in the conduct of international negotiations. Sustained, direct contact over a number of years has also created a cadre of Soviet foreign policy officials familiar with and cognizant of a number of Members of Congress and their potential for the considerable wielding of power.

The House and Senate Arms Control Observers Groups were created in 1985 by separate resolutions in both Houses of Congress. The purpose of the groups is to provide bipartisan monitoring of the conduct and progress of the ongoing Geneva arms control negotiations on intermediate nuclear, strategic nuclear, and space defense weapons, in the hopes that active consultations between the U.S. negotiators and Members of Congress will help shape a more politically-sustainable arms control negotiating position. Given failure to obtain Senate ratification of SALT II and two nuclear testing treaties concluded with the Soviet Union in the mid-70s, congressional and executive branch supporters of the Observer Groups argue their existence will help smooth subsequent legislative approval of prospective arms control agreements. The House Observers Group is composed of 20 members, 10 from each party with no formal chairmen. The Senate Observers Group is composed of 12 Senators, 6 from each party, with Senators Sam Nunn (D-Ga.), Claiborne Pell (D-R.I.), Ted Stevens (R-Alas) and Richard Lugar (R-Ind.) serving as co-chairmen.

The two Groups have made numerous visits to Geneva since their creation. In addition to meeting with the U.S. negotiating team, regular meetings have been conducted with Soviet representatives to the Geneva negotiations, including Heads of Delegations. The Reagan Administration has regarded the Groups and their conduct favorably, and the House and Senate Groups have been careful not to criticize the negotiating positions taken by the executive branch in the negotiations. For example, Senator Dole, the Senate Majority Leader at the time the Senate Observers Group was created, remarked that the purpose of the Senate Observers Group would be to establish a "mechanism for appropriate and responsible Senate input into the negotiating process."[26] Senators would not be negotiators but would serve as a "channel for information and feedback as formal negotiations ensue, so that the Senate could more knowledgeably play the ratifying or other role which might later be required."[27] For its part, the Reagan Administration has welcomed the Groups and has argued that they can "facilitate and enhance our consultative process and help establish the kind of unity which our nation needs as we approach this issue of great importance."[28]

The establishment of the Observers Groups is a potentially far-reaching development for Congress' role in U.S.-Soviet relations. The current head of the U.S. delegation, Ambassador Max Kampelman, has encouraged the advice of Members on negotiating strategy so that they will be "intimately involved in the negotiating process from the start instead of merely voting on a package deal at the end."[29] The Senate Observers Group even has small office space in Geneva and a budget of $500,000 for administrative and staff support. The Senate Observers Group is also being given access to negotiating cable traffic when Senators are in Washington.

Moreover, both the House and Senate Observers Groups include senior Congressional leadership figures and arms control experts, including the chairmen and ranking members of the House Foreign Affairs and Senate Foreign Relations Committees and the House and Senate Armed Services Committees. It is unlikely that this group will merely monitor negotiating developments without making suggestions of their own. Many of the Members of these Groups have supported radically different negotiating strategies opposed by the Reagan Administration, including a comprehensive bilateral nuclear weapons freeze and comprehensive nuclear test ban negotiations. Should negotiations become stalemated for a long period of time, it is likely that alternative negotiating strategies will be expressed directly to U.S. negotiators in Geneva.

For its part, Soviet leaders, tired of past Congressional rebuffs on arms control agreements negotiated with the U.S. executive branch, have accepted the Groups' existence and have granted access not only to the Soviet negotiating team, but also visiting members of the Soviet leadership, including Marshall Sergei Akhromeev, the head of the Soviet Armed Forces. One participant in the Senate Observer Group meetings with Soviet officials reported to me repeated exchanges between Senators and Soviet arms control negotiators on the details of both Soviet and American arms control negotiating positions, and it is believed these discussions are reported to the Soviet leadership.

This development demonstrates how far Soviet leaders have come in recognizing Congress' foreign policy powers. Soviet leaders now appear to recognize the old adage that to avoid a Congressional crash landing, Congress must be in on the takeoff. The Arms Control Observer Groups represent, like the Commission on Security and Cooperation in Europe, fora for enduring Soviet contact with and exposure to Congress' role in U.S.-Soviet relations.

In addition to exposure to Members of Congress through negotiating fora, the accession of Gorbachev as General Secretary and Dobrynin as head of a revitalized Central Committee International Department has brought new direct interactions with the Congress. These new interactions are of a qualitatively higher level and have included (1) Soviet testimony before a committee of Congress; (2) an on-site Congressional visit to a sensitive Soviet radar installation long regarded by American policymakers as a violation of the ABM Treaty; and (3) a periodic television dialogue between Members of Congress and the USSR Supreme Soviet.

The Soviet nuclear accident at Chernobyl in April, 1986 prompted worldwide fears concerning the safety of nuclear power. In particular, in contrast to the stated goals of Gorbachev to become more open about discussing and revealing internal political, economic, and social developments in the Soviet Union, the Soviet Union was intensely criticized for not immediately alerting international authorities about the accident and then minimizing the loss of life and potential health effects in Eastern and Western Europe resulting from nuclear fallout from the accident. Perhaps in part because of this pressure, Second Secretary of the Soviet Embassy in Washington Vitalii Churkin (now a key staff member of the Central Committee International Department) was allowed to make an unprecedented appearance before the House Committee on Energy and Commerce's Subcommittee on Energy Conservation and Power, which was holding hearings in early May 1986 on the accident and its implications for the nuclear power industry in the United States. Churkin appeared at the request of the Subcommittee.

Since the accident was less than a week old when Churkin testified, the informational aspects of his testimony were not especially revealing. On a number of technical questions Churkin could not provide answers. He essentially repeated the essence of the Soviet Union's public posture at the time on the accident which included the following elements: (1) the situation around Chernobyl had stabilized; (2) the accident had resulted in only 2 deaths and 150 injuries and the level of contamination did not require special measures to protect the population; (3) there was no need for special assistance from foreign countries to clean up the accident or assist the injured; (4) the Soviet Union had been forthcoming in notifying neighboring countries of the accident and that no real health effects had occurred; (5) the Soviet Union was interested in any international measure that could help prevent a reoccurence of such an accident anywhere in the world and; (6) criticisms of the Soviet handling of the accident and its notification procedure to other countries were unfounded and not consistent with the facts.[30]

Despite the formalistic nature of Churkin's testimony, it represented the first time a request by a Congressional committee for testimony by the Soviet Embassy had been accepted. It now appears that the Soviet Union is no longer merely content to gather information from Congress through hearings, publications, intelligence recruitment attempts, Congressional visits to the Soviet Union, and Soviet delegation visits to the United States. Where possible, the Soviet foreign policy apparatus is ready to engage Congress directly on its own ground: the hearing rooms of Congressional committees.

Another unique form of direct interaction emerged in August-September 1987 with the invitation by the USSR Supreme Soviet for three House Members, Rep. Thomas J. Downey (D-N.Y.), Rep. Bob Carr (D-Mich.), and Rep. Jim Moody (D-Wisc.), to visit the site of an air defense radar facility at Krasnoyarsk in Western Siberia. The Krasnoyarsk radar has been a controversial military facility ever since the Reagan Administration first contended in 1983 that the radar's purpose, when fully constructed, is to be a battle management radar to be used for anti-ballistic missile purposes in violation of the ABM Treaty. That Treaty permits only one such ABM complex for both the United States and the Soviet Union and the Soviet Union already has one ABM complex on the outskirts of Moscow.

The Downey delegation received unprecedented access to parts of the Soviet Union never before visited by Americans, let alone a Congressional delegation. The Krasnoyarsk installation is located in a restricted military area where the Soviet military is instructed to shoot intruders without warning. The delegation was told that the top authorities of the Ministry of Defense, with the concurrence of the Politburo, gave approval for the delegation to visit the Krasnoyarsk facility. Downey's delegation took thousands of pictures, made audio and visual tapes, took notes and drew diagrams. Soviet authorities did not interfere with this process in any way. Some picture-taking on some aspects of the site were prohibited and while most questions asked of Soviet military authorities on the radar site were answered fully, some questions about the radar's technical operations received vague answers. In addition to a visit to the Krasnoyarsk site, the delegation also carried on a number of very detailed and open discussions on the Krasnoyarsk radar and other U.S.-Soviet arms control issues when the group was in Moscow.

The delegation reached a number of conclusions about the Krasnoyarsk controversy. First, the delegation speculated that the radar's construction could well be the result of a failure of coordination within the Soviet foreign policy and national security apparatus. The delegation was told by Soviet officials that the radar was for early warning and space-tracking purposes. The ABM Treaty permits early warning radars of the Krasnoyarsk type to be deployed only on the periphery of national territory pointed outward. Space-tracking radars are not restricted by the Treaty in any way. If the radar has a dual purpose, it could be a violation of the ABM Treaty because Krasnoyarsk in not located on the Soviet Union's periphery. When the U.S. first raised the Krasnoyarsk issue in 1983, Soviet officials told the delegation, the Reagan Administration had already begun its plans to move forward with space-based defense weapons research under the SDI program, which if eventually pushed to weapons deployment would clearly violate the ABM Treaty.

The Downey delegation also concluded that whatever the purpose of the Krasnoyarsk radar, it was years from being operational and therefore is not a violation of the ABM Treaty until it is made so. There appeared to be no evidence of 'hardening' to protect the complex, casting doubt that its construction is a priority asset in a conscious policy to break out of the ABM Treaty, a charge leveled by the Reagan Administration. The physical state of radar construction and the lack of certain characteristics and facilities made it an unlikely candidate to be an ABM battle management radar complex, which the Reagan Administration had also contended. In the judgment of the delegation, the Krasnoyarsk radar was not even an effective early-warning radar. The delegation also recommended that on-site inspections of the Krasnoyarsk radar complex should continue so that any future new developments concerning the radar's construction or purpose could be verified.

Why this particular delegation received such exceptional treatment is open to speculation. The delegation was originally invited to the Soviet Union under the auspices of the Natural Resources Defense Council (NRDC), a private American group composed of natural scientists and other professionals which has conducted a cooperative program with members of the USSR Academy of Sciences designed to demonstrate the feasibility and verifiability of a comprehensive nuclear test ban. Under NRDC auspices, Soviet authorities originally agreed to let the delegation visit a Soviet nuclear testing site. Upon its arrival in the Soviet Union, the delegation pressed Soviet officials to also let the group observe the Krasnoyarsk facility as evidence of Soviet willingness to permit on-site inspection of sensitive military facilities. Since such inspection would be an intrinsic part of future arms control agreements, the Downey delegation tried to convince Soviet military and foreign policy officials of the perceived Soviet need to be forthcoming on on-site inspection, if only to disprove the Reagan Administration's allegations that the Krasnoyarsk radar violated the ABM Treaty. After a few days of deliberations, Soviet officials agreed.

There is some evidence to suggest that at least one reason for the decision to let the delegation visit Krasnoyarsk was sensitivity to the need to influence

Congressional deliberations on arms control issues. During meetings in Moscow, delegation members explicitly queried Soviet officials as to why Gorbachev in the fall of 1986 had proposed a summit in Reykjavik when such a proposal at that particular time fatally undermined efforts by the House to impose a series of arms control restrictions on President Reagan. After this exchange, at least two Soviet arms control experts, IMEMO's Alexei Arbatov and ISKAN's Andrei Kokoshin, told one member of the Downey delegation that they would urge the Soviet leadership to devote more careful consideration to the issue of how Soviet foreign policy initiatives toward the United States affect legislative actions designed to encourage arms control progress, even if those actions were opposed by the Reagan Administration. If in fact Soviet leaders directly pursue such a strategy, it would represent an unprecedented effort to try to influence Congress' role in U.S.-Soviet relations.

Another qualitative leap in direct interactions developed in late 1987 with the initiation of a direct televised exchange via satellite between Members of the USSR Supreme Soviet and the U.S. Congress. The so-called Capitol to Capitol programs, televised by the U.S. commercial network the American Broadcasting Corporation (ABC) and the Soviet State Committee for Television and Radio (Gostelradio) have involved direct exchanges on three major issues affecting U.S.-Soviet relations: mutual security, human rights, and regional conflicts. The exchanges are conducted from actual legislative offices of the Congress and the Supreme Soviet.

The Capitol to Capitol exchanges were set up through the initiative of Rep. George Brown (D-Calif.), a long-time proponent of peaceful uses of outer space. The programs were the result of a four-year effort undertaken by Brown and his staff to create a direct television linkup between Members of Congress and Soviet policymakers to discuss key issues between the superpowers. Working in cooperation with Internews, a mixed profit, non-profit corporation headquartered in San Francisco and New York, Rep. Brown and his staff made several visits to the Soviet Union to elicit positive Soviet interest.

In 1986, after a friendly intervention by Speaker O'Neill with Soviet Ambassador Dobrynin in support of the project, the Supreme Soviet sent a delegation to the United States later that year to make arrangements for the satellite hookup and agree on the substantive agenda. An initial program shown only in the Soviet Union was produced in April, 1987. Internews succeeded in persuading ABC to broadcast three subsequent programs in September, October, and November of 1987. Another three shows are scheduled for sometime in 1988. ABC News Correspondent Peter Jennings and Gostelradio Correspondent Leonid Zolotarevskii are co-moderators for the program.

The Capitol to Capitol initiative has not received formal sanction from either the executive branch or the Congress and individual Members of Congress express their own personal views on the shows. Nonetheless, a number of Members have participated either as panelists or as questioners from the studio audience. Participants have included Brown, Rep. Claudine Schneider (R-R.I.), Brown's Republican program cosponsor, Rep. Jim Leach (R-Ia.), Rep. Downey, Rep. Clay Shaw (R-Fla.), Rep. Les Aspin (D-Wisc.), chairman of the House Armed Services Committee, Sen. Nunn, chairman of the Senate Armed Services Committee, Sen. Bill Bradley (D-N.J.), Sen. Nancy Kassebaum (R-Kans.), Sen. Daniel Moynihan (D-N.Y.), Rep. Trent Lott (R-Miss.), the House Minority Whip, Rep. Steny Hoyer (D-Md.), chairman of the Commission on Security and Cooperation in Europe, Rep. Benjamin Gilman (R-N.Y.), ranking minority member of the House Foreign Affairs Committee's Subcommittee on Europe and Middle East, Rep. Gerald Solomon (R-N.Y.), ranking minority member of the House Foreign Affairs Committee's Subcommittee on Human Rights and International Organizations, Rep. George Gekas (R-Pa.), and Rep. Robert Dornan (R-Calif.).

The Soviet participants have included a number of influential policymakers such as Vadim Zagladin, first deputy chief of the Central Committee International Department, Ivan Laptev, editor-in-chief of the Soviet government newspaper *Izvestia*, Georgii Zhukov, political observer for the Communist Party newspaper *Pravda*, and Evgenii Primakov, director of IMEMO.

Despite the lack of official U.S. government sponsorship, or perhaps because of it, the Capitol to Capitol initiative has in the view of its promoters helped to bring about some important breakthroughs in the agenda of superpower relations. First, the programs have been carried live and unedited in the Soviet Union even as the participants held extremely frank and freewheeling debates on such issues as human rights repression in the Soviet Union and the Soviet invasion of Afghanistan. Second, perhaps because of the airing of these programs, Soviet authorities have taken the opportunity to announce the resolution of some family reunification and emigration cases. This has provided piecemeal but concrete progress on human rights disputes, progress which might otherwise not have been possible in the normal exchange of correspondence between Members of Congress and the Soviet leadership.

Third, informal but candid dialogue has been the norm in these programs, enabling Soviet policymakers and Members of Congress to part with set speeches and take direct measure of each other on such issues as: (1) Soviet political repression and the use of torture and psychiatric hospitals to punish political dissent; (2) the arbitrary application of Soviet laws to arrest dissidents and deny emigration requests; (3) the suppression of religion and individual expression in the Soviet Union; (4) health care deficiencies, homelessness, unemployment, and other human rights issues in the United States; (5) the differences in political processes in the two countries, including the lack of competitive elections in the Soviet Union; (6) the Soviet invasion of Afghanistan and the U.S. support of the anticommunist rebels in Nicaragua and; (7) Soviet perceptions of the potentially destabilizing elements of the U.S. SDI program and the Reagan Administration's efforts to reinterpret the ABM Treaty to elude the Treaty's ban on developing and testing SDI-type space defense systems.

By permitting this type of direct informal interaction, the Capitol to Capitol program gives Members of Congress and their Soviet counterparts a rare opportunity to probe each other's policy preferences and intentions. Like other direct interactions, the Capitol to Capitol program represents one more developing and qualitatively different form of Soviet-U.S. Congress diplomacy on issues affecting superpower relations.

Parliamentary Exchanges

Another source of information available to the Soviet leadership on Congress' role in foreign policy is parliamentary exchanges. Since 1974, the year the Jackson-Vanik amendment was adopted, the USSR Supreme Soviet has conducted an ongoing series of parliamentary exchanges with the U.S. Congress. The attention and priority given to regular exchanges with high-level Congressional delegations is itself evidence of the importance attached to Congress' role in U.S. foreign policy.

Leaders of the Supreme Soviet have repeatedly pressed Congressional leaders for the establishment of formal relations between the Congress and the Supreme Soviet similar to those established between the Congress and the parliaments of Canada, Mexico, the European Parliament, and NATO member countries. While congressional leaders have not acted on this proposal, they have been amenable to regular exchanges. Since 1978, the House Majority Whip has taken informal responsibility for establishing periodic exchange visits to the Soviet Union and the reception of Supreme Soviet delegations to the United States. While no similar structure exists in the Senate, Senator Byrd, whether as majority or minority leader of the Senate, has arranged for several visits of high-ranking Senate delegations to the Soviet Union.

The Supreme Soviet itself has only a symbolic role in the Soviet political system. It meets twice a year with sessions lasting only a few days. It plays a legitimizing function, serving as "a ceremonial forum where the regime can announce its programs."[31] While in theory vested with all legislative power, it in fact stays in session only long enough to approve what its Presidium and the Council of Ministers has already done in its name.

The Supreme Soviet is a bicameral national legislature with one house, the Council of the Union, elected from single-member constituencies, and the other the Council of Nationalities, elected proportionately by union republic, autonomous republic, autonomous oblast, and national district. Like other organs of Soviet government, the Supreme Soviet has had an over-representation of party members when compared to the ratio of party members to the general population. The Supreme Soviet has also had uncontested elections, and party control of nominations.

Most of the Soviet political leadership is elected to the Supreme Soviet. As mentioned earlier, the Supreme Soviet has standing committees, including foreign affairs committees, which in recent years have been headed by a Politburo member. Standing committees are more active than the Supreme

Soviet as a whole. They work out proposals for consideration by the Presidium and exercise control over government ministries and agencies within their jurisdiction. With respect to this last function, in the foreign affairs area there is no evidence to suggest that the Foreign Affairs Commissions have had any thorough supervisory control or oversight responsibilities over the Ministry of Foreign Affairs.

Quite typical of Soviet political institutions, the Presidium of the Supreme Soviet is a more powerful organization than its parent body. The chairman is the ceremonial head of state and the current chairman, Andrei Gromyko, has a wealth of experience in dealing with Members of Congress. The Presidium has the authority to issue decrees, ratify treaties, and appoint ministers. However, since the chairman has traditionally been a full Politburo member, the Presidium actually legitimates decisions made in other Party and government institutions. However, because the power of judicial review in the Soviet political system rests with the Presidium, and the USSR Supreme Court and the Procurator-General are subordinate to the Presidium, the Presidium does have importance in dealing with human rights cases of interest to Members of Congress. Furthermore, since the accession of Dobrynin to the chairmanship of the Council of the Union's Foreign Affairs Commission, a separate entity has been established under Supreme Soviet auspices to deal with human rights cases and communicate directly with Members of Congress on cases of interest.

The Presidium is a body of about 40 members, with only a few members regularly present in Moscow. Because it exercises its powers daily, even though the full Presidium only meets formally every two months, the Politburo and Central Committee Secretariat usually make decisions that are then legitimized by the Supreme Soviet. This process points to the Presidium as an additional source reinforcing party control over all political decisions, including those in the foreign policy realm.

Nonetheless, the tasks of official head of state, foreign travel, receiving foreign dignitaries and ambassadors etc., provide the chairman of the Presidium with visibility. This visibility clearly advanced the career of Brezhnev, who held the position in the early 1960s and used it to enhance his prestige and foreign policy experience, assets which were useful in his becoming General Secretary in 1964. Brezhnev later reclaimed the chairmanship for himself in 1977. On the other hand, the chairmanship has also been known to be an emeritus position for past service rendered. This clearly appears to be the case for its current occupant.

Given the often ceremonial, largely truncated powers of the Supreme Soviet, its standing committees, and its Presidium, the political importance of parliamentary exchanges between the Congress and the Supreme Soviet comes not because Soviet delegates are represented in that body, but because of the party rank of Supreme Soviet delegations visiting the Congress or hosting Congressional delegations. Supreme Soviet sponsorship of these exchanges provides the official protocol mechanism for the exchange of views on foreign policy issues between 'legislatures,' fictional though that may be in the Soviet case. Nonetheless, though the Soviet legislature may have extremely limited powers, the representation of high-ranking party officials in the legislature and its delegations suggests parliamentary exchanges are taken very seriously and demonstrates the importance Soviet policymakers attach to Congress' role in foreign policy.

Moreover, the Supreme Soviet bureaucracy, particularly its International Department, is often crucial to the success of congressional delegations visiting the Soviet Union. Their logistical capability in terms of extending a formal invitation and servicing a delegation's logistical needs is critical, particularly since the fall of 1986 when the U.S. embassy began operating without the use of Soviet personnel. Given virtually non-existent Embassy assets for logistical support of congressional delegations, it is not an exaggeration to say that without a formal Supreme Soviet invitation, a congressional visit to the Soviet Union is very difficult. The Supreme Soviet is also not without considerable power in choosing what delegations it will host and at what level. It is not accountable to the wishes of the Ministry of Foreign Affairs and appears to have considerably greater logistical assets for hosting congressional delegations. It has been known to clash with the Ministry over whether and how to receive delegations and will defer only to the Central Committee International Department on this issue.

The Supreme Soviet also has considerable substantive capabilities. The Supreme Soviet's Parliamentary Group, which organizes foreign travel and contacts for Soviet legislators, includes a number of notable policymakers who serve as spokesmen for Soviet foreign policy positions in meetings with Members of Congress and can be influential in arranging other high-level meetings for congressional delegations.

In 1974 and 1978, Supreme Soviet delegations visiting the United States were headed by Boris Ponomarev, a candidate member of the Politburo. The 1974 visit represented a major new initiative on the part of Soviet political leaders who began to realize the need during the Jackson-Vanik debate in Congress of opening relations with Congress "which the Soviet leadership had not previously deigned to recognize officially."[32] In 1985, a similar delegation visiting the United States was headed by Shcherbitskii, a full member of the Politburo. Reciprocal visits were made by Congressional delegations headed by Rep. Carl Albert (D-Okla.), then Speaker of the House of Representatives, in 1975, by Senators Hubert Humphrey (D-Minn.) and Hugh Scott (R-Pa.) in 1975, Rep. John Brademas (D-Ind.) then the House Majority Whip in 1979, Senator Abraham Ribicoff (D-Conn.) in 1978, Rep. Thomas Foley (D-Wash.), the then House Majority Whip and now House Majority Leader, in 1983, former Speaker O'Neill in 1985, and Speaker Wright in 1987. As a testament to the high rank of these delegations, many of these parliamentary exchanges resulted in meetings between the Party General Secretary and American delegations. In addition, a number of visits by Members of Congress that were not billed as full-blown parliamentary exchanges have occurred in the last 14 years.

An examination of Soviet delegations that took part in parliamentary exchanges attests to their importance and the high party rank of the delegates.

For example, the 1985 Shcherbitskii delegation also included the following Soviet officials who held the following positions at the time: Vladimir Alkhimov, chairman of the board of the USSR State Bank and a Central Committee member; Boris Paton, deputy chairman of the Council of the Union and President of the Ukrainian Academy of Sciences and a Central Committee member; and Boris Stukalin, chairman of the Propaganda Department of the Central Committee.

The delegation was also supported by a number of americanists, including: Arbatov; Alexander Bessmertnykh, then Chief of the USA Department of the MFA; Col. Gen. Nikolai F. Chervov, Directorate Chief, General Staff of the USSR Armed Forces, who accompanied Gorbachev on his visit to the United Kingdom in December, 1984; Vitaliy Kobysh, Chief, U.S. Sector, International Information Department of the Central Committee; Stanislav Kondrashev, a 'political observer' for *Izvestia;* and Valentin Zorin, a 'political observer' for the USSR State Committee for Television and Radio Broadcasting, and a member of the editorial board of ISKAN's monthly journal.

The O'Neill delegation, in its meetings with the Supreme Soviet, also were confronted with a high-ranking delegation including the following Soviet officials holding the following positions at the time: Lev Tolkunov, chairman, Council of the Union (the protocol equivalent of the Speaker of the House), and a member of the Central Committee and chairman of the Supreme Soviet's Parliamentary Group; August Voss, chairman of the Council of Nationalities (protocol equivalent of the Senate Majority Leader), deputy chairman of the Parliamentary Group and a member of the Central Committee; Zagladin, first deputy chief of the Central Committee International Department and secretary of the Foreign Affairs Commission of the Council of the Union; Stukalin, already described above; Alexander Chakovskii, editor-in-chief of *Literaturnaia Gazeta;* Richard Kosolapov, editor-in-chief of *Kommunist,* the Party's main ideological journal. Arbatov, Chervov, and Iakovlev also supported the Supreme Soviet delegation for the O'Neill visit.

Parliamentary exchanges have gradually developed a quadrapartite framework of discussions on issues affecting U.S.- Soviet relations: arms control, human rights, trade, and regional issues. While discussions often involve only an exchange of official positions on these issues on both sides, well-prepared delegations on both sides, together with agreements by the respective chairmen of the delegations to limit the time of individual presentations, can produce useful discussions. Members of Congress who oppose certain aspects of the executive branch's foreign policy can occasionally explore the flexibility or lack of it in the Soviet position on various issues affecting U.S.-Soviet relations. At the same time, opposition Members have been very careful to dispel the impression that they are vulnerable to Soviet attempts to divide them from the American administration.

Objectives of Parliamentary Exchanges

From the perspective of Soviet foreign policymakers, parliamentary exchanges serve a number of objectives. First, these exchanges can be thought of as serving an intelligence collection purpose. The first-hand personal exchanges with high-ranking Members of Congress in both professional and social settings provide extremely valuable information on a whole range of critical political issues. For example, inside information on the likely direction of legislative action on defense and foreign policy programs, attitudes toward expanded U.S.-Soviet trade and on what terms, attitudes toward cultural, educational, and scientific exchanges, attitudes toward human rights issues, and political trends including electoral strategies and the current political standing of the President or the Congressional leadership might well be gleaned from sustained contact with Members of Congress. This type of contact complements intelligence on critical questions that is gathered by the MFA and KGB, and analyzed in amerikanistika.

The second Soviet objective served by parliamentary exchanges is to provide alternate, redundant channels of communication to top American policymakers when U.S.-Soviet relations have deteriorated. Influential Members who participate in parliamentary delegations are given full exposure to Soviet positions on a variety of issues and are treated as foreign dignitaries in an effort to create as favorable impression as possible. Soviet delegates try to convince Members that improved relations are possible if only the 'dangerous' aspects of U.S. policy toward the Soviet Union are reversed.

The ability of Soviet policymakers to relate to and possibly influence a powerful foreign policy institution like the Congress is demonstrably advanced by parliamentary exchanges, particularly when channels of communication with the executive branch are largely stymied. This 'parliamentary strategy' is most graphically demonstrated by the fact that while there were no meetings between the American and Soviet heads of state from July 1979 to November 1985, most of the House and Senate leadership, influential committee chairmen, and other influential Members visited the Soviet Union and were received by the Soviet General Secretary.

It should be pointed out that like Soviet policymakers, the executive branch may utilize the Congress as well for U.S. foreign policy purposes during these parliamentary exchanges. Letters from Presidents to the Soviet General Secretary are often carried by Congressional delegations. For example, an exchange of letters between Reagan and Gorbachev regarding preparations for the November, 1985 summit was facilitated by O'Neill's meeting with Gorbachev in April of that year. A similar purpose was achieved regarding preparations for the next Reagan-Gorbachev summit by a letter from Reagan carried by Reps. Fascell and William Broomfield (R-Mich.), the chairman and ranking minority member of the House Foreign Affairs Committee, who visited with Gorbachev in early 1986. Such indirect communications are often preferred by the executive branch during times of poor relations. Thus, the executive branch, as well as Soviet policymakers, have endorsed parliamentary exchanges.

In addition, it is normal practice for visiting Congressional delegations to be briefed by the State Department, the Defense Department, and the CIA before their departure. Extensive briefing books are given to the delegations, outlining U.S. and Soviet positions on foreign policy issues, with suggestions as to what points Members should stress in their meetings with Soviet officials. High-level Administration officials often give these briefings, and stress the need for Congress and the President to "speak with one voice" on issues affecting U.S.-Soviet relations. Sensitivity is high among Members concerning the need for bipartisanship in foreign affairs and the need to avoid any deliberate undermining of current U.S. foreign policy positions during their visit. Thus, successive executive branches have supported U.S.-Soviet parliamentary exchanges as a means of demonstrating to the Soviet leadership the degree of solidarity between the Administration and Congress on the direction of U.S. policy toward the Soviet Union.

Furthermore, congressional delegations afford access for top U.S. Embassy officials to meet with Soviet leaders, access which would otherwise be denied them. It is customary for Congressional delegations to include the U.S. Ambassador in its meetings with the Soviet Foreign Minister and Party General Secretary. This inclusion provides the Ambassador greatly increased access to the Soviet leadership, and enhances the Embassy's understanding of the views of the Soviet leadership on critical issues in U.S.-Soviet relations. By contrast, requests through diplomatic channels for the Ambassador to see the Soviet leadership without the presence of Congressional delegations are usually not successful.

In addition, parliamentary exchange visits often include social gatherings at the homes of high party officials who may be influential in foreign policy but who have no contact with the Embassy because these officials hold party, not government positions. Reports on these gatherings provided by Members extend Embassy knowledge and understanding of the Soviet foreign policy process. Thus, it can be easily argued that parliamentary exchanges provide practical benefits not only to Soviet but also American foreign policymakers.

From a Soviet perspective, the final objective served by parliamentary exchanges is the opportunity afforded for Soviet foreign policymakers to 'lobby' Members of Congress on critical foreign policy issues. The word lobby should be used carefully in this case because the effort undertaken by Soviet parliamentary exchange participants rarely involves direct efforts, as characterized in American-style lobbying, to affect or change votes on specific legislation that may be pending before the House or Senate. Rather, the effort is directed at demonstrating Soviet foreign policy positions in their most positive light and stressing areas of commonality with positions taken by Members of Congress visiting the Soviet Union.

This type of lobbying takes several forms. For example, in May, 1974, a Supreme Soviet delegation led by Ponomarev visited the United States "for the expressed purpose of lobbying the Congress on the trade bill."[33] The effort came too late and was largely an exception to the overreliance placed by the Soviet leadership and then Ambassador Dobrynin in Washington to negotiate trade and emigration issues solely with the executive branch. As a result, the Jackson-Vanik amendment linking trade concessions with liberalized Soviet emigration policies was enacted.

In the months leading up to the signing of the SALT II Treaty, a number of House and Senate delegations, particularly a high-ranking group of Senators led by Senator Ribicoff who were undecided on whether to vote for advice and consent, were exposed to extensive discussions with a high-ranking Supreme Soviet delegation in the Soviet Union, as well as meetings with Brezhnev and Gromyko. SALT II approval was clearly the objective of Soviet participants as "military and arms control issues dominated most of the formal discussions between the delegation and Soviet officials. Most prominent among these issues was the SALT II Treaty."[34]

In July, 1979, Senator Byrd visited the Soviet Union with the primary purpose of discussing the SALT II Treaty as well as the Senate's constitutional role in the treaty process. Byrd was accorded exceptional treatment including a meeting at Brezhnev's summer retreat in the Crimea. Brezhnev stressed his opposition to "amendments and demands which, he said, could mean almost a replay (of the negotiations) from the beginning."[35] At a subsequent meeting with Gromyko in Moscow, Gromyko stressed that "when he heard some political figures in the United States say that the Kremlin underrates the role of the Senate, he felt such statements were misdirected."[36]

In 1983, a group of influential Democratic senators led by Senator Claiborne Pell (D-R.I.), the then ranking minority member and now chairman of the Senate Foreign Relations Committee, had extensive sessions with Supreme Soviet representatives of high-party rank and was also the only Congressional delegation to have met with Yuri Andropov when he was General Secretary. During the visit, a Soviet moratorium on anti-satellite weapons testing was announced. A U.S.-Soviet moratorium on anti-satellite testing was known to be supported by Pell and other Democratic Senators on the trip. The offer is believed by a Senate staff member interviewed to have been timed to the Pell visit.

In 1983, the delegation to the Soviet Union led by Rep. Foley was requested to attend a late-night meeting with ISKAN director Arbatov to discuss the impending NATO decision to modernize its theater nuclear weapons, a decision the Soviet Union had launched an unprecedented political campaign in Europe to stop. Arbatov stressed to the delegation that the impending decision would seriously degrade U.S.-Soviet relations, lead to a possible Soviet walkout from the Geneva arms control talks, and create incentives for Soviet opponents of detente to gain control of Soviet foreign policy and usher in a sustained period of antagonism. Andropov's illness and an admission that he would "not be around much longer" were also acknowledged. While the meeting had little effect, and elements of propaganda and disinformation could well have been present, some aspects of the meeting were judged by one participant to have been quite candid.

In 1985, during Speaker O'Neill's visit to the Soviet Union, Gorbachev announced in an interview with *Pravda* a proposal for a comprehensive freeze on U.S.-Soviet nuclear arsenals. The 13-person delegation included several Members who had consistently supported Congressional resolutions calling for a U.S.-Soviet freeze on nuclear weapons. It is clear from the statements of Supreme Soviet delegates during that parliamentary exchange that this was known to the Soviet leadership.

Thus, parliamentary exchanges are useful in the making and conduct of Soviet foreign policy for a number of reasons. In addition to buttressing with direct personal contact, intelligence collection and amerikanistika, such exchanges are a form of diplomatic back channel to the American foreign policy machinery when normal channels are closed or atrophied. Exploitation of divisions between some elements of Congress and the President, as well as the opportunity to create movement in areas of U.S.-Soviet relations where stalemate has set in, further advances Soviet foreign policy objectives. The fact that the American executive branch also uses these exchanges for many of these same purposes helps to explain their staying power as a unique instrument of U.S.-Soviet diplomacy.

Notes

1. Shevchenko, p. 249.
2. Teddy J. Uldricks, "The Tsarist and Soviet Ministry of Foreign Affairs," in *The Times Survey of Foreign Ministries of the World*, ed. Zara Sterner (London: Time Books, 1982): 533-534.
3. Ibid., p. 534.
4. Hough, *Soviet Leadership in Transition*, p. 128.
5. Ibid.
6. For more on the Byrd-Dobrynin meeting, see Robert G. Kaiser, "To Save SALT, Sen. Byrd Huddled in Secret with Soviet," *Washington Post*, 28 October 1979.
7. For a thorough discussion of Soviet-sponsored front organizations and their role in supporting Soviet foreign policy initiatives in Western Europe and the United States, see U.S. House, Permanent Select Committee on Intelligence, *Soviet Active Measures*, Hearings, 97th Cong. 2nd Sess., 1982; see also Kitrinos, pp. 57-59.
8. Shevchenko, p. 262.
9. Ibid., p. 375.
10. Shevchenko writes: "Although some understanding (by the leadership) of the relationship between Congress and the President has developed recently, there is still little grasp of the relationship of American congressmen to the constituencies, the real role of public opinion, and that worst bugaboo, freedom of information, which they see as a threat to security . . . The great gap in Soviet understanding of U.S. policies and practices sometimes means that even experienced message carriers and advisors like Dobrynin do not necessarily convey accurate information." (Shevchenko, p. 375.)
11. Richelson, p. 102.
12. Ibid., p. 121.
13. Howie Kurtz, "Soviet Agents Busy on Hill, Where Information Abounds," *Washington Post*, 28 March 1982.
14. U.S. Congress, Senate, Select Committee on Intelligence, *Meeting the Espionage Challenge: A Review of United States Counterintelligence and Security Programs*, 99th Cong., 2d sess., 1986, p. 136.
15. For more detail on these recommendations see *Meeting the Espionage Challenge*, pp. 139-141.

16. Margaret Gentry, "Ex-Aide Says He Was Double Agent." *Washington Post*, 12 March 1976.

17. Jon Margolis and James Coates, "Senator's Aide—Good Friend or Bad Spy," *Chicago Tribune*, 28 April 1982.

18. Kurtz, "Soviet Agents,".

19. Richelson, p. 196.

20. For additional information on the internal organizational structure of the KGB and the GRU, see Richelson, pp. 21-39.

21. Ibid., p. 51.

22. Ibid., p. 54.

23. For more on Bogdanov's KGB connections, see *Soviet Active Measures*, pp. 70, 73.

24. For further information on KGB organizational structure in Soviet embassies and consulates, see Richelson, pp. 77-80.

25. Ibid., p. 80.

26. U.S. Congress, Senate, *Report of the Senate Arms Control Observer Group Delegation to the Opening of the Arms Control Negotiations with the Soviet Union in Geneva, Switzerland,* 99th Cong., 1st sess., 1985, p. 10.

27. Ibid.

28. Ibid., pp. 13-14.

29. William Drozdiak, "Senators Take Part at Geneva," *Washington Post*, 19 March 1985.

30. For full details on the Churkin testimony see U.S. Congress, House, Committee on Energy and Commerce, *Soviet Nuclear Accident at Chernobyl*, Briefing and Hearing Before the Subcommittee on Energy Conservation and Power, 99th Cong., 2d sess., 1986, pp. 25-49.

31. Darrel P. Hammer, *USSR: The Politics of Oligarchy* (Boulder, Colo., Westview Press, 1986): 102.

32. Stern, p. 138.

33. U.S. Congress, House, Committee on Foreign Affairs, *Soviet Diplomacy and Negotiating Behavior,* by Joseph Whelan of the Senior Specialists Division, Congressional Research Service, Library of Congress (Washington: Government Printing Office, 1979), p. 423. (See footnote 102 on that page.)

34. U.S., Senate, *Report to the United States Senate of the Senate Delegation on Parliamentary Exchange with the Soviet Union,* 96th Cong., 1st sess., 1979, p. 3.

35. U.S., Congress, Senate, Senator Byrd speaking on his trip to the Soviet Union and Western Europe, 96th Cong., 1st sess., 20 July 1979, *Congressional Record*, 1628: 19722.

36. Ibid., p. S19725.

6

Leadership Attitudes

As Chapters 4 and 5 have amply demonstrated, a vast array of information from a variety of sources is available to the Soviet leadership concerning Congress' role in U.S. foreign policy. However, analyzing leadership attitudes in light of the availablility of this information is a much more difficult proposition.

Unlike americanists, the Soviet leadership does not publish extensively its views on Congress and foreign policy. At best, passing references can be found in prepared statements by Soviet leaders during visits of Congressional delegations. These statements point to the importance of parliamentary exchanges as one of the means of strengthening U.S.-Soviet relations and the general atmosphere in which relations are conducted.

Shevchenko provides some clues to leadership attitudes from his own personal experiences with the Soviet leadership. For example, Brezhnev is believed to have regarded one of the important aspects of the SALT process to be that it could put pressure on Congress to reduce military spending. Brezhnev, however, "could not comprehend how the United States Congress had the power to block implementation of presidential promises to the USSR regarding the coveted most-favored nation status."[1] Shevchenko also recounts that Andropov supposedly was "opposed (to) the agreement on ending the (Vietnam) war because he believed that pressure from . . . the Congress would eventually force the President to withdraw."[2]

Given the relative lack of information the most valuable source available on leadership attitudes comes from the reports of Congressional delegations to the Soviet Union that have met with members of the Politburo and the Central Committee Secretariat. Reports from these delegations, together with interview research conducted with some of the participants, is the basis for the following appraisals of Soviet leadership attitudes.

Since 1974, when parliamentary exchanges and Congressional travel to the Soviet Union became greatly intensified, Members of Congress have held meetings on foreign policy issues with the following current or former members of the Politburo and Central Committee Secretariat in alphabetical order: Yuri Andropov, Leonid Brezhnev, Anatolii Dobrynin, Mikhail Gorbachev, Andrei Gromyko, Aleksandr Iakovlev, Aleksei Kosygin, Vasilii Kuznetsov, Egor Ligachev, Viktor Nikonov, Boris Ponomarev, Grigorii Romanov,

Eduard Schevernadze, Vladimir Shcherbitskii, and Lev Zaikov. The attitudes of these Soviet leadership figures will be analyzed below, with the exception of Dobrynin, whose attitudes toward the Congress have been described earlier in this chapter.

Only one Congressional delegation, the Pell delegation in August, 1983, met with Andropov when he was General Secretary and none met with him during his previous years on the Politburo. A delegation participant interviewed said he saw no evidence of any thorough understanding on Andropov's part of Congress' powers in foreign policy but neither was there a sense of a refusal or inability to differentiate between the powers of the Congress and that of the President in foreign policy. The participant was convinced however, that the delegation's wholly Democratic membership was well-known to Andropov. What was also clear to this participant was that Andropov put forth a message of reasonableness, and expressed a desire through contacts with Members of Congress, to break the logjam on U.S.-Soviet relations that existed at the time.

In fact, judging from Andropov's opening statement to the delegation, there appeared to be some indications of at least surface understanding of Congress' role in foreign policy. Andropov remarked that:

> The fact that representatives of one political party—in this case the Democratic party—are present here is in principle of no significance to us. Do not take me wrong. We see you as responsible public figures of the United States of America having an influence on the formation of policy. Everything I say to you I would say to Republican Senators.[3]

The above passage indicates an acknowledgement of the importance of Congress' role in foreign policy, as well as an apparent understanding that the mere fact that the Pell delegation was composed entirely of Democrats did not mean they would automatically oppose the foreign policy of the Reagan Administration. Thus, a surface understanding of both the separation of powers and the two-party system and its effects on Congress' role in foreign policy can be detected. Moreover, as discussed in chapter 3, the announcement of a Soviet moratorium on anti-satellite weapons testing at the time of the Pell visit, as well as Andropov's endorsement of a bilateral nuclear weapons freeze during the meeting with Pell's delegation, could well have been calibrated to the fact that many members of the delegation generally supported these proposals.

The remainder of Andropov's meeting with the Pell delegation, however, reflected a more rigid litany of Soviet foreign policy positions. Andropov argued that: (1) the United States was seeking military superiority; (2) by contrast, the Soviet Union sought good relations on the basis of mutual benefit; (3) the NATO deployment of new nuclear missiles would have profound consequences for the United States as well as Europe; (4) the Soviet Union's arms control proposals have been rebuffed and ignored by the United States and that the Soviet Union will not make unilateral concessions or arms control agreements that force the Soviets to restructure their forces while not requiring the United States to do the same; (5) U.S. policy attempts to explain away every international problem, particularly in the Third World, as the fault of Soviet intrigue and plots when what is needed is a U.S. commitment to political settlements and resolving conflicts by peaceful means; (6) the U.S. and the Soviet Union have different definitions of human rights and that Soviet dissidents had been properly imprisoned; and (7) since 1945 over 250,000 Jews had been permitted to emigrate and nearly all applications had been processed favorably, with the remaining few not allowed to leave because of their access to state secrets or because they were serving prison sentences.[4]

During his long tenure as General Secretary, Brezhnev met with many Congressional delegations. Two in particular provide some insight. The Ribicoff delegation in November, 1978 witnessed a presentation by Brezhnev that not surprisingly stressed SALT ratification. However, Brezhnev's understanding of the Senate's role in that process was questionable. The few remaining issues in the completion of the SALT II negotiations, and American concerns about them which were raised by the delegation, were dismissed as unsubstantiated excuses to criticize the Soviet Union.

During the Byrd visit in July, 1979, after SALT II negotiations had been concluded, and shortly before Senate consideration was to begin, Brezhnev took an uncompromising line on senatorial prerogatives that did not indicate a thorough understanding of the Senate's treaty powers. After endorsing SALT II as a major step in reducing the arms race, Brezhnev proceeded to tell Byrd that there seemed to be some in the United States who wanted, so to speak, to "correct" the treaty in their own favor during the process of ratification. Brezhnev pointed out that for the Soviets, only the treaty signed in Vienna would be accepted by the Soviets. Brezhnev regarded any Senate amendments as evidence that the U.S. was not a serious negotiating partner and that such amendments would put an end to the treaty.

Byrd was told further that "those who harbor hopes of introducing amendments or reservations should carefully reflect on the grave responsibility that will be theirs if the treaty does not enter into force."[5] While Brezhnev ended his remarks to Byrd by stressing that he believed that the U.S. Congress wanted good relations with the Soviet Union, its willingness would be measured by the Senate's position on SALT II.

An apparent lack of understanding of Congress' role in foreign policy was even more striking for Kosygin and Romanov. The Ribicoff delegation had extensive contact with Kosygin during its 1978 visit. When told of the possibility of Senate rejection of SALT II, Kosygin angrily responded that if the Senate rejected the treaty, then it will have joined the side of war. Kosygin chided the Senators that "surely your electorates did not elect you to vote for war, and I cannot believe they would keep in office anyone who did."[6]

When Kosygin received questions about treaty verification, land-based missile vulnerability, which would increase under the treaty and was one of the principal criticisms against the treaty, and the status of the Backfire bomber, a Soviet medium-range bomber with some strategic capability that was not included in SALT II limitations, Kosygin was clearly provoked. He replied that he did not really expect to see members of the U.S. Senate "come here to engage in complex technical discussions related to SALT. I thought that you would address yourselves to the more fundamental problems of peace."[7]

Romanov's encounter with the Ribicoff delegation, the only Congressional delegation with whom he had extended contact, also showed little understanding of the Congress' foreign policy powers. While endorsing peaceful coexistence, the rejection of military superiority, and the need for the SALT II agreement, Romanov was one of many Soviet officials who met with the Ribicoff delegation who stated that they were aware of a congressional faction opposed to SALT II. Romanov was seen by Senators as one who would dismiss concerns of delegation members over the issues as "either irrelevant–therefore casting suspicions on the motivations of those who regarded them as issues–or as adequately safeguarded in the treaty."[8]

In an encounter with Senator John Glenn (D-Ohio), a member of the delegation, Glenn told Romanov that some Democrats in the Senate might vote against a new SALT II Treaty even if their own party chief President Carter favored it. Romanov asked in astonishment, "But can't you discipline them?" The Ribicoff delegation was particularly disturbed by Romanov's ignorance "with respect to the role of the Senate in the treaty process."[9]

The official report of the delegation appears also to have been influenced by Romanov (as well as other Soviet leaders) perception of Congress' role in foreign policy:

> Throughout the delegation's discussions with Soviet officials, it was apparent that the Soviet side found it difficult if not impossible to grasp the reality that a SALT treaty negotiated in good faith and supported by the United States government could be defeated by the Senate. The Soviet side repeatedly questioned the grounds upon which individual Senators can challenge the judgment of the Executive Branch in various substantive issues addressed by the treaty, and tended to ascribe to those in the United States who opposed SALT, or were skeptical of its benefits to the United States, motives ranging from unfounded distrust of the Soviet Union to a calculated desire to resume the Cold War. Although the Soviet side recognized the constitutional authority of the Senate to refuse its consent to the ratification of any treaty, Soviet officials appeared to be baffled over how the Senate can possibly have any reservations over an agreement which in their view was self-evidently beneficial to the interests of both the United States and the Soviet Union.[10]

Like Brezhnev, Gromyko also visited with numerous Congressional delegations. For example, the negative effects of the Ribicoff visit were apparently of such concern to the Soviet leadership that during Byrd's visit several months later, Gromyko specifically pointed out that the Soviet leadership understood the role of the Senate, that it was not trying to pressure or threaten the Senate, that the Soviet leadership was speaking its mind on the need for quick and favorable action by the Senate with no amendments attached and that such opinions were not a form of intimidation.

Gromyko's impressively conciliatory stance with Byrd was a deft piece of diplomacy not practiced by other Politburo members, who apparently had deeply alienated the Ribicoff delegation, a delegation which contained a number of swing votes on SALT II advice and consent. The meeting between Gromyko and Byrd also tended to confirm assessments of Gromyko as a "dogged and crafty practitioner, constantly seeking advantage for the Soviet Union, but also willing to accommodate Western interests in whatever measure the tactical situation dictates."[11] At a crucial juncture in U.S.-Soviet relations, Gromyko was demonstrating his profound interest in preserving detente with the United States, a policy with which he was clearly recognized as chief Soviet protagonist.

As for Gromyko's understanding of Congress' role in foreign policy, the evidence is less impressive. In his conciliatory meeting with Byrd, Gromyko pointed out that the Soviet leadership thought the treaty was completed and did not want protracted Senate debate that would delay the treaty implementation. Byrd responded that from the Senate's perspective "the negotiation process had taken 7 years. The second half of our constitutional process—of equal importance—would probably take 4 to 6 months."[12] Thus, while Gromyko was willing to show deference and respect, there appears to be either a lack of understanding or unwillingness to accept Congress as an equal partner to the President in foreign policy, with considerable powers in its making and conduct.

Other encounters between Gromyko and Members of Congress are less revealing of his understanding of its role in foreign policy but do validate Shevchenko's characterization of Gromyko as being at that time "unreservedly devoted to the Soviet political system, a fundamental element of the system— one of its most powerful driving forces—at once its product, and one of its supreme masters."[13] Like other Soviet leadership figures, Gromyko subjects Members of Congress to a long defense of existing Soviet foreign policy positions.

For example, during the O'Neill visit, Gromyko delivered a wide-ranging broadside against U.S. arms control and foreign policy positions. He stated that: (1) the U.S. has refused to negotiate on the issue of space weapons, including restraints on the Strategic Defense Initiative, which Gromyko saw as a clearly offensive-oriented concept that would force the Soviet Union to increase rather than decrease its strategic weapons; (2) the U.S. has refused to enter negotiations for a comprehensive test ban, a comprehensive freeze on nuclear weapons, or an agreement on no first use of nuclear weapons; and (3) the Soviet Union favors increased cultural, economic, and trade relations but the U.S. has imposed artificial restraints in these areas and has imposed "mountains of sanctions" against the Soviet Union which made improvements in trade and cultural areas impossible. Nonetheless, during Gromyko's visit with the Wright delegation, the former Foreign Minister did appear to understand Congress' independent foreign policy powers. He stated that the Congress has the power to change the Reagan Administration's arms control policy and that if it did so the Soviet Union would be ready to achieve arms control agreements.

Two other Brezhnev Politburo holdovers, Kuznetsov, a candidate member, and Shcherbitskii, have also had contact with the Congress. Kuznetsov, served as First Deputy Minister of Foreign Affairs from 1955-1977, and as First Deputy Chairman of the Presidium of the Supreme Soviet (the ceremonial Vice-President of the country) from 1977-1986. Kuznetsov's exposure to the American political system and foreign policy was thus quite extensive. For example, Kuznetsov played a central role in U.S.-Soviet negotiations concerning the Cuban missile crisis and helped arrange President Nixon's visit to the Soviet Union, a visit which culminated in the signing of the SALT I and ABM agreements. Nonetheless, relatively little is known of his views of Congress' role in foreign policy.

One of Kuznetsov's principal duties as First Deputy Chairman was to relieve the chairman (which included at one time or another, Brezhnev, Andropov, Chernenko, and Gromyko under his tenure) of many onerous ceremonial and diplomatic tasks expected of the Presidium's chairman. In August, 1979, a House delegation led by Rep. Lester Wolff (D-N.Y.), was invited to the Soviet Union by the Supreme Soviet and was expecting to see Brezhnev. While Soviet officials cited scheduling conflicts as the reason the delegation did not do so, one participant interviewed said he believed that the strong emphasis on human rights issues which the delegation stressed to Soviet officials led to the cancellation of the Brezhnev meeting. The delegation was given a meeting with Kuznetsov instead.

Kuznetsov's meeting with the Wolff delegation shed little light on his views of Congress' role in foreign policy. Aside from a strong endorsement of SALT, the need for U.S.-Soviet cooperation in a variety of areas, and the usual inventory of standard Soviet foreign policy positions at the time, no specific information about the Congress' foreign policy powers was evident during the meeting. A delegation participant indicated that Members seemed to think Kuznetsov had a working understanding of Congress' role in foreign policy.

As well, little is known about two current Politburo members, Ligachev and Zaikov. Zaikov met with the Fascell delegation when the former was the head of the Leningrad party organization and Zaikov did not deal with foreign policy issues in their discussion. Ligachev, while giving the Wright delegation an extensive briefing on economic reform in the Soviet Union did not dwell on foreign policy issues either beyond reporting Gorbachev's positive feeling about his meeting with the delegation and expressing his (Ligachev's) support for intensified contacts between the Supreme Soviet and the Congress.

More information is available on Shcherbitskii. The 1985 Supreme Soviet delegation which Shcherbitskii headed was the first of its kind to visit the United States in seven years. Moreover, according to House staffers who participated, the visit was in part a reciprocal visit for the Foley delegation visit to the Soviet Union in 1983 but also designed to bring about a future visit at the highest House level by Speaker O'Neill. Shcherbitskii, as a full Politburo member, represented an elevation in the status of Supreme Soviet delegations, which previously had been headed by Ponomarev, only a candidate member of the Politburo.

Shcherbitskii's selection was seen by those interviewed for this study as a compromise choice among Politburo members. He was of full Politburo rank, thereby demonstrating the importance with which Congress and its role in U.S. foreign policy and U.S.-Soviet relations was viewed by the Soviet leadership. At the same time, since Shcherbitskii was not one of the Politburo members residing in Moscow, he was not needed to run the day-to-day affairs of the political system. This factor was critical because the illness of General Secretary Konstantin Chernenko at the time had become acute. This was borne out by the fact that Chernenko died near the end of the delegation's visit, forcing the Shcherbitskii delegation to return home.

Shcherbitskii's public statements during the parliamentary exchange, which covered three lengthy plenary sessions, reflect a surface understanding of Congress' role in foreign policy. Shcherbitskii stressed the importance of U.S.-Soviet parliamentary exchanges for the formation of the two countries' foreign policies. He also noted the presence of Members of Congress who, from his perspective, were in favor of reducing tensions, curbing the arms race, and in general improving relations.

Additionally, Shcherbitskii cited the fact that legislation calling for a U.S.-Soviet nuclear weapons freeze, as well as negotiations for a comprehensive test ban, both of which were opposed by the Reagan Administration, were under consideration in the foreign policy committees of the Congress. He also criticized Congress' position on U.S.-Soviet trade. The Congress, he said has always regarded trade, and particularly so during the last several years, as an element of political pressure to be applied against the Soviet Union and has doled it out in those spheres which it has considered profitable.

Shcherbitskii's public statements concerning Congress' actions on foreign policy issues are impressive when compared to attitudes evident in meetings held with Members of Congress by other Politburo members of the Brezhnev era. He appeared to demonstrate an accurate understanding of liberal arms control initiatives pending in the Congress at the time of his visit, as well as a general understanding of the Committee system and a grudging acceptance of Congress' position regarding the political terms of U.S.-Soviet trade.

Individual assessments of Shcherbitskii's understanding of Congress and foreign policy derived from interview research are somewhat more critical. House staffers participating in the Shcherbitskii visit regarded him as not generally cognizant of Congress' foreign policy powers but possessing instead a more vague understanding of the importance of Congressional leaders. In the opinion of these participants, Shcherbitskii demonstrated little understanding of the separation of powers.

A long meeting with Speaker O'Neill during the visit, at which O'Neill was sharply critical of Soviet foreign policy, particularly with respect to Afghanistan, left an impression upon at least one House staffer that Shcherbitskii had very little conception of Congress' role in foreign policy. To this participant, Shcherbitskii represented a Soviet-style "machine politician," sent because of his Politburo rank to demonstrate to the Congress Soviet recognition of the Congress' importance, but lacking any intellectual capacity to deal with complex foreign policy process questions like the separation of powers.

While current Foreign Minister Shevardnadze has met with relatively few congressional delegations, he seems to have at least a basic understanding of Congress' role in U.S. foreign policy. For example, Shevardnadze told the Wright delegation that Congress carefully takes public opinion into account in its foreign policy actions and that the calibration helped to explain Congress' actions in taking arms control positions different from that of the President. He joked with Speaker Wright that the Republicans at the meeting were not nearly as difficult as the Speaker had said at the outset and suggested that since the delegation was meeting with him in the Office of the Collegium of the Foreign Ministry, the Soviet Union should have a representative in the Congress. Shevardnadze aslo expressed his willingness to examine human rights cases raised by the delegation.

Iakovlev, while the author of many studies on U.S. foreign policy, has given relatively little attention to the Congress. What attention has been given has been a largely polemic-filled analysis that rivals Cold War-era writings on the Congress. Iakovlev appears to be convinced that the "radical right-wing" of the Republican Party has seized control of U.S. foreign policy. With no empirical substantiation, he gives credit to Senator Jesse Helms (R-N.C.) for having organized more than 30 Republican Senators to support his views on a regular basis. Iakovlev also cites the formation of the conservative Republican Study Committee in the House as becoming "one of the most important links in the overall mechanism of right-wing activities among the American ruling elite, connected by thousands of driving belts with other conservative organizations."[14]

The work of Helms' Congressional Club, the Republican Study Committee in the House, and conservative political organizations that lobby the Congress and finance election campaigns are seen by Iakovlev as engaging in "crude, reactionary agitation during election campaigns against liberals."[15] Their success in defeating Democratic Senators in 1980, and their role in bringing Republican control of the Senate, are cited as proof of their commanding influence.

Right-wing representatives in Congress are described by Iakovlev as demanding direct confrontation with the Soviet Union, by renouncing past arms control agreements, seeking increases in defense programs, and an unregulated arms race. Their views on the Soviet Union are described as "permeated with reactionary thinking, chauvinism, anticommunism, and anti-Sovietism, urging Reagan into a new struggle for power and implementation of the program of the Radical Right."[16]

Moreover, as this passage demonstrates, Iakovlev offers the unqualified judgment that the American right-wing has become all powerful with respect to the direction of U.S. foreign policy:

> The very idea of 'adjusting' Reaganism from the 'right' could only emerge in certain conditions. Indeed, the right wing has gained many key positions in American society and the state. If there were any liberals left, they have been forced out. Some of them even joined the Right. Chauvinist, hegemonistic, and aggressive sentiments prevail. The diktat of the monopolies and the military-industrial complex has increased.[17]

Despite Ponomarev's central role in the establishment of quasi-formal ties between the Supreme Soviet and the Congress, and his leadership of Supreme Soviet delegations in 1974 and 1978, little information is available on Ponomarev's views of Congress' role in foreign policy.

Ponomarev has often been described as a genuine believer in Marxist-Leninist ideology, a patron of Mikhail Suslov whose doctrinaire rigidity put him in direct contrast to the pragmatic approach towards U.S.-Soviet relations practiced by Gromyko and the MFA diplomats. Nonetheless, his long tenure as head of the International Department made him a powerful figure in foreign policy outside the realm of U.S.-Soviet relations. The role of the International Department in influencing public opinion in the West, together with his protocol position as chairman of the Council of Nationalities' Foreign Affairs Commission made him a logical choice to head up the 1974 and 1978 delegations, as well as lead the discussions on the Soviet side for reciprocal parliamentary exchanges held in the Soviet Union in 1979 and 1983 and headed on the American side by Reps. Brademas and Foley.

Ponomarev's exchanges with these delegations reveal a fairly unimpressive understanding of the foreign policy prerogatives of the Congress. For example, the 1979 meetings with the Brademas delegation produced the usual endorsement of SALT II as well as a judgment that both the U.S. and the Soviet Union had basically achieved a parity of nuclear forces that would not be radically changed. At the same time, Ponomarev did not diverge from the rigid line articulated by Brezhnev that "the adoption by the Senate of amendments or revisions . . . would amount to the deliberate scuttling of the treaty with all the consequences that this entails."[18] Ponomarev also spoke of the shared concern among Soviet leaders and Members of Congress, that aside from SALT II, little progress was being made in other disarmament negotiations. However, Ponomarev then went to list a standard set of Soviet disarmament proposals as a possible solution. He concluded his remarks by endorsing stepped-up parliamentary exchanges.

Ponomarev's public remarks during the 1974 Supreme Soviet visit to the United States indicate a somewhat confused understanding of the separation of powers. For example, Ponomarev noted that "both the leaders of the governing Republican Party and many leading figures of the Democratic Party in opposition are for the improvement of Soviet-American relations."[19] As one scholar has noted, this formulation "equates the American political system with a parliamentary democracy, regards the control of executive power as dominant and Congress as politically subservient to the President, and overstates the role of party affiliation in foreign policymaking."[20] This reasoning may well explain subsequent Soviet complaints that President Carter had "demonstrated bad faith with regard to SALT II, for if a Democratic president could impose his will on a Democratic Congress, it would be difficult to explain the failure of the Senate to ratify SALT II in any other way."[21]

Nonetheless, one House staffer interviewed regarded Ponomarev, despite a fuzzy understanding of the separation of powers, as understanding that Congress had independent foreign policy powers that had to be respected and, if possible, influenced. This individual also believed that Ponomarev regarded Members not merely as protocol figures (like some of their Supreme Soviet counterparts) but rather powerful policymakers. Ponomarev was seen as recognizing the need to go beyond rhetorical set pieces in exchanges with Members of Congress and engage in substantive exchanges on critical issues in U.S.-Soviet relations.

Nikonov's major exposure to the Congress came during a visit to the United States at the invitation of Rep. Emilio (Kika) de la Garza (D-Tex.), chairman of the House Agriculture Committee. Chairman de la Garza had visited the Soviet Union in 1985 and the House Agriculture Committee had maintained ongoing informal contact with Soviet agricultural officials and the Soviet Embassy for a number of years. After Nikonov was named to the Politburo in June, 1987 and was given overall responsibility for Soviet agriculture, the Soviet Embassy requested that Chairman de la Garza and the House Agriculture Committee staff handle the official program of the visit. De la Garza agreed and Nikonov visited a number of American cities including Washington, Chicago, St. Louis, and Orlando.

Nikonov was on a trade mission and the main focus of his public remarks dealt with ways to promote trade, particularly in agricultural areas, joint ventures between Soviet economic enterprises and private U.S. firms, and the future terms of U.S. grain sales to the Soviet Union. As such, Nikonov did not speak directly of Congress' role in foreign policy. Nonetheless, according to one American participant in the Nikonov visit, the Soviet Politburo member demonstrated what could be called at least a surface understanding of the Congress' foreign policy powers.

For example, the Soviet Embassy and apparently Nikonov himself personally requested that the House Agriculture Committee, not the Departments of State and Agriculture, coordinate the visit, a Soviet recognition of the Committee's considerable power in the making and conduct of U.S. agricultural policy. Nikonov also repeatedly queried de la Garza and the Agriculture Committee staff on how a Member of Congress is appointed to Congressional committees, how one becomes chairman, how the staff is hired, and other detailed questions about the organization of Congress and its legislative business. Nikonov also dispatched different teams of Soviet staff on his delegation to question Members of Congress and staff about its structure and organization and then compared the answers he received.

One American participant saw Nikonov's efforts as a combination of intelligence gathering on the Congress and utilizing the Congress as an alternate channel of communication on critical issues like U.S.-Soviet trade. Such an observation is consistent with the Soviet objectives in parliamentary exchanges outlined in chapter 5. In short, Nikonov appears to have recognized that the Congress is an independent and powerful institution that on specific issues like the economic benefits of grain sales to the Soviet Union, can take positions different from that of the executive branch.

Of all past and present Politburo members who have met with Members of Congress since 1974, Gorbachev has easily demonstrated the most impressive understanding of Congress' foreign policy powers. The amount of time devoted to meetings with Members, the number of groups with whom Gorbachev has been willing to meet, and his apparent understanding of Congress' role in foreign policy have been verified by a number of Members across the ideological spectrum. One House Member interviewed said that unlike Brezhnev and Kosygin, Gorbachev clearly understood the importance of the Congress. Whereas Brezhnev and Kosygin, in the view of this Member, regarded meetings with the Congress as ceremonial, and tended to equate Congress' power in the American political system with the power of the Supreme Soviet in the Soviet system, Gorbachev viewed Members as powerful foreign policymakers.

Another House Member interviewed tended to confirm this. He believed Gorbachev clearly understood Congress' place in the process of foreign policymaking and even grudgingly accepted the proposition that attempts to divide the Congress from the President on foreign policy issues for purposes of advancing Soviet foreign policy objectives would be unsuccessful. At the same time, another observer of Gorbachev's dealings with the Congress pointed out that his willingness to devote much more attention to the Congress was part of a larger public strategy to meet with various American institutions and groups that had taken foreign policy positions opposed to the Reagan Administration. This observer also argued that the Democratic takeover of the Senate in 1986 would further intensify attention devoted to Congress.

The trip report of the delegation that visited the Soviet Union in August-September 1985, headed by Senators Byrd and Strom Thurmond (R-S.C.), then chairman and ranking minority member of the Senate Judiciary Committee, also mentions apparent grasp of Congress' foreign policy powers. Gorbachev's 3½ hour meeting with the delegation revealed "a significant departure from the style of previous Soviet leaders, who were more formal and less versatile in their dealings across the table with American officials."[22] Gorbachev was described as displaying "substantial knowledge of American politics and society," although the delegation was unclear as to whether Gorbachev had developed a genuine understanding of the American political system.

Furthermore, Gorbachev's style in meetings with Members also projects an apparent understanding of legislative prerogatives as well as Congress' ongoing oversight activities in foreign policy. For example, introductory remarks made by Speaker O'Neill during his meeting with Gorbachev included the fact that given the reality of a Republican President and Republican-controlled Senate, O'Neill was the leader of the political opposition in the U.S.. Gorbachev remarked sardonically that from Moscow's perspective, it was not always easy to distinguish the policy perspectives of the opposition from those of the Administration.

Gorbachev continued this type of informed banter and discussion with the Wright delegation. During their 1987 visit, Gorbachev suggested that every time he met with Secretary of State Shultz, the Secretary suggested that Soviet concessions on the INF negotiations were necessary because otherwise Congress would not approve any subsequent INF agreement. Gorbachev told Wright he was not aware that Members of Congress were demanding bloodthirsty concessions. At the same time, Gorbachev did chide the Congress for its criticism of the Soviet Union for purposes of domestic consumption and expressed fears that the 1988 election would frustrate further progress in U.S.-Soviet relations. Gorbachev was careful to acknowledge, however, that Congress did differ from the President on a variety of issues including arms control. He acknowledged Congress' role on issues such as the status of the SALT II Treaty, where attempts had been made to force continued compliance by the Reagan Administration. He was frustrated, however, by what he termed "threat-mongering" by the Administration to get weapons programs through the Congress. Gorbachev expressed his willingness to examine the list of human rights cases submitted by the delegation and expressed the hope that through continued meetings with the congressional leadership, both the Congress and the Soviet leadership could get to know each other better and anticipate each other's reactions to actions either had taken.

Gorbachev also had a wide-ranging discussion with the bipartisan House and Senate leadership during the Washington summit. He prodded Members of Congress to seek improvements in bilateral relations and to tone down criticism of the Soviet Union on the issue of human rights, calling for meetings of U.S. and Soviet leaders to resolve differences on this subject. On regional issues, Gorbachev was noncommittal concerning Soviet policy on Afghanistan, the Persian Gulf, and Central America but did express his interest in resolving these disputes in the near future. Gorbachev also appeared to downplay the failure of Congressional leaders to gain consensus within Congress to enable Gorbachev to address a joint session of Congress. Such a move had been opposed by conservative Republicans in the House, but Gorbachev dismissed the controversy over the proposal as "perhaps just a sign of our difficult times."[23]

Members of Congress attending the meeting described the discussions as "remarkable and stunningly frank." The impending debate over Senate ratification of the INF Treaty was discussed, with Members assuring Gorbachev that treaty ratification would be forthcoming. However, Gorbachev rejected what he called "ultimatums from Congress" about emigration and internal political change. At the same time, House Minority Leader Michel emerged from the meeting convinced that Gorbachev was "very attuned to our system, (and) how it operates."[24]

Additionally, unlike Brezhnev, Gorbachev does not rely on assistance from staff during meetings with Members. He refers to Congressional documents, including reports on defense legislation as well as the comprehensive studies of the Joint Economic Committee on the Soviet economy. While this type of literacy on the Congress is impressive, it is also somewhat selective. For example, Gorbachev was not aware of a well-known study done by the Congress' Commission on Security and Cooperation in Europe that refuted Soviet charges about human rights violations in the United States.

Nonetheless, the fall of 1987 brought perhaps the most direct evidence of Gorbachev's understanding of Congress' role in U.S.-Soviet relations. In a speech in Murmansk on October 1, Gorbachev made a reference to hearings conducted by the Joint Economic Committee on the implications of Gorbachev's economic reform program for U.S. national security interests. After initially praising testimony before the Committee that internal economic reform would reduce the risk of U.S.-Soviet nuclear confrontation, Gorbachev then attacked other testimony that argued that successful Soviet economic reforms would strengthen the Soviet Union's political and military position, threaten U.S. national security and the political solidarity of the NATO alliance, expand Soviet economic and military influence in the Third World, and lead to expanded Soviet influence in international economic institutions.

Gorbachev attacked proponents of this view of the possibilities of Soviet economic reform. He also claimed in the Murmansk speech that the testimony in question before the Joint Economic Committee proposed countervailing U.S. policy options to frustrate reforms including (1) bringing about Soviet economic collapse by pressing ahead with expensive weapons programs like SDI, which would force the Soviet Union to alter its economic reform programs by greater military spending for its own space defense systems; (2) increasing military assistance to anticommunist resistance forces and; (3) preventing expansion of East-West trade by tightening export controls on high-technology products and vetoing Soviet membership in international economic organizations. Gorbachev regarded such policy advice as reflecting the views of the "military-industrial complex" in the United States, and the product of "militarist and anti-Soviet forces (who) are evidently worried that the interest in the people and political circles of the West at what is now happening in the Soviet Union . . . wipes away the artificially-created image of an enemy, the image of which they have now been unscrupulously exploiting for decades."[25]

The reference to the Joint Economic Committee hearings prompted a response from Sen. William Proxmire (D-Wisc.), chairman of the Subcommittee on National Security Economics, the panel which held the hearings to which Gorbachev referrred. Proxmire, in an October 3 letter to Gorbachev, argued that the testimony in question, from a Department of Defense witness, did not in fact argue for pursuing a policy of forcing Soviet economic collapse. Nor did the testimony in question call for increased SDI spending to force a similar Soviet response. While Proxmire acknowledged that the DOD witness did state that a successful Soviet economic reform program would produce a more dynamic and powerful adversary, Proxmire argued that official Soviet secrecy about its own defense programs made it more difficult for U.S. policymakers to decide what should be spent for SDI and other military programs as well.

Proxmire also tried to correct other statements made by Gorbachev about the Subcommittee testimony. The DOD testimony did recommend against Soviet membership in the General Agreement on Tariffs and Trade (GATT) and the International Monetary Fund (IMF), not because of an interest in Soviet economic isolation but because the Soviet command economy was inconsistent with the free trade principles of the GATT and because of disruptive Soviet behavior in other international organizations, exemplified by such actions as its support for expelling Israel from the United Nations. Proxmire also defended DOD's policy of tight control on high-technology exports to Warsaw Pact countries as necessary given thefts and other illegal acquisitions of Western technology by those countries. Proxmire argued that the Reagan Administration had loosened export controls on nonstrategic trade with the Soviet Union, and that the DOD witness did not call for economic warfare against the Soviet Union. Proxmire concluded his letter by asking Gorbachev to provide better insights and an ongoing dialogue on Soviet policies and intentions.[26]

Gorbachev's response to the Proxmire letter came in the form of a visit to Proxmire's office during the Washington summit by Abel Aganbegian, a top-ranking official of the USSR Academy of Sciences and generally regarded as one of Gorbachev's principal advisers on internal economic reform. During a one and one half hour meeting with Aganbegian, Proxmire discussed the problem of obtaining reliable data on Soviet defense spending and its effects on the Soviet economy, the effects of U.S. export controls on U.S.-Soviet trade, and the status of internal political opposition to Gorbachev's economic reforms. Aganbegian expressed the view that their dialogue should continue, and the Joint Economic Committee staff is currently pursuing the possibility of inviting Aganbegian to testify before the Subcommittee's 1988 hearings on the Soviet economy.

The Gorbachev-Proxmire exchange is an indication of how carefully the Soviet leadership is now following the proceedings of Congress in its foreign policy oversight activities. Never before has a Soviet General Secretary directly referred to Congressional testimony in his public statements and such attention validates what is believed to be Gorbachev's growing interest and knowledge of Congress' foreign policy responsibilities and activities.

Finally, despite general agreement that Gorbachev's understanding of Congress' role in foreign policy is unprecedented for a member of the Soviet leadership, this did not mean that the style of his predecessors in citing the standard Soviet foreign policy positions while severely criticizing U.S.

foreign policy positions had been jettisoned altogether. The O'Neill, Fascell, and Byrd-Thurmond delegations all were given lengthy lectures about: (1) the U.S. unwillingness to improve relations on a mutually-beneficial basis; (2) the deliberate deterioration by the U.S. of economic, cultural, and scientific relations; (3) the offensive nature of SDI and the American unwillingness to negotiate SDI restraints at the Geneva arms control negotiations; (4) the American refusal to respond to Soviet proposals for a nuclear freeze and a comprehensive test ban treaty; and (5) the belief in some circles in the U.S. that the U.S. could militarily and economically exhaust the Soviet Union into political submission or fundamental political change and the futility of attempting such a strategy.

Overall Assessment of Leadership Attitudes

Despite the somewhat scarce and largely impressionistic information on Soviet leadership attitudes toward the Congress, a number of judgments are possible. First, there is tendency by all Soviet leaders to employ a style of presentation that refuses to accept shared responsibility for downturns and deterioration in U.S.-Soviet relations. This style, which is unmistakable to anyone who has witnessed or participated in meetings between Members and the Soviet leadership, cannot merely be dismissed as the instinct of all politicians to avoiding taking blame for bad news. It has been colorfully described by former Senator Henry Bellmon (R-Okla.) as a tendency on the part of Soviet leadership figures to believe that "everything they do in the world is for peace, stability, purity and that we shouldn't even suspect their motives or challenge them."[27]

The refusal to accept even shared responsibility for downturns and deterioration in U.S.-Soviet relations, and to often blame Congress for such periodic declines, indicates the effects of an official ideology professing regime infallibility. This manifestation is particularly apparent in the views of Brezhnev, Kosygin, Romanov, and Iakovlev, and to a lesser extent Ponomarev in their meetings with Members of Congress.

On the other hand, the comprehension gap that existed between amer-ikanistika on Congress' role in foreign policy, and Soviet leadership attitudes concerning that role appears to have narrowed considerably. Understanding is clearly much greater now than in the late 1970s, on such questions as the separation of powers, and the two-party system. Also notable is an awareness of the committee system, legislative efforts by Members either consistent or inconsistent with Soviet foreign policy positions, and a seeming awareness of Congressional publications and oversight efforts.

At least at the level of General Secretary, this type of sophistication seems to have evolved slowly with Brezhnev knowing little of Congress' operations or prerogatives, to Andropov who seemed to have some surface understanding, to Gorbachev who appears to have clear understanding. Other attitudes, such as those of Gromyko and Shcherbitskii, appear more calculated to the achievement of system goals and objectives that intersect with the interest of Members of Congress at a particular time and place. Thus, Gromyko's interest in gaining SALT II ratification by the Senate and Shcherbitskii's mission to elevate and strengthen parliamentary exchanges as alternate means of communication to American policymakers at a time relations with the executive branch were poor led them both to develop some appreciation of Congress' role in foreign policy. Finally, the importance of the Congress in the making and conduct of foreign policy appears to be no longer in question in the minds of the Soviet leadership. Both the House and Senate leadership, Democratic and Republican, have met with Gorbachev in lengthy sessions that bear no resemblance to the often ceremonial visits given by Brezhnev. The chairman and ranking member of the House Foreign Affairs Committee have also been given a lengthy session by Gorbachev. A wide range of Politburo members met with the Wright delegation. At all of these meetings, a wide range of issues covering numerous aspects of U.S.-Soviet relations was discussed. The ritualistic character of meetings that was evident under Brezhnev was kept to a minimum.

Moreover, Soviet leaders appear to know who the influential Members of Congress are, and that such Members must be reckoned with if U.S.-Soviet relations are to be advanced. Interview research presented in this chapter offers convincing evidence that the Soviet leadership, recognizes Congress' extensive power, independent of the executive branch, to either improve, or set back U.S.-Soviet relations. It therefore behooves the Soviet leadership to seek to bring about the former rather than the latter. Perhaps the amerikanistika outlined in chapters 2 and 3, as well as the multiple sources of information on Congress' role in foreign policy outlined in Chapters 4 and 5, have begun to influence Soviet foreign policymakers at the pinnacle of the Soviet political system.

Notes

1. Shevchenko, p. 386.
2. Ibid., p. 288.
3. U.S. Congress, Senate, *Dangerous Stalemate: Superpower Relations in Autumn 1983*, Report of a delegation of eight Senators to the Soviet Union to the United States Senate, 98th Cong., 1st sess., 1983, p. 25.
4. For further comments and analysis on Andropov and the Pell delegation's responses, see *Dangerous Stalemate*, pp. 5-23, 29-33.
5. Byrd, p. S19723.
6. *Senate Delegation on Parliamentary Exchange*, p. 6.
7. Ibid., pp. 6-7.
8. Ibid., p. 7.
9. *Soviet Diplomacy and Negotiating Behavior*, p. 423.
10. *Senate Delegation on Parliamentary Exchange*, pp. 11-12.
11. Shevchenko, p. 200.
12. Byrd, p. S19725.
13. Shevchenko, p. 192.
14. A.N. Iakovlev, *On the Edge of an Abyss*, (Moscow: Progress Publishers, 1985), p. 149.

15. Ibid.

16. Ibid., p. 158.

17. Ibid.

18. U.S. House, *House Delegation Trip to the Soviet Union.* 96th Cong., 1st sess., 1979, p. 26.

19. U.S. International Communications Agency, *Soviet Elite Perceptions of the U.S.: Public Statements of Soviet Leaders,* by Stanley H. Kober, Research Report No. R-12-80 July 1980, p. 7-8.

20. For further information, see Kober, pp. 7-8.

21. Kober, p. 8.

22. U.S. Senate, *The Superpowers at a Crossroads: Soviet-American Relations in the Autumn of 1985.* 99th Cong., 1st sess., 1985, p. 31.

23. Helen Dewar "Hill Leaders Hold Freewheeling Debate with Soviet," *Washington Post,* 10 December 1987.

24. Joel Brinkley, "Soviet Visitor is Turning on All His Charm," *New York Times,* 10 December 1987.

25. Foreign Broadcast Information Service, trans., "Speech by Mikhail Sergeevich Gorbachev, General Secretary of the CPSU Central Committee, at presentation of Order of Lenin and Gold Medal in Murmansk," October 2, 1987.

26. The author is indebted to Richard Kaufman, staff member of the Joint Economic Committee for the text of the Proxmire letter to Gorbachev.

27. *Soviet Diplomacy and Negotiating Behavior,* p. 423 (see footnote 99 on that page).

7

Conclusion

At the outset of this study, it was established that an exploration of a largely undiscovered subject matter in Soviet foreign policy research, namely, Soviet perspectives on the role of Congress in U.S. foreign policy, could contribute inductively to the establishment of a widely accepted perspective on how Soviet foreign policy is formulated and carried out. It was noted that new analysis on a fresh subject matter offered the potential for enhanced theory-building in American studies of Soviet foreign policy. It was also argued that Soviet views of the Congress had far-reaching foreign policy implications since a "Congress factor" as described by Soviet scholars might well indicate a major effort by the Soviet leadership to take a close account of Congress' influence on the making and conduct of U.S.-Soviet relations.

As such, this study has set out in a detailed fashion an examination of Soviet attitudes on the role of Congress in U.S. foreign policy. Amerikanistika, the perspectives of foreign policy institutions like the MFA, the Central Committee International Department, and the KGB, and the Soviet leadership have been analyzed. Direct interactions including numerous meetings between the Soviet leadership and Members of Congress have been examined. The theoretical and practical implications of Soviet views of the U.S. Congress for the conduct of superpower relations and the study of Soviet foreign policy can now be described.

At the outset, one must concede that attempting to evaluate Soviet attitudes on Congress' role in U.S. foreign policy and relating those attitudinal evaluations to the validity of existing Western perspectives of Soviet foreign policy is a highly difficult task. The most notable difficulty is the inescapable problem of levels of analysis within which attitudes are filtered.

Several levels of analysis in some way shape attitudes: the level of decisionmaking; the level of bureaucracy; the nature and state of domestic politics; the international environment and; the level of personal beliefs and images.[1] Evidence which seems to provide support for one of the competing Western perspectives of Soviet foreign policy may in fact have been filtered through one or more of these levels of analysis. For example, bureaucratic-level considerations such as ISKAN's institutional role in promoting a pragmatic approach to U.S.-Soviet relations, the domestic political level requirement in the Soviet Union that scholarship serve policy objectives, the complex international environment level in which Congress' actions on foreign policy are shaped, and personal-level differences of opinion in evaluating Congress' policymaking role are all different levels of analysis which affect Soviet attitudes toward the Congress.

As such, there are legitimate reasons to be cautious about the evaluation of Soviet attitudes with a view toward testing validity of differing Western perspectives on Soviet foreign policy. Given the difficulties described, one can legitimately ask whether the empirical effort will yield any theoretically-useful results. Is the game worth the candle?

If the answer is yes, one must acknowledge that evaluating the validity of existing perspectives has explicit value connotations. As one scholar has thoughtfully stated, in measuring and evaluating Soviet reality, "both opponents and proponents of the use of pluralism in Soviet studies took as their yardstick the concept of pluralism current in the study of American politics."[2] The adherents to the pluralist perspective and to a lesser extent the subsequent corporatist perspective were in one sense scholarly rebels seeking to break the hold of the totalitarian perspective, which had previously dominated Soviet studies in the postwar period. The commitment by some scholars to reject the totalitarian perspective was "tantamount to a decision to reorient the study of Soviet politics."[3]

Thus, while value connotations cannot be denied, the new subject matter and information contained in this study also reflects the disciplinary and theoretical goals of the Soviet studies field. By evaluating the validity of existing perspectives of Soviet foreign policy, this study has tried to achieve some of the field's principal empirical goals, including finding "good starting points for breaking the system down into its essential elements," and "highlighting key characteristics of the Soviet system."[4]

In short, we are paralyzed both in terms of theory-building and policymaking unless we are willing to evaluate the actions of Soviet foreign policymakers with an eye towards identifying organizing elements and key characteristics of Soviet foreign policy and analyzing their implications for the making and conduct of Soviet policy toward the United States. It is in this vein that the following conclusions are offered.

First, it is apparent that particularly with respect to amerikanistika, the pluralist perspective on Soviet foreign policy has wide-ranging explanatory capability. In the ten subject areas of amerikanistika on Congress and foreign policy, areas which are a fully representative cross-section of Congressional activity in foreign policy, the type of informed debate, use of Western concepts of political science, and rejection of rigid, orthodox Stalinist analysis identified in the pluralist perspective of Soviet foreign policy predominated the discussion. This was clearly the case in part or all of seven of those areas. Pluralist images were clearly present in discussions on Congress' role in U.S. policy toward Western Europe, arms sales to the Middle East, and defense and arms control policy. They were also prevailing in the discussions on the separation of powers, the two-party system, the organization of Congress with respect to foreign policy, and pressure groups. Each of these discussion areas will be considered in turn.

For example, concerning the case studies in chapter 3, the discussion of Congress' role in U.S. policy in Western Europe demonstrated an ability to perceive realistically differences between the executive branch and the Congress on how U.S. policy should be conducted. It included an understanding of constituent politics with respect to U.S. policy in the region as well as accurate descriptions of the policy differences on issues such as the Soviet gas pipeline and U.S. foreign assistance to Greece and Turkey. The same can be said for the discussion of Congress and U.S. arms sales to the Middle East, where one finds overall analytical quality to be quite good on such issues as the type of political lobbying, the substantive arguments used by proponents and opponents of particular sales, and executive-legislative negotiations on the scope and manner of arms sales made to the region. The discussion of Congress' role in U.S. defense and arms control policy is also of exceptionally high standards showing an impressive ability to follow the intracacies of legislative consideration of issues as well as a sometimes harsh, unfair, but thorough judgment concerning the results of Congress' efforts to be a "political barometer of the changing mood in American society" on issues of war and peace.

Validating evidence for the pluralist perspective is also evident on the process and procedural aspects of Congress' role in U.S. foreign policy discussed in chapter 2. The bulk of amerikanistika concerning the concept of separation of powers is clearly pluralist in tone, with deep and spirited debates among Soviet scholars concerning the type, scope, and manifestations of legislative powers in foreign policy, the root causes of recent legislative activism in foreign policy as well as its positive and negative effects, and the implications of such activism for the making and conduct of U.S. foreign policy. Concerning the two-party system, a rather complex understanding of the operational aspects of the two-party system, the role and nature of bipartisanship in foreign policy, and the relatively greater importance of factions crossing party lines is apparent. With respect to the organization of Congress on foreign policy issues, one also sees a largely straightforward discussion of legislative structure and the increasingly fractionated process of Congress' foreign policymaking. Finally, regarding pressure groups, americanists demonstrate for the most part a respectable level of discussion and debate on such issues as the effect of public opinion on Congress, the role of elections and the electoral factor, and the executive branch as a pressure group.

In some ways, the conclusion that americanists' scholarly effort appears to support the pluralist perspective of Soviet foreign policy is hardly startling. Other American scholars have pointed out that americanists at the foreign policy research institutes of the Academy of Sciences have been in the forefront of rejecting analysis of U.S. foreign policy based on simplistic economic determinism. These scholars have also pointed out the trends in amerikanistika that (1) favor an analysis of the U.S. foreign policy "mechanism" that treats separately the politics of foreign policy from its economic substructure; (2) recognize the pluralism of various sectors of the ruling class, enabling some political elites and factions to impose their will even on major "business circles,"; and (3) accept ambiguity, inconsistency, and complexity in describing the operation of U.S. foreign policy, including Congress'·role in that policy.[5]

Americanists have also been described as the "scholar-publicists" and "salesmen" of detente, whose views in the intensely political atmosphere of Soviet scholarship are designed to foster a moderate Soviet foreign policy course with respect to relations with the United States. Their intellectual commitment, and the research empires americanists have created are designed to promote such a course. A return to Cold War-style relations with the United States could well harm the institutions americanists work for and produce a downturn in their own personal career advancement. Hostile superpower relations have often been associated in the Soviet Union with internal repression of international studies. One need only recall the barren scholarly climate of the late Stalin period to appreciate how much americanists have at stake in promoting improved U.S.-Soviet relations.

Amerikanistika on Congress' role in U.S. foreign policy has fallen almost exclusively into what one scholar has called the third and current phase of post-war Soviet studies of the United States.[6] In this third phase, americanists began to grasp the importance of electoral factors in shaping Congressional actions in foreign policy, and the complexity and effects of organizational factors and cross-party factions. Consequently, americanists have recognized the futility of analysis which defines Congress solely as a progressive institution against an executive power dominated by monopoly capital.

One cannot help but be struck by the level of sophistication now present in amerikanistika on a number of issues. Soviet scholars recognize the ability of Congress to work with the NATO allies to smooth out differences caused by an American executive branch. They point out the inconsistencies of legislators who vote for both the MX missile and legislation calling for a nuclear freeze. Finally, the open admission by scholars operating within a Marxist-Leninist conceptual framework that Congress is a "mirror of American politics," and a "political barometer" of changing political moods suggests even a willingness to acknowledge Congress' representative nature. This is a truly startling admission given the operational environment, described in chapter 4, within which americanists must perform their research.

In the opening chapter, the assumptions of the pluralist school of Soviet foreign policy were examined. Some of these assumptions include the stress on significant feedback from abroad in the making and conduct of Soviet foreign policy, intense informed discussion, debate, and disagreement on foreign policy issues, the absence of a "blueprint" for foreign policy, and support among Soviet elites for improved U.S.-Soviet relations if reciprocated by American policymakers.

An analysis of amerikanistika on Congress' role in U.S. foreign policy helps to support these assumptions. The precise, often impressive analysis of both contemporary, and process and procedural issues concerning Congress and foreign policy clearly support the notion of significant feedback from abroad. Debates over the meaning and significance of Congress' actions in U.S. defense and arms control policy, and the relevance of the two-party system or the separation of powers for an operational understanding of U.S. foreign policy clearly indicate intense, informed discussion, debate, and disagreement on foreign policy issues. The chagrin among americanists for Congress' inconsistency in foreign policy, and the shift in attitude among americanists from widespread support for Congress' role in foreign policy to one of widespread concern supports the assumption of no blueprint in Soviet foreign policy. Finally, the identification of actions by Congress and factions in Congress that support advances in arms control and improvement in U.S.-Soviet relations suggests that Soviet americanists are seeking a reciprocal response to their interest for more cooperative, less conflictual U.S.-Soviet relations. Thus, amerikanistika on Congress' role in U.S. foreign policy supports in large measure the assumptions of the pluralist perspective on Soviet foreign policy. Nonetheless, the validation of the pluralist perspective is not complete. For the evidence from this study leads to a second conclusion: that attitudes toward Congress' role in foreign policy among Soviet foreign policymaking institutions and the presumptions and conclusions of amerikanistika on some issues affecting Soviet foreign policy are best explained by the corporatist perspective of Soviet foreign policy.

Unlike americanists in the foreign policy research institutes, practitioners of Soviet foreign policy, particularly in the MFA, do not enjoy even a quasi-academic atmosphere to consider alternatives to an existing political line or strategy regarding Soviet relations with the United States. While sharing with americanists (indeed many MFA diplomats are themselves americanists) a commitment to improved U.S.-Soviet relations, Party and MFA diplomats are much more attuned to short-term considerations of policy implementation. They are also much more vulnerable to the inevitable political accountability that comes with the success or failure of a current policy.

Furthermore, given the past predictive failures of Soviet scholars concerning Congress' actions on Jackson-Vanik, SALT II ratification, and other issues, policy practitioners in the MFA and the Central Committee International Department should be skeptical of the explanatory power of amerikanistika. As such, MFA diplomats in Washington and Moscow, as well as their counterparts in the Central Committee International Department, have a thoroughly utilitarian understanding of Congress' role in foreign policy. Those Embassy diplomats processing Congressional visits to the Soviet Union have an understanding of foreign policymakers in Congress that is concerned among other things with the issue of whether those proposed travels, and Embassy recommendations as to whether visas should be approved and who the delegation should see, will enhance or degrade Embassy prestige in Moscow. Similarly, the Central Committee International Department must judge carefully whether Embassy recommendations are accurate, and if so, at what level congressional delegations should be received. The same is true to a lesser extent for the International Department of the Supreme Soviet. None of these institutions wants to be associated with recommending leadership attention to Congressional delegations that prove inimical to advancing Soviet foreign policy objectives.

The Soviet Embassy's extensive network of contacts, as well as KGB operations and the long experience of Dobrynin, are designed to provide the best intelligence possible for Soviet policymakers making and conducting Soviet policy toward the United States. While the Embassy and the MFA's USA Department undoubtedly support improved U.S.-Soviet relations and believe some (not all) Congressional visits to the Soviet Union may contribute to such an improvement, policy implementation takes precedence over policy prescription. Concerns for Embassy and Ministry prestige and influence, as well as the stress on implementation rather than initiation, falls into system maintenance behavior articulated in the corporatist perspective of Soviet foreign policy.

This same concern for policy implementation also appears to be operative in amerikanistika on a number of issues relative to Congress' role in foreign policy. As has already been pointed out, Soviet scholars are bound by the principle of konkretnost, which stresses the performance of services for policymakers and the making of scientific efforts relevant to policymaking needs. On some issues affected by Congress' role in foreign policy that are particularly relevant to policymakers, such as U.S.-Soviet trade or Congress' current attitude regarding its war powers prerogatives (a barometer of legislative attitudes toward the use of force in U.S. foreign policy), amerikanistika seems analytically subordinated to whether Congress' actions— serve or detract from Soviet foreign policy objectives. This is also true to a lesser extent in other discussion areas including the separation of powers, the two-party system, and the organization of Congress and its effects on U.S. foreign policy. A brief examination of amerikanistika in these areas helps prove this point.

For example, in the discussion on Congress' role in U.S.-Soviet trade, the value of Congress' actions in contributing to existing Soviet policy objectives in such trade appears to be the analytical barometer of amerikanistika, a trend conforming to the system maintenance emphasis described in the corporatist perspective on Soviet foreign policy. In the discussion on constitutional responsibilities concerning war powers and treaties, stress on the argument that treaties and executive agreements are equally binding, as well as the general disappointment over the ability of the War Powers Resolution to restrain the use of U.S. military power suggests that for americanists, "the question in their mind is political—what its policy implications are for the USSR—not constitutional (considerations)."[7] Soviet interpretation regarding the equally-binding effect of treaties and executive agreements is consistent with the traditional interpretation of international law on this question. However, it also appears that analysis is being subordinated to pure consideration of Soviet interests alone.

Furthermore, while the pluralist perspective carries the most explanatory capability on the process and procedural issues discussed in chapter 2, some phenomena supporting the corporatist perspective are present as well. For example, the criticisms of legislative activism in U.S. foreign policy that threaten detente and the improvement of U.S.-Soviet relations, and the alternating approval of such activism on other issues such as ending the Vietnam War or denying aid to anticommunist rebels in Angola, tends to support system maintenance motivations that are a principal feature of the corporatist perspective. The same can be said for some aspects of the discussion of the two-party system, when bipartisanship is either castigated or praised depending on whether a bipartisan approach to a particular foreign policy issue is consistent with Soviet foreign policy objectives.

Some amerikanistika regarding the negative effects of the organization of Congress on foreign policy issues is also best explained by the corporatist perspective. Dating from the late 1970's when a conservative mood in Congress buried detente and its most visible symbol, the SALT II agreement, americanists have had concerns about fragmentation of foreign policy decisionmaking and the parochialism of Congress' foreign policy concerns. They have also developed growing sympathy with the argument that Congress is better at obstructing executive foreign policy initiatives that it is at proposing its own. The switch of preference among many americanists to the executive during this period was no accident and clearly reflected, in part, a disillusionment with Congress' attitude on crucial aspects of U.S.-Soviet relations. As a result, those institutions more closely associated at any given time with a more "sober" outlook in foreign policy (i.e. exhibiting less overt hostility to the USSR) "have as a rule been presented as more responsible, more rational, more far-sighted components of the system."[8] This tendency in americanist analysis also conforms to the main features of the corporatist approach to the study of Soviet foreign policy.

As such, it appears that the effects of konkretnost on some central foreign policy issues distorts the dual role of americanists in "justifying a particular set of policies and recommending their development in one direction or another."[9] Apparently, because of the centrality to Soviet foreign policy objectives of some issues like U.S.-Soviet trade and American constitutional responsibility on the decision to go to war, americanists are not allowed, as they have on other issues of Congress' role in U.S. foreign policy, to make subtle policy recommendations. Analysis is only permitted to justify existing policy positions.

Finally, the element of clientelism that is an important part of the corporatist perspective on Soviet foreign policy can also be identified in the types of services performed by americanists for the Soviet leadership. The preparation of policy-relevant studies on Congress' role in U.S. foreign policy, propaganda and legitimation functions performed through participation in mass media press articles and television and radio appearances, participation in parliamentary exchanges, the training of foreign policy cadres for Party and government institutions, and patron-client relationships established between Soviet leaders and key americanists, all suggest a type of clientelism designed to maintain the prevailing power structure, in keeping with the assumptions of the corporatist perspective.

The third conclusion of this study is that the totalitarian perspective continues to have limited application concerning Soviet views of the U.S. Congress. The totalitarian perspective on Soviet foreign policy, largely discredited by American scholars but still widely accepted by American foreign policymakers, continues to have residual explanatory power. Amerikanistika on Congress' and U.S. policy toward Eastern Europe, as well as difficulties in grasping in the deepest conceptual sense the separation of powers as anything beyond a tactical outgrowth of ruling class political control are examples of phenomena explained by the totalitarian perspective. As well, the search for the monopoly summit orchestrating the two-party system, and the simplistic analysis of defense and ethnic group lobbies tends to support the assumptions of the totalitarian perspective.

Brief illustrations augment this conclusion. Americanist analysis of Congress' role in U.S. policy in Eastern Europe is so polemical as to be devoid of any serious discussion of Congress' involvement in that policy. The replacement of rational discussion by simplistic nostrums is what one would expect from the Soviet foreign policy outlook described in the totalitarian perspective. The same can be said of the failure to come to grips fully with the separation of powers and the analytical fallback to an often crude class analysis that tries to explain complex institutional foreign policy relationships between the executive and legislative branches. Further evidence supporting the totalitarian perspective can be found in the effort on the part of some americanists to see the real role of the two-party system as servicing "monopoly capital." The same can be said for simplistic descriptions of defense and ethnic lobby groups as "tools of the military-industrial complex," or "agents of Zionism."

One must also acknowledge that KGB intelligence collection efforts concerning Congress' foreign policy activities are also consistent with the totalitarian approach. The KGB's primary institutional purposes, which include ensuring the Communist Party's political predominance, taking all necessary actions no matter how intrusive to advance the objectives of the Party leadership, and verifying day-to-day loyalty of government institutions to the Soviet political system tend to validate the element of police state control in the totalitarian perspective on Soviet foreign policy. In dealing with the Congress, both in Washington and Moscow, the KGB's willingness to use personal recruitment, intimidation, harassment, and blackmail to preserve and advance the power of the Soviet political system tends to validate the obsession with security and generated hostility associated with the totalitarian perspective.

Several factors account for the enduring, albeit limited, explanatory capability of the totalitarian perspective. First, official Soviet ideology creates the need to fit all the detailed information concerning the U.S. "into an all-embracing Marxist-Leninist framework (which) imposes a rigidity and uniformity on American public life which can only be regarded as, at best, simpleminded."[10] Second, rigid adherence to an official ideology, a cardinal tenet of the totalitarian perspective, invariably affects the analytical quality of amerikanistika on Congress' role in foreign policy. To demonstrate ideological reliability, americanists must sometimes complement their often sophisticated discussion of such issues as the two-party system, the role of partisanship, and cross-party factional groupings in Soviet foreign policy, with a resort to ritual dogmas about the controlling interest of the ruling class.

Thus, amerikanistika on Congress and foreign policy, even as it grows in sophistication, has not been able to escape the propagandistic function that is required of its authors, including "the perpetuation of useful myths and distortions (that) inhibit theoretical development."[11] A complete debate over Marxist- Leninist assumptions about the liberal state and its political superstructure, the nature of the separation of power and pluralistic power hierarchies, and the reality or facade of a multi-party political system are apparently still too politically hot to handle in Soviet academic circles. Such a debate, as one scholar has pointed out, could "provoke awkward speculation among readers about the relationship between their own state and its ruling class (that is, the working class)."[12] Thus, the "internal dynamics of the Soviet political system place a high premium on doctrinal orthodoxy and continuity."[13]

Third, there also appear to be foreign policy issues so critical to questions of Soviet national security that analysis of Congress' role concerning these issues cannot go beyond simplistic caricature. Thus, as we have seen, the depiction of Congress' role concerning U.S. policy toward Eastern Europe lacks any sense of analytical balance and the extent of alleged Congressional perfidy can only be described as bizarre. As in the case of certain process and procedural issues which have uncomfortable domestic implications, contemporary issues like Congress' role in potentially loosening Soviet control of Eastern Europe hits too close to home to allow americanists to produce more sober analysis.

Finally, while a number of americanists acknowledge the requirements of official ideology with mere lip service at the outset of their articles and books, for some americanists a Marxist-Leninist analytical framework is not only required, but is an intellectually-sound basis for explaning Congress' role in foreign policy. In addition to remaining orthodox scholars who still adhere to a state monopoly capital approach to the study of the Congress, many americanists still proceed from an approach based more generally on historical materialism. Also quite relevant are the enduring effects of the Soviet-Russian political culture. Thus, the recurring references in amerikanistika to the increasingly frenetic, disjointed, and disorganized process of Congressional consideration of foreign policy issues stems in part from cultural-bound assumptions that bargaining, temporary victories, pragmatic compromises, and ambiguous results are more likely to produce disorder than sound policy.

The Soviet-Russian political culture, as one scholar has noted, has had a "tradition of positively rejecting interest groups."[14] It has been reinforced by the Leninist rejection of the notion of interest groups as entities that serve as surrogates for broad societal groups and political parties as entities that broker interest group demand rather than dictating public policy. This underlying assumption of the concept of pluralism as applied to American politics (and adapted to the Soviet Union by scholars in the pluralist school) is, in the view of adherents to the totalitarian perspective inconsistent with rigid party discipline and the tenets of democratic centralism. With a historical development that throws "grave doubt on the emergence of even a limited pluralism in the Soviet system in the coming decades," scholars supporting the totalitarian perspective argue that the Soviet system's "stability and dynamism (or lack of dynamism) are centrally related to the weakness of groups, not to inchoate group activity."[15]

In describing the remaining usefulness of the totalitarian school, some have regarded it as valuable in explaining the "remaining obstacles, both institutional and ideological, to change of a pluralist kind."[16] This formulation is quite useful for it helps to explain how two tenets of the totalitarian approach to the study of Soviet foreign policy, an official ideology and party control of communications, have distorted elements of amerikanistika on Congress' role in foreign policy and prevented lines of scholarly inquiry from being pursued that would have enriched its theoretical development. It can be rightly stated that, after "a decade and a half of applying pluralism to the study of Soviet politics, any epitaph for totalitarianism would be premature."[17]

Nonetheless, the constraints on the analytical quality of amerikanistika appears to be diminishing because this study has produced convincing evidence for a fourth conclusion that the comprehension gap between the Soviet leadership and americanists concerning Congress role in foreign policy has narrowed, with images of all three Western perspectives of Soviet foreign policy present in both the Soviet leadership and among americanists.

The pervasive ignorance that seemed to characterize the views of the Soviet leadership concerning Congress and foreign policy in the mid and even late 1970's can no longer be supported by the available evidence. Interview research and Congressional reports on meetings with the Soviet leadership show an apparent understanding, albeit perhaps only at a surface level, of the separation of powers concept in U.S. foreign policy, the two-party system, the committee system, the views of individual Members on foreign policy issues and Congress' oversight responsibilities through the process of hearings and publications. This understanding is indeed a far cry from Brezhnev's refusal to accept any Congressional changes in the SALT II Treaty. It is also quite distant from Kosygin's inability to understand Congress' interest in the details of the Treaty or Romanov's incredulity at the temerity of Democratic senators opposing a treaty negotiated by their party boss. By contrast, Gorbachev and the current leadership have developed a vastly expanded network of contacts with the Congress involving not only increased parliamentary exchanges, but direct interaction and even diplomacy through direct televised contacts, testimony before a committee of Congress and working directly with congressional representatives to international conferences and negotiations.

Unlike the late 1970's, when the Soviet leadership attitudes conformed primarily to the totalitarian perspective, we now find behavior predicted by all three perspectives on Soviet foreign policy. While one must clearly be careful with impressionistic interview research and Congressional reports of meetings with the Soviet leadership, such sources provide valuable insights. For example, one such participant interviewed felt that the surface understanding of Congress' role in foreign policy constituted a "politician's understanding" of that role, not conceptually rich but basically sound. Indeed, Gorbachev appears to have an informed, articulate understanding of the scope and range of Congressional activities in foreign policy, as well as an apparent grasp of crucial issues such as bipartisanship and the futility of blatant Soviet efforts to divide the President from the Congress. This type of political outlook clearly supports the assumptions of the pluralist perspective of Soviet foreign policy. For those supporting that approach, Gorbachev personifies a more self-confident Soviet leadership able to deal with and understand the complexities of the American political system and the making and conduct of U.S. foreign policy. There is evidence from Gorbachev's meetings with Congressional delegations to suggest that this outlook is in fact well in place. Gorbachev not only appears to have surface understanding of the Congress but now may even actually study legislative oversight activities as evidenced by his references to the Joint Economic Committee hearings on the Soviet economy. This is clearly a startling change from Brezhnev-era leaders.

Behavior predicted by the corporatist perspective on Soviet foreign policy is also present in the Soviet leadership. Narrow, utilitarian understanding, calibrated according to time and place, to achieve specific foreign policy objectives appears to be evident in Gromyko and Shcherbitskii and based on available evidence, Shevardnadze and Nikonov. Tactical knowledge designed to gain policy advantage by diplomacy, deference, protocol and other means is clearly a corporatist image and the behavior of Gromyko in particular, much like Dobrynin and the Embassy diplomats, seems to validate that image.

Finally, as in the case of amerikanistika, totalitarian images endure in the Soviet leadership. The outlook of Iakovlev, who seems convinced the American right-wing dominates Congress' actions in foreign policy, is unmistakably totalitarian notwithstanding his role as a major supporter of internal political and economic reform and his emergence as one of Gorbachev's principal foreign policy advisors. The style of presentation by the Soviet leadership, which professes regime infallibility and refuses to accept shared responsibility for deterioration in U.S.-Soviet relations, is also a trait that is stressed by the totalitarian perspective.

The presence in both amerikanistika and Soviet leadership attitudes of images from all three Western perspectives raises an important point about efforts to build theories of Soviet foreign policy. Writing on the scholarly debates on the proper conceptualization of the Soviet political system, one scholar has commented on criteria for the usefulness of such conceptualizations for building knowledge and understanding:

The kind of models or ideal-types that we use can serve a number of functions. . . . However, the most useful formulation in terms of advancing understanding is to highlight phenomena and relationships that were poorly understood in the past, to raise questions that lead to new and productive research.

From this perspective, incompleteness of a model is not necessarily harmful. A model or concept that *de facto* deals only with the input or output side of politics, that highlights unexpected similarities or differences between political systems, may be enormously useful in stimulating research and analysis that would not otherwise be undertaken. Moreover, the usefulness of a model can depend on the framework in which it arises. A confused or ambiguous concept or model which corresponds to the conventional wisdom and which only obscures problems may be useful for ideological purposes, but it is worthless from a scientific point of view. The very same ambiguous model which illuminates neglected phenomena or relationships or raises unexpected questions may be extremely valuable.[18]

This study has attempted to meet these criteria for conceptual usefulness. By demonstrating at what points and with which institutions, issues, and individuals the existing Western perspectives of Soviet foreign policy have explanatory power, phenomena and relationships poorly understood have been highlighted. The value of using several perspectives to analyze the same evidence has been demonstrated. As such, we do not have to rely on only one of the differing perspectives on Soviet foreign policy. Each perspective offers valuable insights sometimes obscured by other perspectives. Finally, through an examination of the existing perspectives of Soviet foreign policy, a "Congress factor" in Soviet calculations was discovered, illuminating a neglected phenomena of Soviet foreign policy and raising unexpected questions about the effects of that factor on U.S.-Soviet relations.

While this study did not resolve the debate over the explanatory power and value of existing perspectives of Soviet foreign policy, it did demonstrate new research on this vital theoretical question. Hopefully, this study will stimulate further research and analysis on a heretofore unknown but far-reaching question facing the study of Soviet foreign policy.

The development in the Soviet leadership of images from all three Western perspectives also suggests two other significant insights. First, the very existence of a much more sophisticated outlook regarding Congress' role in U.S. foreign policy suggests that amerikanistika, which largely shares this outlook, may be having a permeating effect at the top of the Soviet political system. The evidence is problematic as indicated by the lack of clearcut, unambiguous americanist influence on such issues as the Soviet response to the defense and arms control debate in Congress discussed in chapter 3. Nonetheless, as Soviet leadership sophistication regarding Congress' role in foreign policy grows among Soviet leaders, American scholars will have to pay increasing attention to amerikanistika as a source of policy information.

Secondly, the growing sophistication in the Soviet leadership regarding Congress' role in foreign policy raises the question posed by adherents to the pluralist perspective on Soviet foreign policy as to whether "a correlation exists between improved perceptions on the one hand and attitudes towards the United States on the other."[19] Does moderation in leadership views of Congress' role in foreign policy suggest a more moderate view of U.S. policy toward the Soviet Union more generally? Given Congress' unpredictability in foreign policy issues, and the poor record of the predictions of Soviet (and indeed American) scholars concerning the direction of Congress' actions in this area, does an increasingly sophisticated view of the Congress by Soviet leaders lead to moderation and conflict limitation? Or conversely, does uncertainty and confusion about what a complex foreign policy institution like the Congress will do lead to frustration, arrogance, and miscalculation?

As stated at the conclusion of chapter 1, this study is also a study for policymakers. Both the executive branch and Congress must be more aware of the varied and intense ways the Soviet foreign policy apparatus seeks the best information available on legislative actions in U.S. foreign policy. The scope and intensity of this effort by both Soviet scholars and policymakers as described in this study serves a policy purpose. Obviously, as we saw on the issue of legislative action on defense and arms control issues, Soviet leaders will not make policy decisions regarding the critical aspects of U.S.-Soviet relations only on the basis of its knowledge of what Congress may do. A host of domestic and international factors, as seen from both Washington and Moscow will be involved. But now more that ever before, Soviet leaders appear to grasp the "Congress factor" in U.S. foreign policy. This recognition poses new challenges and responsibilities for both American scholars and Members of Congress and staff, a subject which is the basis of our final conclusion, namely that growing Soviet recognition of the role of Congress will have new and significant effects on the conduct of U.S.-Soviet relations.

This study has shown that Soviet leaders, after Jackson-Vanik and the demise of SALT II, have learned from bitter experience that the Congress has significant foreign policy powers that can be thoroughly disruptive of Soviet foreign policy calculations. As changes in leadership attitudes have become more detectable, evidence grows that this lesson is being learned. The Soviet leadership is pushing hard for the formalization of parliamentary ties between the USSR Supreme Soviet and the Congress, and have welcomed scores of visiting Congressional delegations. Such ties with the Congress are seen by Soviet leaders as a means of shaping legislative attitudes on U.S.-Soviet relations to a more positive direction. The Soviet leadership has had too much rueful experience to any longer permit its ignorance to harvest bitter Congressional fruit.

Since the political shock of Jackson-Vanik, the Soviet leadership and foreign policy apparatus has slowly gained more experience in dealing with the Congress on foreign policy matters. One House staffer who has participated in Congress' relations with the Soviet foreign policy machinery has presciently observed that the Jackson-Vanik experience above all else proved to Soviet leaders that their conduct of relations with the United States could not be focused on the executive branch alone.

The diplomatic back-channel, controlled by Gromyko, Dobrynin, Nixon, and former Secretary of State Henry Kissinger, was clearly preferred by

Brezhnev-era Soviet leaders in their dealings with the United States. But in the view of the House staffer interviewed, Kissinger's own disdain of Congress' foreign policy powers led him to ignore the Congress whenever possible. Kissinger is also thought to have created the impression in the minds of Soviet leaders that the Congress was not a significant factor in U.S.-Soviet relations. When Kissinger could not "deliver" the Congress, Soviet leaders for a long-time suspected trickery and machinations orchestrated from the White House but also slowly moved to develop their relations with the Congress.

Since that time, contacts between Soviet foreign policymakers and Members of Congress have grown steadily. Members and staff have been a central element of U.S. delegations to the review conferences mandated by the Conference and Security and Cooperation in Europe (CSCE). They have also actively participated in contentious CSCE review meetings in Belgrade, Madrid, and now Vienna concerning Soviet compliance with the human rights provisions of the CSCE agreement.

Moreover, in recent years, the Soviet leadership under Gorbachev has intensified contacts with Congress to a truly unprecedented level. The scope and extent of parliamentary exchanges cosponsored and encouraged by the Soviet Union have grown rapidly. While this study has analyzed a representative cross-section of these visits, there have been many more. By the time this study is published, several more congressional delegations will have visited the Soviet Union. While President Reagan and General Secretary Gorbachev have now met annually from 1985-1988, congressional summits occur with even greater frequency. The House and Senate leadership, both Republicans and Democrats, have met with Gorbachev, Gromyko, Shcherbitskii, and other Soviet leaders. Influential committee chairmen have also met on several occasions with Soviet leaders.

But Soviet foreign policymakers have not stopped at parliamentary exchanges. Freewheeling exchanges on issues have occured in meetings with the House and Senate Arms Control Observer Groups. Televised exchanges have occured through the Capitol-to-Capitol program. A House delegation has been given access to one of the most sensitive defense facilities in the Soviet Union. A Soviet diplomat has testified before a congressional committee. Teams of experts from the Ministry of Foreign Affairs and the Central Committee International Department have directly briefed Members of Congress on internal political developments in the Soviet Union. Even on the formerly off-limits subject of human rights, the Supreme Soviet has proposed the establishment of a joint commission with the Congress to investigate individual human rights abuses. Compared to the limited, frosty relationship between the Brezhnev leadership and the Congress, the Gorbachev leadership effort to establish a comprehensive network of contacts with the Congress is truly remarkable. Soviet leaders now appear to recognize the old adage that to avoid a congressional crash landing, Congress must be in on the takeoff stage of initiatives in superpower relations.

Thus, Members of Congress find themselves the subject of increasing attention by Soviet foreign policymakers. Whether for purposes of information gathering, direct human intelligence, an alternate channel of communication when relations with the executive branch are poor, or as a means to conduct a subtle, indirect form of lobbying to bring about changes in U.S. policy, the Soviet leadership is actively seeking the widest possible contacts with the Congress.

As such, like it or not, ready or not, Soviet leaders have come to accept Members of Congress as foreign policymakers. This raises several interesting issues and challenges that Congress as an institution has not faced before this time.

One scholar has put forth the hypotheses that "the more perceptive an individual's stated view of the adversary, the less hostile his apparent feelings toward it, and the more he was inclined to urge policies of conflict limitation and agreement."[20] If we accept the growing evidence that the Soviet leadership is becoming more perceptive of Congress' role in foreign policy, Members of Congress share a greater responsibility for attempting "to increase the authority of the more 'realistic,' less militant elements (of the Soviet leadership) and at the same time to weaken the position of the more conservative, ideologically orthodox groups."[21]

Such a responsibility is indeed fraught with difficulties. Projecting a willingness to recognize Soviet moderation while not in the process promoting the perception in the minds of Soviet leaders that Congress will hamstring the executive branch's approach to U.S.-Soviet relations will be hard to pull off. At the same time, members may be increasingly called on by the executive branch, as they have in the past, to project a willingness to do business with the Soviet leadership on crucial issues in U.S.-Soviet relations.

Evidence in this study shows impressively the ability of Soviet leaders to recognize Congressional viewpoints that diverge from current executive branch policy and their willingness to try and exploit these differences. Members and staff will no doubt have to be sensitive to this Soviet effort to gain tactical advantage and play off the executive branch against the Congress. On the other hand, Members of Congress cannot and will not simply parrot executive branch positions in their meetings with Soviet leaders. Congress must make independent foreign policy judgments and maintain its essential integrity in the U.S. foreign policymaking process. As both the Soviet leadership and the American executive branch have realized, Members of Congress can serve as useful intermediaries in breaking logjams on often critical issues. Since Congress' approval, particularly in supporting appropriations, is required for much of the stuff of which U.S.-Soviet relations is made, an intermediary role seems eminently reasonable and practical.

Moreover, this study has demonstrated that Soviet specialists on the Congress, and Soviet leaders, understand that Congress' involvement in foreign policy is a complex phenomena which cannot be easily manipulated by Soviet leaders or foreign policy actions. Ignorance of Congress' role in foreign policy has been replaced by a recognition that the complexity of Congressional involvement makes successful attempts at manipulation at best problematic. Recognition of Congress' role is being accompanied by a growing acceptance of the likely failure of efforts to attempt openly to divide Congress from the President on foreign policy issues.

Congress' growing activism in foreign policy has not always been accompanied by a commitment to educate itself about the issues to which it is becoming increasingly involved. From the author's own experience, the questions most frequently asked by Members visiting Soviet leaders and foreign policymakers are "Who are these people? What do these people think of us? What do they know about the Congress? What will be their approach in meetings with us?"

This study, the first of its kind, has attempted to answer those questions by examining amerikanistika across a broad range of foreign policy issues in which Congress has been involved. The attitudes and activities of the Soviet foreign policy apparatus in dealing with Congress, the new types of direct interaction with Members, and Soviet leadership attitudes have been examined.

But clearly more needs to be done. In-depth studies of Soviet views of each of the subject areas covered by this effort, as well as other subject areas could be written. The new information on leadership attitudes that has been revealed by this study will have to be updated continually and elaborated upon further.

In short, Soviet attitudes toward the role of Congress in U.S. foreign policy are taking on increasing importance and represent an emerging new factor in the conduct of U.S.-Soviet relations. The challenge for American scholars of the Soviet Union, as well as Members of Congress and their staffs, is to provide further contributions to knowledge and be cognizant in their policy dealings of a new element in the policymaking process which has growing theoretical and practical importance for the study and conduct of U.S.-Soviet relations.

Notes

1. For a full description of the role of the levels of analysis in affecting decisionmaking perceptions of international politics, see Robert Jervis, *Perceptions and Misperceptions in International Politics*, (Princeton, N.J.: Princeton University Press, 1976), pp. 4-31, particularly p. 28.

2. Solomon, p. 5.

3. Ibid., p. 23.

4. Bunce and Echols, p. 2.

5. For more on these points, see Schwartz, *Soviet Perceptions of the United States*, pp. 152-159.

6. For a full discussion of the three evolutionary phases in Soviet views of the American political system, see Malcolm, pp. 151-152.

7. Schwartz, p. 49.

8. Malcolm, p. 148.

9. Ibid., p. 160.

10. Schwartz, *Soviet Perceptions of the United States*, p. 147.

11. Malcolm, p. 155.

12. Ibid.

13. Schwartz, *Soviet Perceptions of the United States*, p. 148.
14. Odom, p. 562.
15. Ibid., p. 565.
16. Brown, *Soviet Politics*, p. 41.
17. Solomon, p. 24.
18. Hough, "Pluralism, Corporatism, and the Soviet Union," p. 50.
19. Schwartz, *Soviet Perceptions of the United States*, p. 159.
20. Ibid.
21. Ibid., p. 164.

8

Epilogue

The Congress' critical role in U.S.-Soviet relations was once again demonstrated in the first half of 1988, with the extended and ultimately favorable consideration of the Intermediate-range Nuclear Forces (INF) Treaty. Because this study was completed before Senate consideration of the Treaty, this Epilogue will deal briefly with that consideration and with Soviet views of the Congressional debate.

Because the Reagan Administration chose to negotiate the INF accord as a treaty, only the Senate was directly involved in the formal approval process. The Senate's lengthy consideration of the INF Treaty tended to belie what most observers believed would be inevitable advice and consent by a comfortable margin. This is not to say, however, that treaty consideration was not without its controversies.

Some treaty skeptics feared that the Treaty's basic provisions banning all nuclear missiles with ranges between 300 and 3,400 miles would remove classes of nuclear weapons that the NATO alliance and its member states had expended considerable political capital to deploy. Other skeptics worried that removing intermediate-range nuclear missiles undermined a credible NATO deterrent to Soviet conventional military attack in Western Europe, and left that deterrent principally in the hands of strategic nuclear missiles based in the United States.

Some opponents of the Treaty were deeply concerned about its verification provisions, particularly those dealing with data supplied by the Soviet Union on the precise size of its missile inventories to be destroyed under the Treaty, provisions in the Treaty to distinguish Soviet missiles covered by the Treaty from similar strategic nuclear missiles which were not covered, and the treatment of "futuristic" weapons in the 300-3400 mile range specified by the Treaty.

Finally, Senate Democrats, while overwhelmingly supportive of the Treaty, insisted on the inclusion of a provision in the resolution of ratification that bound the Reagan Administration and future Administrations to the interpretation of the Treaty's terms established at the time of Senate advice and consent. This provision was designed to prevent a reoccurence of the Reagan Administration's practice of reinterpreting treaties to suit current policy objectives long after the Senate had acted on a particular treaty. This occurred with respect to the ABM Treaty, when in 1985 the Administration had argued that the ABM Treaty permitted development, testing, and deployment of space-based strategic defense systems envisioned under the Strategic Defense Initiative (SDI) program. The Senate debate on advice and consent to the ABM Treaty in 1972 was conducted under an interpretation which prohibited all but research on SDI-type systems.

In the end, all of these controversies were resolved to the satisfaction of the vast majority of Senators. Those concerned about the political and military effects of the Treaty in Europe became convinced that to reject the Treaty in the face of clearcut West European support would be too harmful to contemplate. Concerns about a loss of deterrence were filtered into an argument for modernization and improvement of NATO's conventional forces and battlefield nuclear weapons not covered by the Treaty. Such modernization, it was argued, would provide a useful replacement of INF systems in the effort to deter any possible Soviet military attack against Western Europe.

The concerns about terms of verification were assuaged as well. As Senators delved into the details of the Treaty's verification provisions, most became convinced that adequate safeguards against noncompliance had been established by American negotiators. Finally, while having to swallow hard on the "reinterpretation" provision, Senate Republicans grudgingly accepted this amendment after a compromise which allowed the executive branch more latitude in interpreting provisions of the Treaty for which no authoritative understanding was established during the Senate debate. It was also agreed "futuristic" weapons in the range covered by the Treaty would be banned. After months of hearings by three Senate committees, and many days of lengthy floor debate, the Senate on May 27 rewarded the Reagan Administration's intense lobbying efforts on behalf of the Treaty and supported advice and consent by a margin of 93-5, far more than the two-thirds support required.

Soviet americanists, while largely sharing the view of most American observers that the INF Treaty would ultimately be approved by the Senate, were nonetheless uneasy about the length of the debate and the potential of the opposition to frustrate and complicate Senate approval. Thus, while amerikanistika on the Senate debate was largely straightforward, apprehension was apparent in the description of the slow process leading to eventual approval.

Some analysis dwelled on the lengthy consideration of the Treaty, and how delays might result in the gradual and eventually fatal loss of support, as in the case of the SALT II Treaty. Americanists also expressed the fear that the Treaty's approval might be delayed by linkages to other issues like the impending Soviet withdrawal from Afghanistan. This concern became particularly acute when Senate Majority Leader Robert Byrd, concerned that the Reagan Administration might cut off assistance to the anti-Communist rebels in Afghanistan in order to get Soviet troops out of that country, threatened to hold up consideration of the INF Treaty until he received assurances that the rebels were not being cut off prematurely. When Byrd received such assurances, INF consideration in the Senate was back on track.

Even the "reinterpretation" provision, which americanists supported in principle, raised concerns because Senate Republican opposition could lead to delays in approval. Nonetheless, americanists were favorable to the "reinterpretation" provision, perhaps because of its possible effects on limiting the SDI program, and were sympathetic to the role of the Senate in the treaty-making process, a role which was being undermined by executive branch reinterpretation efforts.

Soviet analysis devoted attention and praise to the steady stream of high-ranking executive branch and private witnesses appearing before Senate committees in support of the INF Treaty. The statements of Secretary of State George Shultz, Chairman of the Joint Chiefs of Staff William Crowe, and even former Secretary of Defense Caspar Weinberger were cited with approval. However, americanists also focused on the somewhat lonely efforts of Sen. Jesse Helms (R-N.C.) to defeat the Treaty. Helms was castigated as stopping at nothing to wreck the Treaty, as being part of a "war party" in the Senate, using "scare tactics," delays, and procrastination to introduce extraneous arguments that would undermine the solid majority support for the Treaty.

Americanists also presciently argued that the main purpose of Helms' opposition was to retard the prospects, because of election-year pressures and scheduling distractions, of Senate consideration of a strategic nuclear weapons agreement should the Reagan Administration be successful in concluding one. ISKAN director Georgii Arbatov directly brought up this point in a February 19 interview with Moscow television in which he argued that Senate conservatives wanted the INF Treaty to remain as "an isolated episode rather than be the first step in the process which would . . . [take] us away from being on the verge of a nuclear war and crazy spending on armaments."

Americanists were also concerned that one of the political prices paid for Senate approval of the INF Treaty would be increased budgetary support for NATO's conventional forces and tactical nuclear weapons not covered in the INF Treaty. This effort was viewed as seeking new pretenses to increase defense spending and arresting increased support for disarmament efforts by replacing INF weapons with new nuclear and conventional weapons, rather than pursuing disarmament and a balance of forces at a lower level.

Parliamentary exchanges also played their usual role in providing important information to the Soviet leadership on Senate consideration of the INF Treaty. In late January, a Supreme Soviet delegation led by Lev Tolkunov, the chairman of the Council of the Union and protocol equivalent of the Speaker of the House of Representatives visited the United States, in large part to assess the prospects for INF approval. Meetings with the Senate Foreign Relations Committee and individual Senators appeared to have confirmed judgments that the Senate would eventually act favorably. Tolkunov left Washington with the view that the Senate would approve the treaty.

This assessment, of course, proved to be accurate. As Senate Majority Leader Byrd and Senate Minority Leader Robert Dole worked through a procedural thicket of amendments and towards final approval, americanists praised the bipartisan efforts of the Senate leadership to block a Helms-led filibuster on the Senate floor that threatened to prevent President Reagan and General Secretary Gorbachev from exchanging the official instruments of ratification at the Moscow summit in late May. With final Senate approval on May 27, americanists hailed the Senate action as representing a strengthening of trust between Moscow and Washington and a consolidating of strategic stability. Senators were praised for taking seriously their foreign policy responsibilities. Symbolizing the central role played by the Congress in the making and conduct of superpower relations, Senators Byrd and Dole flew to Moscow to participate in the official ratification ceremony for the INF Treaty, the first treaty on U.S.-Soviet arms control to be approved by the Senate in over fifteen years.

One other development bears mentioning. Perhaps because of a growing appreciation of the role national legislatures can play in the formulation and implementation of a nation's foreign policy, or perhaps because of Central Committee International Department (ID) head Anatolii Dobrynin's efforts (discussed in detail in chapter 5) to resuscitate the credibility of the Supreme Soviet in foreign policy, the Soviet Union conducted its own extended legislative debate of the INF Treaty.

Shortly after the approval of the INF Treaty at the Washington summit in December 1987, a Preparatory Commission with members drawn from the Foreign Affairs Commissions of the two houses of the Supreme Soviet was established to begin the ratification process on the Soviet side. The Commission, headed by deputy ID chief Georgii Kornienko, included some rather notable members including Politburo leader Egor Ligachev; Dobrynin; Marshall Sergei Akhromeev, head of the Soviet Armed Forces; and Roald Sagdeev, director of the Space Research Institute of the USSR Academy of Sciences. The Commission's deliberations were lengthy, detailed and exhaustive by past Soviet standards.

Unlike the ritualized consideration by the Supreme Soviet of past international agreements, consideration of the INF Treaty involved hearing from a whole range of public officials, scientific experts, cultural figures, and private citizens. In an apparent attempt to emulate U.S.-style legislative oversight, Foreign Minister Eduard Shevardnadze and Defense Minister Dmitrii Iazov, as members of the Soviet government, were also called before the Commission to defend the Treaty.

The Commission's deliberations received unprecedented television and radio coverage in the Soviet Union. In the spirit of glasnost, some criticisms of the Treaty were also discussed, with references made to critical letters received by constituents of Supreme Soviet members. These criticisms included the fact that the Treaty required greater Soviet missile reductions than were required of the United States, that British and French intermediate-range missiles were not included in the accord, and that the provisions for verification were insufficient to deter American noncompliance.

Soviet government witnesses appearing before the Commission, most notably Shevardnadze and Iazov, responded to these arguments in public sessions televised nationwide. They stressed that the overall nuclear balance remained at essential parity and that the Treaty did produce an equal result on INF-range missiles between the United States and the Soviet Union. As for the British-French missile issue, government spokesmen stressed that to demand their inclusion would have produced a stalemate which would frustrate arms control progress over missiles which were not critical to the overall military balance with the NATO countries. On the issue of verification, Shevardnadze argued that thoroughly elaborate, unprecedented compliance provisions were mandated by the Treaty to insure unambiguous verification.

The Preparatory Commission, after several months of meetings and public hearings, recommended to the two Foreign Affairs Commissions of the Supreme Soviet in early May that the Treaty be ratified. On May 23, the Foreign Affairs Commissions recommended that the Presidium of the Supreme Soviet exercise its responsibilities under the Soviet Constitution to ratify the Treaty. On May 28, the Presidium approved formal ratification.

Obviously, too much can be made of the vastly-enhanced ratification effort by the Supreme Soviet. The type of oversight conducted and the amount of criticisms leveled against the Treaty pale by comparison to the laborious, detailed oversight work done by the Senate on the Treaty. Nor can it be said the outcome of Soviet legislative consideration was ever in doubt.

Nonetheless, the ongoing efforts by Dobrynin to elevate the significance of the work of the Supreme Soviet suggests that one element of political reform efforts in the Soviet Union includes the replacement of a nominal legislature with a more powerful and effective one. Gorbachev's own proposals at a special Communist Party conference in late June to make the Supreme Soviet a much more powerful representative body validates the strengthening of the legislature as a leadership objective and priority.

As such, perhaps the argument of some americanists discussed in this study that the U.S. Congress plays an important systemic role in reflecting public opinion and generating public support for both domestic and foreign policy goals may now have reached the consciousness of the Soviet leadership. Led by Gorbachev, who appears to understand the role of the U.S. Congress in the American political system better than anyone in the Soviet leadership, Soviet decisionmakers may be seeking to apply these virtues of genuine legislative involvement in policymaking to their own political system. Should this development take place, Soviet views of the U.S. Congress will be important not only because of their impact on superpower relations but also as a barometer of the condition of internal political reform efforts in the Soviet Union. The subject of this study therefore takes on ever greater significance for the study and conduct not only of U.S.-Soviet relations but also of the Soviet political system as a whole.

Appendix:
List of Interviews

The author is indebted to the following individuals, who in agreeing to be interviewed in connection with this study, offered a number of highly useful insights, perspectives, and experiences:

Werner W. Brandt, Legislative Assistant to Rep. Thomas S. Foley (D-Wash.), Majority Leader, U.S. House of Representatives;

Mario A. Castillo, Assistant to the Chairman and Chief of Staff, Committee on Agriculture, U.S. House of Representatives;

Rep. Silvio O. Conte (R-Mass.), Ranking Minority Member, Committee on Appropriations;

Richard C. D'Amato, Counsel and Deputy Staff Director for Foreign and Defense Policy, Senate Democratic Policy Committee;

Richard D. DiEugenio, Senior Legislative Associate, House Committee on Education and Labor;

T.Z. Dzhaparidze, Senior Researcher, Domestic Policy Department, Institute of the USA and Canada, USSR Academy of Sciences;

John Elliff, Professional Staff Member, Senate Select Committee on Intelligence;

Rep. Dante B. Fascell (D-Fla.), Chairman, Committee on Foreign Affairs;

Gary Harter, Special Agent, Federal Bureau of Investigation;

Thomas Hansen, Political Officer, U.S. Embassy, Moscow;

T.N. Iudina, Senior Research Fellow, Institute of the USA and Canada, USSR Academy of Sciences;

Iu. A. Ivanov, Section Chief, Political-Military Department, Institute of the USA and Canada, USSR Academy of Sciences;

Jamie Jameson, Vice-President, Research Associates International;

I.O. Karaganova, Researcher, Domestic Policy Department, Institute of the USA and Canada, USSR Academy of Sciences;

A.A. Mishin, Professor of Constitutional Law, Faculty of Law, Moscow State University;

Cheryl Mendonsa, Office Administrator, Office of Representative George E. Brown, Jr. (D-Calif.);

Christopher D.W. Nelson, Vice-President, Teramura International, formerly Subcommittee Staff Associate, Subcommittee on Asian and Pacific Affairs, House Committee on Foreign Affairs;

A.S. Nikiforov, Senior Researcher, Institute of State and Law, USSR Academy of Sciences;

L. Kirk O'Donnell, Director, Center for National Policy, formerly General Counsel, Office of the Speaker of the House of Representatives;

R. Spencer Oliver, Chief Counsel, House Committee on Foreign Affairs, formerly Staff Director, Commission on Security and Cooperation in Europe;

John B. Ritch, II, Professional Staff Member, Senate Foreign Relations Committee;

V.A. Savel'ev, Senior Research Fellow, Institute of the USA and Canada, USSR Academy of Sciences;

James Schoellaert, Foreign Service Officer, Bureau of Economic and Business Affairs, Department of State, formerly Staff Consultant, House Committee on Foreign Affairs;

Robert Sherman, Legislative Assistant, Office of Representative Les AuCoin (D-Ore.);

Iu. A. Shvedkov, Senior Researcher, Political-Military Department, Institute of the USA and Canada, USSR Academy of Sciences;

Martin Sletzinger, Staff Consultant, House Committee on Foreign Affairs, formerly Staff Assistant, Commission on Security and Cooperation in Europe.

V.A. Tumanov, Section Chief, Comparative Law Department, Institute of State and Law, USSR Academy of Sciences;

N.A. Ushakov, Section Chief, International Law Department, Institute of State and Law, USSR Academy of Sciences; and

E.M. Veremeva, Researcher, Domestic Policy Department, Institute of the USA and Canada, USSR Academy of Sciences.

Bibliography

Non-Soviet Sources

Abshire, David M. and Nurnberger, Ralph eds. *The Growing Power of Congress.* Beverly Hills: Sage Publications, 1981. Almond, Gabriel and Powell, G. Bingham. *Comparative Politics.* Boston: Little, Brown & Co., 1966.

Arnold R. Douglas. *Congress and the Bureaucracy: A Theory of Influence.* New Haven: Yale University Press, 1979.

Aspaturian, Vernon V. "Soviet Foreign Policy." In *Foreign Policy in World Politics.* 2d ed., pp. 112-145. Edited by Roy C. Macridis. Englewood Cliffs: Prentice Hall Inc., 1962.

Barghoorn, Frederick C. "The Security Police." In *Interest Groups in Soviet Politics,* pp. 93-129. Edited by H. Gordon Skilling and Franklin Griffiths. Princeton, N.J.: Princeton University Press, 1973.

Bax, Frans R. "The Legislative - Executive Relationship in Foreign Policy: New Partnership or New Competition?" *Orbis* 20 (Winter 1977): 881-904.

Beloff, Nora. "Escape from Boredom: A Defector's Story." *The Atlantic Monthly.* November 1980, pp. 42-50.

Bennet, Douglas J. Jr. "Congress in Foreign Policy: Who Needs It?" *Foreign Affairs* v.57, (Fall, 1978), pp. 40-50.

Brinkley, Joel. "Soviet Visitor is Turning On All His Charm." *New York Times.* 10 December 1987.

Brown, Archie. "Pluralism, Power, and the Soviet Political System: A Comparative Perspective." In *Pluralism in the Soviet Union,* pp. 61-107. Edited by Susan Gross Solomon. New York: St. Martin's Press, 1983.

———. *Soviet Politics and Political Science.* London: MacMillan Press Ltd., 1974.

Bunce, Valerie and Echols, John M., III. "Soviet Politics in the Brezhnev Era: Pluralism or Corporatism?" In *Soviet Politics in the Brezhnev Era,* pp. 1-26. Edited by Donald R. Kelley. New York: Praeger Publishers, 1980.

Christopher, Warren. "Ceasefire Between the Branches: A Compact in Foreign Affairs." *Foreign Affairs* 60 (Summer 1982): 989-1005.

Crabb, Cecil V. Jr. and Holt, Pat M. *Invitation to Struggle: Congress, the President and Foreign Policy.* Washington: Congressional Quarterly Press, 1980.

Cronin, Thomas E. "A Resurgent Congress and the Imperial Presidency." In *Perspectives on American Foreign Policy,* pp. 320-345. Edited by Charles W. Kegley and Eugene R. Wittkoff. New York: St Martin's Press, 1983.

Dahl, Robert A. *Who Governs?* New Haven, Conn.: Yale University Press, 1961.

Dallin, Alexander and Lapidus, Gail. "Reagan and the Russians: United States Policy Toward the Soviet Union and Eastern Europe." In *Eagle Defiant: U.S. Foreign Policy in the 1980s,* pp. 191-236. Edited by Kenneth A Oye, Robert J. Lieber and Donald Rothchild. Boston: Little, Brown & Co., 1983.

Destler, I.M. "Trade Consensus, SALT Stalemate: Congress and Foreign Policy in the 1970s." In *The New Congress*, pp. 329-359. Edited by Thomas E. Mann and Norman J. Ornstein. Washington: American Enterprise Institute, 1981.

———. and Alterman, Eric R. "Congress and Reagan's Foreign Policy." *Washington Quarterly* 7 (Winter 1984): 91-101.

Dewar, Helen. "Hill Leaders Hold Freewheeling Debate with Soviet." *Washington Post*, 10 December 1987.

Divine, Robert A. "Congress and the President: The Struggle Over Foreign Policy." In *The Presidency and Congress: A Shifting Balance of Power?* pp. 166-181. Edited by William S. Livingston, Lawrence C. Dodd, and Richard L. Schott. Austin, Texas: Lyndon B. Johnson School of Public Affairs, 1979.

Drozdiak, William. "Senators Take Part at Geneva." *Washington Post*, 19 March 1985.

Easton, David. "The Analysis of Political Systems." In *Comparative Politics: Notes and Readings*, pp. 93-106. Edited by Roy C. Macridis and Bernard E. Brown. Homewood, Ill.: The Dorsey Press, 1977.

Edwards, George C. *Presidential Influence in Congress*. San Francisco: W.H. Freeman and Co., 1980.

Eran, Oded. *The Mezhdunarodniki*. Ramat Gan, Israel: Turtledove Publishing, 1979.

Fascell, Dante B. "The Crucial Importance of the War Powers Resolution." *Miami Herald*, 31 March 1986.

Fisher, Louis. *The Constitution Between Friends: Congress, the President, and the Law*. New York: St. Martin's Press, 1978.

Fisher, Louis. *The Politics of Shared Power*. Washington: Congressional Quarterly Press, 1981.

Fleron, Frederick J. Jr. ed. *Communist Studies and the Social Sciences*. Chicago: Rand McNally and Company, 1969.

Franck, Thomas M. and Weisband, Edward. *Foreign Policy by Congress*. New York: Oxford University Press, 1979.

Friedrich, Carl J. and Brzezinski, Zbigniew. *Totalitarian Dictatorship and Autocracy*. New York: Praeger Publishers, 1956.

Garthoff, Raymond L. "The Soviet Military and SALT." In *Soviet Decisionmaking for National Security*, pp. 136-161. Edited by Jiri Valenta and William Potter. London: George Allen and Unwin, 1984.

Gentry, Margaret. "Ex-Aide Says He Was Double Agent." *Washington Post*, 12 March 1976.

Golan, Galia. "Soviet Decisionmaking in the Yom Kippur War, 1973." In *Soviet Decisionmaking for National Security*, pp. 218-237. Edited by Jiri Valenta and William Potter, London: George Allen and Unwin, 1984.

Greenstein, Fred. "The Impact of Personality on Politics: An Attempt to Clear Away Underbrush." *American Political Science Review* (September 1967): 629-642.

Gregorian, Hrach. "Assessing Congressional Involvement in Foriegn Policy: Lessons of the Post-Vietnam Period." *Review of Politics* 46 (January 1984): 91-112.

Hammer, Darrell P. *U.S.S.R.: The Politics of Oligarchy*. Hinsdale, Ill.: The Dryden Press, 1986.

Henkin, Louis. *Foreign Affairs and the Constitution*. New York: Norton, 1975.

Hinckley, Barbara. "Congress and Foreign Policy." In *Stability and Change in Congress*, 2d ed., pp. 167-194. Edited by Barbara Hinckley. New York: Harper and Row, 1978.

Hough, Jerry F. "Pluralism, Corporatism, and the Soviet Union." In *Pluralism in the Soviet Union*, pp. 37-60. Edited by Susan Gross Solomon. New York: St. Martin's Press, 1983.

———. *Soviet Leadership in Transition.* Washington, D.C.: The Brookings Institution, 1980.

———. *The Soviet Union and Social Science Theory.* Cambridge, Mass.: Harvard University Press, 1976.

———. "The Soviet System: Petrification or Pluralism." *Problems of Communism* (March-April 1972): 25-45.

Janos, Andrew C. "Interest Groups and the Structure of Power: Critique and Comparisons." *Studies in Comparative Communism,* XII (Spring 1979): 3-27.

Jervis, Robert. *Perception and Misperception in International Politics.* Princeton, N.J.: Princeton University Press, 1976.

Kaiser, Robert. "To Save SALT, Sen. Byrd Huddled in Secret with Soviet." *Washington Post,* 28 October 1979.

Kanet, Roger E. and Menon, M. Rajan. "Soviet Policy Toward the Third World." In *Soviet Politics in the Brezhnev Era,* pp. 235-262. Edited by Donald R. Kelley. New York: Praeger Publishers, 1980.

Kanet, Roger E. ed. *The Behavioral Revolution and Communist Studies.* New York: The Free Press, 1971.

Katzenstein, Peter J. *Corporatism and Change: Austria, Switzerland, and the Politics of Industry.* Ithaca, N.Y.: Cornell University Press, 1984.

Kegley, Charles W. and Wittkoff, Eugene R. "The Role of Congress in Making Foreign Policy." In *American Foreign Policy: Pattern and Process,* pp. 393-433. Edited by Charles W. Kegley and Eugene R. Wittkoff. New York: St. Martin's Press, 1982.

Kelley, Donald R. "Toward a Model of Soviet Decision Making: A Research Note." *American Political Science Review* (June 1974): 703-706.

Kitrinos, Robert W. "International Department of the CPSU." *Problems of Communism* (September-October 1984): 47-75.

Kolkowicz, Roman. "The Military." In *Interest Groups in Soviet Politics,* pp. 131-171. Edited by H. Gordon Skilling and Franklin Griffiths. Princeton, N.J.: Princeton University Press, 1973.

Kurtz, Howie. "Soviet Agents Busy on Hill Where Information Abounds." *Washington Post,* 28 March 1982.

Latus, Margaret Ann. "Assessing Ideological PACs: From Outrage to Understanding." In *Money and Politics in the United States: Financing Elections in the 1980s,* pp. 142-171. Edited by Michael J. Malbin. Washington: American Enterprise Institute, 1984.

Leyton-Brown, David. "The Role of Congress in the Making of Foreign Policy." *International Journal* 38 (Winter 1982-1983): 59-76.

Lodge, Milton. "Soviet Elite Participatory Attitudes in the Post-Stalin Period." In *The Behavioral Revolution in Communist Studies,* pp. 79-101. Edited by Roger Kanet. New York: The Free Press, 1971.

Malcolm, Neil. *Soviet Political Scientists and American Politics.* London: MacMillan Press, Ltd., 1984.

Mansfield, Harvey C. Sr., ed. *Congress Against the President.* New York: Praeger Publishers, 1975.

Margolis, Jon and Coates, James. "Senator's Aide—Good Friend or Bad Spy?" *Chicago Tribune,* 28 April 1982.

Mayhew, David R. *Congress: the Electoral Connection.* New Haven: Yale University Press, 1974.

Mills, Richard M. "One Theory in Search of Reality: The Development of United States Studies in the Soviet Union." *Political Science Quarterly* LXXXVII (March 1972): 63-79.

Neustadt, Richard E. *Presidential Power: The Politics of Leadership from FDR to Carter.* New York: John Wiley and Sons, 1980.

Odom, William E. "A Dissenting View on the Group Approach to Soviet Politics." *World Politics* (July 1976): 542-567.

Pike, Frederick B. and Stritch, Thomas. eds. *The New Corporatism: Social-Political Structures in the Iberian World.* Notre Dame: University of Notre Dame Press, 1974.

Podhoretz, Norman. "The Future Danger." *Commentary*, (April 1981), pp. 29-47.

Remnek, Richard B. "Soviet Scholars and Soviet Policy Toward India." In *Social Scientists and Policy Making in the USSR*, pp. 86-107. Edited by Richard B. Remnek. New York: Praeger Publishers, 1977.

Richelson, Jeffrey T. *Sword and Shield: Soviet Intelligence and Security Apparatus.* Cambridge, Mass.: Ballinger Publishing Co., 1986.

Rosenau, James. "Pre-theories and Theories of Foreign Policy." In *Approaches to Comparative and International Politics*, pp. 29-92. Edited by R. Barry Farrell. Evanston, Ill.: Northwestern University Press, 1966.

Schmitter, Phillipe. "Still the Century of Corporatism." *Review of Politics* 36 (January 1974): 85-131.

Schwartz, Joel J. and Keech, William R. "Group Influence and the Policy Process in the Soviet Union." *American Political Science Review* (September 1968): 840-851.

Schwartz, Morton. "The Americanists." *Across the Board* 16 (August 1979): 50-61.

_____ . *Soviet Perceptions of the United States.* Los Angeles: University of California Press, 1978.

Shevchenko, Arkady. *Breaking with Moscow.* New York: Balantine Books, 1985.

Simes, Dmitri. "The Politics of Defense in the Brezhnev Era." In *Soviet Decisionmaking for National Security*, pp. 74-84. Edited by Jiri Valenta and William Potter. London: George Allen and Unwin, 1984.

Sinclair, Barbara. *Majority Leadership in the U.S. House.* Baltimore: The Johns Hopkins Press, 1983.

Skilling, H. Gordon. "Pluralism in Communist Societies: Straw Men and Red Herrings." *Studies in Comparative Communism* XIII (Spring, 1980): 82-88.

_____ . "Interest Groups and World Politics." *World Politics* (April 1966): 435-451.

Soll, Richard S.; Zuehlke, Arthur A., Jr.; and Foster, Richard B. *The Role of Social Science Research Institutes in Formulation and Execution of Soviet Foreign Policy.* Arlington, Va: SRI International, 1976.

Solomon, Susan Gross. "'Pluralism' in Political Science: The Odyssey of a Concept." In *Pluralism in the Soviet Union*, pp. 1-36. Edited by Susan Gross Solomon. New York: St. Martin's Press, 1983.

Spanier, John and Nogel, Joseph. eds. *Congress, the Presidency, and American Foreign Policy.* New York: Pergammon Press, 1981.

Spaulding, Wallace. "Shifts in CPSU ID." *Problems of Communism* (July-August 1986): 80-86.

Stepan, Alfred C. *The State and Society: Peru in Comparative Perspective.* Princeton, N.J.: Princeton University Press, 1978.

Stern, Paula. *Water's Edge: Domestic Politics and the Making of American Foreign Policy.* Westport Conn.: Greenwood Press, 1979.

Sundquist, James L. *The Decline and Resurgence of Congress.* Washington: The Brookings Institution, 1981.

Temko, Ned. "It's Not Democracy, But Many Soviets Have a Say." *Christian Science Monitor*, 24 February 1982.

Truman, David B. *The Governmental Process.* New York: Knopf, 1971.

U.S. Congress. House. *House Delegation Trip to the Soviet Union.* 96th Cong., 1st sess., 1979.

U.S. Congress. House. Committee on Energy and Commerce. *Soviet Nuclear Accident at Chernobyl.* Hearings before the Subcommittee on Energy Conservation and Power. 99th Cong., 2d sess.,1986.

U.S. Congress. House. Committee on Foreign Affairs. *U.S. Policy Towards Eastern Europe, 1985.* Hearings before the Subcommittee on Europe and the Middle East, 99th Cong., 2d sess., 1986.

————. *Congress and Foreign Policy, 1984,* by the Foreign Affairs and National Defense Division, Congressional Research Service, Library of Congress. Washington, D.C.: Government Printing Office, 1985.

————. *Foreign Assistance Legislation for Fiscal Years 1986-1987.* Hearings and Markup before the Subcommittee on Europe and the Middle East. 99th Cong., 1st sess., 1985.

————. *The Active Agenda: Outstanding Issues in U.S.-EC Relations.* Report of the Twenty-Fourth and Twenty-Fifth Meetings of Members of Congress and of the European Parliament. 99th Cong., 1st sess., 1985.

————. *The Soviet Union in the Third World: An Imperial Burden or Political Asset?* by Joseph G. Whelan of the Senior Specialists Division, Congressional Research Service, Library of Congress. Washington, D.C.: Government Printing Office, 1985.

————. *Congress and Foreign Policy, 1983,* by the Foreign Affairs and National Defense Division, Congressional Research Service, Library of Congress. Washington, D.C.: Government Printing Office, 1984.

————. *Congress and Foreign Policy, 1982,* by the Foreign Affairs and National Defense Division, Congressional Research Service, Library of Congress. Washington, D.C.: Government Printing Office, 1983.

————. *The United States and Europe: Focus on the Expanding Agenda for the 1980s.* Report of the Twenty-First and Twenty-Second Meetings of Members of Congress and of the European Parliament. 98th Cong., 1st sess., 1983.

————. *The U.S. Supreme Court Decision Concerning the Legislative Veto.* Hearings, 98th Cong., 1st sess., 1983.

————. *Executive-Legislative Consultation on U.S. Arms Sales,* by the Foreign Affairs and National Defense Division, Congressional Research Service, Library of Congress. Washington, D.C.: Government Printing Office, 1982.

————. *Overview of Nuclear Arms Control and Defense Strategy in NATO.* Hearings before the Subcommittees on International Security and Scientific Affairs and on Europe and the Middle East. 97th Cong., 2d sess., 1982.

————. *The War Powers Resolution,* by John Sullivan. Washington, D.C.: Government Printing Office, 1982.

————. *An Assessment of the Afghanistan Sanctions: Implications for Trade and Diplomacy in the 1980s,* by John Hardt of the Senior Specialists Division, Congressional Research Service, Library of Congress. Washington, D.C.: Government Printing Office, 1981.

————. *Soviet Diplomacy and Negotiating Behavior,* by Joseph G. Whelan of the Senior Specialists Division, Congressional Research Service, Library of Congress. Washington, D.C.: Government Printing Office, 1979.

————. *U.S. Relations with the Countries of Central and Eastern Europe,* by Francis Miko of the Foreign Affairs and National Defense Division, Congressional Research Service, Library of Congress. Washington, D.C.: Government Printing Office, 1979.

U.S. Congress. House. Permanent Select Committee on Intellligence. *Soviet Active Measures.* Hearings, 97th Cong., 2d sess., 1982.

U.S. Congress. Senate. *Senator Byrd speaking on his trip to the Soviet Union and Western Europe.* 96th Cong., 1st sess., 20 July 1979. *Congressional Record,* vol. 1628.

———. *Report of the Senate Arms Control Observers Group Delegation to the Opening of the Arms Control Negotiations with the Soviet Union in Geneva, Switzerland.* 99th Cong., 1st sess., 1985.

———. *The Superpowers at a Crossroards: Soviet-American Relations in the Autumn of 1985.* Report by a Senate delegation to Hungary and the Soviet Union led by Senators Robert C. Byrd and Strom Thurmond. 99th Cong., 1st sess., 1985.

———. *Dangerous Stalemate: Superpowers Relations in Autumn 1983.* Report of a delegation of eight Senators to the Soviet Union to the United States Senate. 98th Cong., 1st sess., 1983.

———. *Report to the United States Senate of the Senate Delegation on Parliamentary Exchange with the Soviet Union.* 96th Cong., 1st sess., 1979.

———. Select Committee on Intelligence. *Meeting the Espionage Challenge: A Review of United States Counterintelligence and Security Programs.* 99th Cong., 2d sess., 1986.

U.S. Congress. Senate. Committee on Foreign Relations. *Treaties and Other International Agreements: The Role of the United States Senate,* by Ellen Collier of the Congressional Research Service, Library of Congress. Washington, D.C.: Government Printing Office, 1983.

U.S. International Communications Agency. Office of Research. *Soviet Americanists: A Supplement,* by Steven A. Grant. Research Report No. R-16-82, August, 1982.

———. *Soviet Research Institutes Project.* 3 vols., by Blair M. Ruble. Research Report No. R-5-81, February 1981.

———. *Soviet Elite Perceptions of the U.S.: Public Statements of Soviet Leaders,* by Stanley H. Kober. Research Report No. R-12-80, July 1980.

———. *Soviet Americanists,* by Steven A. Grant. Research Report No. R-1-80, February, 1980.

Uldricks, Teddy J. "The Tsarist and Soviet Ministry of Foreign Affairs," In *The Times Survey of Foreign Ministries of the World,* pp. 514-535. Edited by Zara Sterner. London; Times Books, 1982.

Valenta, Jiri. "Soviet Decisionmaking on Afghanistan, 1979." In *Soviet Decisionmaking for National Security,* pp. 185-218. London; George Allen and Unwin, 1984.

———. "Soviet Decisionmaking on Czechoslovakia, 1968." In *Soviet Decisionmaking for National Security,* pp. 165-185. London: George Allen and Unwin, 1984.

Zablocki, Clement J. "War Powers Resolution: Its Past Record and Future Promise." *Loyola of Los Angeles Review,* 17 (March 1984): 579-598.

Soviet Sources

Abramov, Iu. K. "Richard Lugar—predsedatel' komiteta po inostrannym delam senata SShA." *SShA: ekonomika, politika, ideologiia* (April 1985): 111-112.

———. "Robert Dole, New Republican Senate Majority Leader." Translated by the Joint Publications Research Service. *USSR Report, USA: Economics, Politics, Ideology* 85-006 (March 1985): 77-79.

Arbatov, G.A. "Vneshniaia politika SShA na poroge 80-kh godov." *SShA: ekonomika, politika, ideologiia* (April 1980): 43-54.

Batiuk, V.I. "98th Congress: Debate on Armaments." Translated by the Joint Publications Research Service. *U.S.S.R. Report, U.S.A.: Economics, Politics, Ideology* 85-002 (March 1985): 41-47.

Belonogov, A.M. *Belyi dom i kapitolii. Partnery i soperniki. Prinyatie soedinennymi shtatami Ameriki mezhdunarodnykh obyazatel'stv.* Moscow: Mezhdunarodnye otnosheniia, 1974.

Bol'shakov, S.I. "Congress and U.S. East European Policy: Past and Present." Translated by the Joint Publications Research Service. *U.S.S.R. Report, U.S.A.: Economics, Politics and Ideology* 74072 (August 1979): 106-113.

Chetverikov, S.B. "'Organizational Problems' of Foreign Policy." Translated by the Joint Publications Research Service. *U.S.S.R. Report, U.S.A.: Economics, Politics, Ideology* 63874 (September 1974): 33-41.

————. *Kto i kak delaet politiku SShA?* Moscow: Mezhdunarodnye otnosheniia, 1974.

Dzhaparidze, T.Z. "Mekhanizm svyazi Belogo doma s kongressom." *SShA: ekonomika, politika, ideologiia* (February 1978):124.

Ershova, E.N. "Congress and the Issue of the Nuclear Freeze." Translated by the Joint Publications Research Service. *U.S.S.R. Report, U.S.A.: Economics, Politics, Ideology* 85-013 (December 1985): 42-51.

Galkin, A. "Crisis of Capitalism's Political System." *International Affairs* (January 1977): 49-58.

Gromyko, A.A. *Kongress SShA.* Moscow, 1957.

Guseva, V.S. "The 95th Congress and Domestic and Foreign Policy Issues." Translated by the Joint Publications Research Service. *U.S.S.R. Report, U.S.A.: Economics, Politics, Ideology* 70707 (March 1978): 60-73.

Iakovlev, A.N. *On the Edge of an Abyss.* Moscow: Progress Publishers, 1985.

Iudina, T.N. "Some Foreign Policy Issues in the 98th Congress." Translated by the Joint Publications Research Service. *U.S.S.R. Report, U.S.A.: Economics, Politics, Ideology* 85-004 (May 1985): 40-49.

————. "'Congress Factor' in U.S. Foreign Policy of the 1970's." Translated by the Joint Publications Research Service. *U.S.S.R. Report, U.S.A.: Economics, Politics, Ideology* 71118 (May 1978): 56-65.

Ivanov, Iu. A. "Trudnye problemy kongressa," *SShA: Ekonomika, politika, ideologiia* (April 1987): 69-77.

————. "Samaia dolgaia sessia." *SShA: Ekonomika, politika, ideologiia* (April 1986): 71-78.

————. "Congress and the U.S. Intervention in Lebanon." Translated by the Joint Publications Research Service. *U.S.S.R. Report, U.S.A.: Economics, Politics, Ideology* 85-003 (March 1985): 56-66.

————. "The Honeymoon and After." Translated by the Joint Publications Research Service. *U.S.S.R. Report, U.S.A.: Economics, Politics, Ideology* 90743 (May 1982): 77-85.

————. *Kongress SShA vneshniaia politika: vozmozhnosti i metody vliiania.* Moscow: Nauka, 1982.

————. "Congress: Labyrinths of Power and Foreign Policy-Making." Translated by the Joint Publications Research Service *U.S.S.R. Report, U.S.A.: Economics, Politics, Ideology* 71548 (July 1978): 100-115.

Ivanov, Iu. A.; Silaeva, E.M.; and Dzhaparidze, T.Z. "Peremeny v kongresse." *SShA: ekonomika, politika, ideologiia* (May 1981): 78-83.

Kazakov, Iu. V. "Congress and U.S. Subversive Policy in East Europe." Translated by the Foreign Broadcast Information Service. *Daily Report, U.S.A.: Economics, Politics, Ideology,* 21 October 1981, pp. 2-7.

Kislov, A.K. and Osipova, N.V. "Obsuzhdenie Sinaiskogo soglasheniia." *SShA: ekonomika, politika, ideologiia* (December 1975): 71-77.

Kokoshin, A.A. *SShA: za fasadom global'noi politiki.* Moscow: Politizdat, 1981.

Kondrashev, S.N. "The President's Fist and Unavoidable Compromises." Translated by the Foreign Broadcast Information Service. *Daily Report*, 5 June 1985, p. A1.

Konovalov, D.N. and Savel'ev, V.A. "Action to Limit Presidential War Powers." Translated by the Joint Publications Research Service. *U.S.S.R. Report, U.S.A.: Economics, Politics, Ideology* 61346 (February 1974): 108-116.

Kozlov, V. "U.S. Congress and American Foreign Policy." *International Affairs* (February 1979): 114-118.

Kremeniuk, V.A. "Presidentskie vybory i blizhnyi vostok." *SShA: ekonomika, politika, ideologiia* (July 1973): 71-77.

Lan, V. *Klassy i partii v SShA: Ocherki po ekonomicheskoi i politicheskoi istorii SShA.* Moscow: 1937.

Lebedev, I.V. " 'Split Government' Again?" Translated by the Joint Publications Research Service. *U.S.S.R. Report, U.S.A.: Economics, Politics, Ideology* 58148 (March 1973): 28-40.

Levin, I.D. and Tumanov, V.A. eds. *Politicheskii mekhanizm diktatury monopolii.* Moscow: Nauka, 1974.

Litvinova, M.A. and V.N. Orlov. "Informatsionno-Analitcheskii sluzhbi kongressa." *SShA: Ekonomika, politika, ideologiia* (April 1987): 112-115.

Mikheev, V.S. "Congress and the 'Atlantic Partnership.'" Translated by the Joint Publications Research Service. *U.S.S.R. Report, U.S.A.: Economics, Politics and Ideology* 84-005 (May 1984): 44-53.

Mishin, A.A. "Legal Relations Between the President and the Congress." Translated by the Joint Publications Research Service. *U.S.S.R. Report, U.S.A.: Economics, Politics, Ideology* 84-012 (December 1984): 53-57.

————. *Gosudarstvennoe pravo SShA.* Moscow: Nauka, 1976.

Mosin, I.N. "Krizis amerikanskykh programm 'pomoschi.'" *SShA: ekonomika, politika, ideologiia* (July 1975): 15-26.

Nikiforov, A.S. "Legal Peculiarities of Presidential Authority." Translated by the Joint Publications Research Service. *U.S.S.R. Report, U.S.A.: Economics, Politics, Ideology* 56958 (September 1972): 21-34.

Nyporko, Iu. I. *Constitutional Interrelationships Between the President and the U.S. Congress in the Area of Foreign Policy.* Translated by the Foreign Broadcast Information Service 49112 (May 1980).

Osipova, N.V. "The Senate and the Package Deal." Translated by the Joint Publications Research Service. *U.S.S.R. Report, U.S.A.: Economics, Politics, Ideology* 72348 (December 1978): 104-113.

Pakhomov, N.I. "Trezvyi podkhod." *SShA: ekonomika, politika, ideologiia* (April 1976): 66-69.

Pechatanov, V.O. "Midterm Elections: Results and Prospects." Translated by the Joint Publications Research Service. *U.S.S.R. Report, U.S.A.: Economics, Politics, Ideology* 83559 (May 1983): 21-30.

Popova, E.I. *Amerikanskii senat i vneshniaia politika 1969-1974.* Moscow: Nauka, 1978.

Primakov, E.M. "Pruzhiny blizhnevostochnoi politiki SShA." *SShA: ekonomika, politika, ideologiia* (November 1976): 3-15.

Prokudin, E.V. "Congress and American-Soviet Trade." Translated by the Joint Publications Research Service. *U.S.S.R. Report, U.S.A.: Economics, Politics, Ideology* 85-006 (May 1985): 54-62.

Savel'ev, V.A. "U.S. Approaches to Dialogue with the USSR." Translated by the Joint Publications Research Service. *U.S.S.R. Report, U.S.A.: Economics, Politics, Ideology* 87-002 (November 1986): 1-13.

———. "The President and Congress in an Election Year." Translated by the Joint Publications Research Service. *U.S.S.R. Report, U.S.A.: Economics, Politics, Ideology* 84-011 (November 1984): 1-14.

———. "The Congress in 1979." Translated by the Joint Publications Research Service. *U.S.S.R. Report, U.S.A.: Economics, Politics, Ideology* 75772 (May 1980): 84-90.

———. "Frenk Cherch - predsedatel' senatskoi kommissii po inostrannym delam." *SShA: ekonomika, politika, ideologiia* (April 1979): 115-119.

———. "Zakonodatel'noe veto." *SShA: ekonomika, politika, ideologiia* (March 1979): 119-125.

———. "Foreign Policy and Congress." Translated by the Joint Publications Research Service. *U.S.S.R. Report, U.S.A.: Economics, Politics, Ideology* L/6761 (January 1977): 47-58.

———. "Sluzhebnyi apparat kongressa." *SShA: ekonomika, politika, ideologiia* (March, 1976): 122-127.

———. *SShA: senat i politika*. Moscow: Mysl', 1976.

Savel'ev V.A. and Silaeva, E.M. "New House and Senate Leaders." Translated by the Joint Publications Research Service. *U.S.S.R. Report, U.S.A.: Economics, Politics, Ideology* 69244 (June 1977): 66-79.

———. The Senate: New Faces, Old Problems." Translated by the Joint Publications Research Service. *U.S.S.R. Report, U.S.A.: Economics, Politics, Ideology* L/7024 (April 1977): 46-56.

Sergunin, A.A. "Presidential Lobbying under Ronald Reagan: Patterns and Methods of Influencing the Congress." Translated by the Joint Publications Research Service. *U.S.S.R. Report, U.S.A.: Economics, Politics, Ideology*. 84-005 (May 1984): 61-69.

Shvedkov, Iu. A. ed. *SShA: vneshnepoliticheskii mekhanizm*. Moscow: Nauka, 1972.

———. "The Congress After the Elections." Translated by the Joint Publications Research Service. *U.S.S.R. Report, U.S.A.: Economics, Politics, Ideology* 77507 (March 1981): 34-46.

Silaeva, E.M. "What is New in the 98th Congress?" Translated by the Joint Publications Research Service. *U.S.S.R. Report, U.S.A.: Economics, Politics, Ideology*. 84050 (August 1983): 33-38.

Silaeva, E.M. and Savel'ev, V.A. "Palata predstavitelei: usilenie 'liberal'-nogo kryla." *SShA: ekonomika, politika, ideologiia* (March 1977): 81-86.

Sokov, N.N. "On the Road to the Elections: The Search for an Alternative Foreign Policy." Translated by the Joint Publications Research Service. *U.S.S.R. Report, U.S.A.: Economics, Politics, Ideology* 84-001 (January 1984): 58-62.

Tatarinova, N.B. and Chernov, V.L. "The 97th Congress and Soviet-American Relations." Translated by the Joint Publications Research Service. *U.S.S.R. Report, U.S.A.: Economics, Politics, Ideology* 83788 (June 1983): 57-65.

Trofimenko, G.A. ed. *Mekhanizm formirovannia vneshnii politiki SShA*. Moscow: Nauka, 1986.

———. "Too Many Negotiators." *New York Times*, 13 July 1979.

Tumanov, V.A. and Vail', I.M. eds. *Izbiratel'nye sistemy i partii v burzhuaznom gosudarstve*. Moscow: Institut gosudarstva i prava, 1979.

Verem'eva, E.M. "Kongress i belyii dom." *SShA: Ekonomika, politika, ideologiia* (October 1987): 74-78.

Zolotukhin, V.P. and Linnik, V.A. "Congress After the Elections." Translated by the Joint Publications Research Service. *U.S.S.R. Report, U.S.A.: Economics, Politics, Ideology* 73015 (March 1979): 83-88.

Zorin, V.S. "200-letie i 'konstitutionnyi krizis.'" *SShA: ekonomika, politika, ideologiia* (July 1976): 24-26.

Index

ABC. *See* American Broadcasting
Corporation
ABM Treaty. *See* Anti-Ballistic Missile
Treaty
Academy of Sciences. *See* USSR
Academy of Sciences
Afghanistan, 2, 5, 7, 33, 61, 70, 105,
125, 142, 146, 170
AFL-CIO. *See* American Federation of
Labor and Congress of Industrial
'Organizations
Africa Institute (USSR), 89
Aganbegian, Abel, 148
AIPAC. *See* American Israel Public
Affairs Committee
Akhromeev, Sergei, 121, 172
Albert, Carl, 128
Aleksandrov-Agentov, A. M., 94
Alkhimov, Vladimir, 129
Allen, James, 32
American Broadcasting Corporation
(ABC), 124
American Federation of Labor and
Congress of Industrial
Organizations (AFL-CIO), 63–64
American Israel Public Affairs
Committee (AIPAC), 45, 72–74
Americanists
education and training, 86–91, 94
influence on Soviet leadership, 93–
98, 155, 157–158
See also Amerikanistika
Amerikanistika
on Congress' organization, 27–40
on constitutional prerogatives and
responsibilities, 20–27, 47–51
historical development, 1, 6, 18–20,
91, 154–155
levels of analysis, 152–153
organization and function, 86–93

on pressure group influence on
Congress' foreign policy role, 40–
47
on the separation of powers, 20–27
on the two-party system, 27–33
on U.S. arms sales to the Middle
East, 71–74
on U.S. defense and arms control
policy, 74–83
on U.S.-European relations, 57–67
on U.S.-Soviet trade, 67–71
See also Americanists
Andropov, Yuri, 132, 135–137, 140
Angola, 5, 32–33, 36, 158
Anikin, A. V., 90
Anti-Ballistic Missile (ABM) Treaty,
81, 122–123, 125, 140, 170
Anti-satellite (ASAT) weapons
program, 76–77, 80–81
Arab states. *See* Middle East
Arbatov, Georgii, 90
influence on Soviet leadership, 93–
94
interactions with Congress, 102,
108, 129, 132, 171
Arms control negotiations, 90, 142,
146
Amerikanistiká and analysis, 74–82
and Congressional organization and
prerogatives, 23–24, 27–29, 31–
33, 38
the infuence of americanists on, 3,
97
parliamentary exchange discussion,
129
and Soviet-West European relations,
67
and U.S.-West European relations,
58, 60–62
and Western perspectives on Soviet
foreign policy, 5, 7–8, 10, 153,
156